DIMENSIONS OF SELF EXPERIENCE

Progress in Self Psychology
Volume 5

DIMENSIONS OF SELF EXPERIENCE

Progress in Self Psychology
Volume 5

Arnold Goldberg
editor

THE ANALYTIC PRESS

1989   Hillsdale, NJ   Hove and London

Published by The Analytic Press, Hillsdale, NJ.

Distributed solely by

Lawrence Erlbaum Associates, Inc., Publishers
365 Broadway
Hillsdale, New Jersey   07642

ISBN 0-88163-086-1
ISSN 0893-5483

Printed in the United States of America
10 9 8 7 6 5 4 3 2 1

Progress in Self Psychology
Editor, Arnold Goldberg, M.D.

Contents

Contributors

Lionel Corbett, M.D., Assistant Professor and Clinical Director of Psychiatry, Rush-Presbyterian-St. Luke's Medical Center, Chicago, IL.

Harry Fiss, Ph.D., Professor and Director of Psychology, Department of Psychiatry, University of Connecticut School of Medicine, Farmington.

James L. Fosshage, Ph.D., Cofounder and Board Director, National Institute for the Psychotherapies; Core Faculty, Institute for the Psychoanalytic Study of Subjectivity, New York City.

Ramon Greenberg, M.D., Faculty, Boston Psychiatric Institute; Lecturer, Harvard Medical School and Massachusetts Mental Health Center.

Jerald Kay, M.D., Professor of Child Psychiatry and Director of Residency Training, University of Cincinnati Medical Center.

Charles Kligerman, M.D., Training and Supervising Analyst, Chicago Institute for Psychoanalysis.

Daniel Kriegman, Ph.D., Human Services Cooperative; Codirector, The Cambridge Institute for the Study of Psychoanalysis and Human Evolution.

Paul K. Kugler, Ph.D., Training Analyst, Inter-Regional Society of Jungian Analysts Training Institute; Member of the Center for the Psychological Study of the Arts, State University of New York at Buffalo.

Robert J. Leider, M.D., Training and Supervising Analyst, Chicago

Institute for Psychoanalysis; Assistant Professor of Clinical Psychiatry, Northwestern University Medical School.

Hyman L. Muslin, M.D., Professor of Psychiatry, University of Illinois College of Medicine, Chicago.

Harry Paul, Ph.D., Member, Board of Directors and Faculty, Training and Research Institute for Self Psychology (TRISP); Staff Psychologist, F.D.R. Veterans Administration Hospital.

Susan H. Sands, Ph.D., Clinical Faculty, The Wright Institute, Berkeley, CA; Staff Psychologist, Department of Psychiatry and Behavioral Medicine, Stanford University.

Estelle Shane, Ph.D., Founding President, Center for Early Education and College of Developmental Studies, Los Angeles; Visiting Lecturer, Department of Psychiatry, UCLA.

Morton Shane, M.D., Director of Education, Training and Supervising Analysis in Adult and Child, Los Angeles Psychoanalytic Society and Institute; Associate Clinical Professor, Department of Psychiatry, UCLA.

Malcolm Owen Slavin, Ph.D., Director of Training, Tufts University Counseling Center; Codirector, Cambridge Institute for the Study of Psychoanalysis and Human Evolution.

Robert D. Stolorow, Ph.D., Faculty, Southern California Psychoanalytic Institute; Coauthor, *Psychoanalytic Treatment: An Intersubjective Approach* (The Analytic Press).

Paul H. Tolpin, M.D., Training and Supervising Analyst, Chicago Institute for Psychoanalysis; Senior Attending Psychiatrist, Michael Reese Hospital, Chicago.

Richard B. Ulman, Ph.D., Member, Board of Directors and Faculty, Training and Research Institute for Self Psychology (TRISP); Research Associate Professor of Psychiatry, New York Medical College.

Ernest S. Wolf, M.D., Training and Supervising Analyst, Chicago Institute for Psychoanalysis; Assistant Professor of Psychiatry, Northwestern University Medical School.

Acknowledgment

The preparation of this book was financed by funds from the Harry and Hazel Cohen Research Fund. Ms. Chris Susman provided secretarial and editorial assistance.

Introduction

Robert J. Leider

This fifth volume in the *Progress in Self Psychology* series contains 12 papers and two comments, or "reflections," covering a wide range of subjects: from dreams and dreaming, to the self in Jung and Kohut; from infant and child observation, to the development of the self in girls and women; from the "therapeutic experience," to such specific clinical topics as eating disorders, substance abuse, suicide, and unresolvable fixations; from a biological analysis of the negative therapeutic reaction, to the future of psychoanalysis and the future analyst. These papers, grounded in the accumulated knowledge of the past, represent some of the most recent work in our field and point toward further advances in the future. We believe the reader will be well rewarded by their study.

When Arnold Goldberg asked if I would write this introduction, he indicated that I might, if I wished, reflect generally on the current state of self psychology. Needless to say this was tempting, and not being of an ascetic bent, I resolved on a course of gratification rather than renunciation. It became, therefore, my plan to accept Goldberg's offer and give my perspective on our field of study, in the hope that this would serve as a useful orientation for the reader. In pursuit of this goal, I shall first comment upon the milieu in which self psychology had its origin; then upon current questions, disagreements, and opinions regarding focal points of Kohut's theories; and finally upon the papers published in this volume.

This introduction is a propitious opportunity for such an enterprise, since the volume is largely composed of papers presented at the Tenth Annual Conference (1987) on the Psychology of the Self. That conference, the occasion for Goldberg's offer, stimulated recollections of the first conference, held in Chicago nine years earlier, and of the events leading up to that meeting.

Self psychology had its birth in Chicago almost 25 years ago with the pioneering work of Heinz Kohut. By the time of the first large meeting in Chicago (October 1978), self psychology was vigorously established and developing rapidly. Subsequent annual meetings were held in distant cities, and one could say that the increasing separation from Chicago represented a further step in the development of self psychology—an adolescence, if you will. The return to Chicago for the tenth meeting might be compared to the beginning of vigorous young adulthood. Kohut would, I believe, be well pleased.

As I reflected back over the years, many memories emerged—of Kohut and his ideas, of the intellectual colleagues with whom he discussed his new ideas, and of the gradual evolution of their independent thought. Psychoanalysis and self psychology have come a long way.

Originally Kohut had a small group of colleagues who provided stimulation and regulation as his creative work proceeded. To these were soon added a few others as the import of self psychology became more widely known. These, then junior, are now senior. Most, though by no means all, are still actively identified with self psychology, and their contributions to it continue. This original group has now been enlarged by the addition of new members, whose perspectives challenge old beliefs, introduce new ideas, and test the group cohesiveness. These newer contributors are now well recognized at meetings and in the literature, and their ideas command wide attention and respect. By no means do they repeat or adhere to all of Kohut's opinions. Their questioning expands our knowledge, and their work contributes to the content of this volume.

Kohut's (1959) paper, "Introspection, Empathy, and Psychoanalysis" introduced the first theme in what was to evolve into a complex concerto of new psychoanalytic ideas. Kohut stressed that access to psychological depths could be obtained only through specific modes of observation: *introspection* into one's own subjective state; and vicarious introspection, *empathy*, into that of another. Psychoanalysis, or any depth psychology, was in his view limited to and defined by data collected in this manner.[1]

---

[1]This position on the centrality of empathy was not original and closely followed Freud (1921). See also Basch (1983a).

EPISTEMOLOGY AND METHODOLOGY

The definition of psychoanalysis by its mode of observation and data collection raised a variety of general epistemological questions: Is any observation independent of pre-existing theory? How does theory affect or determine the phenomena recognized and observed? What are the effects of the observer on the observed? How do we judge the "validity" of an observation? What do we mean by "reality," and how do we know it?

Kohut himself was interested in the philosophical principles underlying scientific methodology, and comments reflecting this concern are found throughout his writing. He reluctantly recognized the effect of theory on observation and inference yet continually hoped to make "experience-near" observations (relatively) free of theoretical influence. He constructed "experience-distant" theories, but recognized them to potentially interfere with the experience-near observation he so much valued. In his later works Kohut recognized the relativism of many judgments (e.g. diagnostic categories) and showed an increased concern with objectivism, subjectivism, and relativism.

These epistemological questions continue to command attention, and many within our field have pursued them. Some address abstract philosophical theory and examine hermeneutics, phenomenology, structuralism, empiricism, postempiricism, realism, relativism, and subjectivism; others address less abstract levels and focus greater attention on the epistemological problems in clinical observation and clinical theory.

Most authors now acknowledge the importance of theory to observation, and there is a general agreement in that regard. On the other hand, there is no unanimity of opinion regarding the proper definition of reality for psychoanalysis, or the criteria by which to judge the validity of an observation or the "truth" of an explanation. As Goldberg (1988) so felicitously put it, there is a "tension between realism and relativism in psychoanalysis."

Positions tend to organize about opposite poles; and writers can be characterized as those who adhere to a philosophical position of objectivism or realism, and those who adopt a position of subjectivism or of relativism. The discussions and philosophical arguments make fascinating reading, and an understanding of these issues has an important effect on one's clinical theory and technical approach. (The reader is referred to Atwood and Stolorow, 1984; Basch, 1983a, 1984a, 1986; Goldberg, 1988; Ornstein and Ornstein, 1980; Ornstein, 1983; Stolorow, Brandchaft, and Atwood, 1987; Wolf, 1986, this volume, for more extensive discussions.)

A separate, more specific methodological question is posed by Kohut's definition of psychoanalysis. Should data derived from external (extrospective, nonempathic) observations be integrated into our theories and utilized in our formulations, or should this knowledge be excluded from psychoanalytic explanation?

Perhaps the most consistent attempt at the exclusion of externally derived information, the most rigorous application of Kohut's sharply defined and delimited focus, is found in the intersubjective approach:

> [T]he only reality relevant and accessible to psychoanalytic inquiry . . . is *subjective reality* . . ." (Stolorow et al., 1987 p. 4). "[W]e do not believe that the analyst possesses any 'objective' knowledge of the patient's life or of human development and human psychological functioning" (p. 6).

Yet this position is difficult to maintain, and even adherents of this approach seem to abandon its strict application when they discuss the relevance of developmental research to clinical understanding.

Most authors do not agree with Kohut's early views on this matter or with the intersubjective position just described; they believe, rather, that information obtained through external observational methods should be recognized, correlated, and integrated with empathically derived theories. Basch (1984a, b, 1986) and Goldberg (1988) best represent this epistemological point of view. Papers that address the tasks of correlation and integration are discussed in the following section.

PSYCHOLOGICAL DEVELOPMENT

A new theme was introduced into psychoanalytic theory when Kohut (1966) asserted that normal development was not marked by a conversion of narcissistic cathexes into object cathexes or of narcissism into object love, as Freud (1914) had postulated, but rather by the *separate* development of each.

This revision of Freud's developmental scheme was followed by an expanded description of childhood development made possible by the subsequent delineation of the selfobject transferences (Kohut, 1971).[2] Examination of these transferences permitted Kohut to con-

---

[2]The discovery of selfobject transferences was considered by Kohut to be his most important contribution to psychoanalytic knowledge (Kohut, 1984, p. 104).

struct an outline presumed to describe the normal development of the self and its component structures.

Others, stimulated and informed by Kohut's findings, continue the task of elaborating our picture of human psychological development. Efforts extend in two directions: one, the expansion of developmental reconstructions derived from empathic observation of transference configurations; the other, the correlation and integration of information derived from infant and child developmental observation, ethology, neurophysiology, linguistics, and other scientific disciplines.

The similarity of data obtained by these disparate methodological approaches is striking, providing a welcome corroboration of self-psychological theory and permitting refinement and correction as incongruities are detected, examined, and understood (Basch, 1976; Beebe and Lachmann, 1988; Bowlby, 1969; Demos, 1988; Lichtenberg, 1983, 1985, 1988; Papousek and Papousek, 1979; Ornstein, 1981; Shane and Shane, 1980, 1986, this volume; Stern, 1985; Stolorow et al., 1987; Tolpin, 1971, 1978, 1986; Tolpin and Kohut, 1979; Wolf, 1983.)

STRUCTURALIZATION AND TRANSMUTING INTERNALIZATION

Kohut believed that experiences of "optimal frustration," the optimal disruption and repair of the empathic bond between child and caretaker, lead to the development of tension regulating structures by a process he called transmuting internalization. This concept, based on mechanisms originally described by Freud (1917) is central to Kohut's theory of structure formation, normal psychological development, and the cure. Over the entire span of his writing, Kohut did not alter his view of the importance of this process, nor of the central role of frustration in its operation (1971, pp. 47–50; 1977, pp. 86–88; 1984, pp. 98–110).

The belief that optimal frustration and transmuting internalization are essential for structuralization has been questioned by a number of authors on the basis of clinical observation and infant developmental studies. They doubt that frustration (optimal or not) provides the sole, or even the major, stimulus for structure formation; and they consider that structuralization is more likely to occur in situations of optimal gratification or optimal responsiveness. Though an increasing number of authors have begun to comment on this issue, Bacal

(1985, 1988) and Terman (1988), have presented the most detailed systematic expositions of this position.

MODELS OF THE MIND

A watershed in the evolution of self psychology and psychoanalysis was reached when Kohut (1977) publicly asserted that a satisfactory understanding of development, psychopathology, and the therapeutic process could not be encompassed within the framework of classical drive theory and the structural model of the mind.[3]

Kohut proposed an astounding theoretical revision. He suggested that developmental schemata should be conceptualized and organized about the development of the self, its motivational (selfobject) needs, and the dangers that threaten its organization and "cohesion"; rather than around the drives and their vicissitudes. Drives, conflict, and the oedipal period were no longer seen as the exclusive, or even the main, factors in psychological development and psychopathology. A new model, the *bipolar self*, was advanced to supplant the tripartite structural model that psychoanalysis had used for 50 years.

This new model raised questions: Is it superior to the previous structural model, and can it replace it? Does it satisfactorily encompass conflict and guilt, addressed by the structural model? Do we retain both models and shift from one to the other depending on the type of pathology under consideration—a "complementarity" of theories? Do we strive for a more inclusive model?

Kohut (1977) addressing these issues, said that oedipal neuroses might be better "explained" by the older, drive-conflict model and that complete psychoanalytic understanding might require different, and complementary theories. This opinion, however, was advanced when Kohut had just introduced the new bipolar model; and whether it was a politic statement, a transitional position, or his final view is in dispute. More important is whether or not it was correct.

Several answers to this question are to be found in the literature. Goldberg (1988), taking a philosophical path, treats us to an illuminating discussion on the evolution of knowledge and the relationship between theories. Shane and Shane (1988) remain consistent proponents of complementarity and vigorously assert its value. Stolorow

---

[3]Models, as meant here, are abstract metapsychological constructions designed to provide a description or analogy intended to represent another abstraction, in this case the mind. They include a system of data, assumption, and inference (often not distinguished) that function to organize observation and provide a framework for explanation and prediction.

(1988) and Stolorow et al. (1987) present yet another perspective, and another solution: that the transference is marked by a continual oscillation between selfobject and conflictual dimensions. The multiplicity of proposed solutions suggests that a satisfactory resolution has yet to be reached.

THERAPEUTIC PROCESS AND THE THEORY OF THE CURE

Kohut's work came to an end with his death in 1981 and the posthumous publication (1984) of *How Does Analysis Cure?* The major intent of this work was to clarify ideas previously expressed, with particular attention to his understanding of the curative process. Few theoretical revisions were introduced.[4]

In general, Kohut's ideas were more sharply articulated and his meaning more clear, for example in his discussions of empathy, castration anxiety, and oedipal conflict. Kohut, however, wished to answer the question, How does analysis cure? and in this he fell short of his mark.

The riddle of the psychoanalytic cure has eluded a satisfactory solution for decades. Answers are imbricated with current or favored theory (abreaction, changing unconscious mental content to conscious, structural reorganization through insight, increasing cohesion of the self via transmuting internatlization, and so on), and none has achieved a sustained acceptance.

In the context of the theory of the self, the question may be succinctly put. Does repair of the self occur as a result of a lengthy immersion in an empathic milieu, "understanding"; or is "explanation" the crucial curative agent? Or are both required, and if so, what are their respective functions?

Kohut (1977, 1984) addressed this problem many times, yet his position remained ambiguous and, I believe, ambivalent. His final published statement (1984) was that empathy alone was not curative; that the therapeutic process requires a phase of understanding, sometimes very protracted, *necessarily* followed by a phase of explanation. But the matter remains unsettled, characterized by a conspicuous lack of consensus.

[4]One significant exception regarded the twinship transference. This transference, previously considered a subtype of the mirror transference, was now considered a major transference in its own right, corresponding to the mirror and idealizing transferences. The model of the mind was analogously modified and said to have three poles: a tripolar self.

Some consider these questions to be spurious, the result of a false dichotomy between affect and cognition. Others believe empathic emersion to be *the* curative factor, explanation being an intellectual epiphenomenon serving only to reduce the therapist's or patient's guilt about not being interpretive and analytic. Yet, others, like Kohut, consider the explanatory phase essential to cement the beneficial effects of empathic understanding. (Many have addressed these matters and specific references are beyond the scope of this introduction.)

A related issue regards the proper stance of the therapist, the ambience of the treatment, and the roles of neutrality and abstinence.

Freud (1915) recommended that treatment be conducted from a position of abstinence and neutrality and (Freud, 1912) that the analyst assume a surgeonlike attitude of emotional coldness and distance. These recommendations have been widely misunderstood and contributed to many difficulties in treatment. Over the years many have come to recognize this misunderstanding of Freud's meaning, and a more responsive, human attitude is now frequently recommended.

The question is thus transformed. How much, in what manner, to what purpose, and to what effect is the analyst more responsive? The answer depends on, among other things, the view taken of the meaning of neutrality, and the role of abstinence, optimal frustration, and optimal responsiveness in the cure (Bacal, 1985, 1988; Basch, 1981, 1983b, 1984b; Kohut, 1977, 1984; Leider, 1983; Ornstein, 1984; Ornstein and Ornstein, 1980; Wolf, 1976, 1983, this volume; Stolorow et al., 1987).

Another critical question relates to transference and transference interpretation—significant to psychoanalytic theory and practice whether one is self-psychologically or classically informed. As Cooper (1988) recently observed, "transference interpretation seems to have replaced self psychology as the encompassing topic . . ." (p. 78).[5]

In a long clinical vignette Kohut (1984, pp. 178–184) explains his perspective on transference evolution and also illustrates the techniques of understanding and explanation he advocates.[6] Two critical issues are delineated. (1) What "truths" are reflected in the transference? Do transferences arise solely from forces within the patient and

[5]Whether or not this is true is hard to judge, and may well be relative to geographical location.
[6]Kohut did not often use the term transference neurosis. In this vignette, *transference neurosis* might better have expressed his meaning.

accurately reflect aspects of his or her past; or to what degree is the transference determined by factors in the present, especially attitudes and actions of the therapist? (2) What judgments, if any, should we make regarding reality or distortion inherent in the transference.

Most current authors no longer adhere to the view that the transference arises solely and independently from within the patient. The form and content of transference phenomena are, in varying degrees, recognized to be influenced and codetermined by the therapist. Yet unanimity ends as opinions diverge regarding the extent and effect of this factor.

The second question, whether to consider the patient's subjective reality a distortion of a more objective reality is important, more controversial, and unsettled. Crucial differences in the goals of treatment are defined by the answer. To sharpen my meaning and illustrate the controversy, I shall recount a recent discussion.

A highly regarded analyst of modern theoretical bent asked, with an air of incredulity, "Arnold, do you really mean what you say, that your goal is 'ultimately to disabuse patients of their mistaken notions'?" And Goldberg answered, with at least as much disbelief, that indeed he did! He meant what he said! A private correspondence ensued, until both participants had exhausted their arguments and energy.[7]

Goldberg (1988) is unambiguous:

> Rather than impose our truths upon patients, initially we view the world from their perspectives. This, however, is but a first step in a process designed ultimately to disabuse patients of their mistaken notions, revealed in the transference—a situation in which we assume privileged access and knowledge [p. 57].

Many agree with this position. Many do not. Perhaps the most clear, and equally emphatic, exposition of the opposite view point is to be found in the following statement: "[I]nvoking the concept of objective reality, along with its corollary concept of *distortion*, obscures the subjective reality encoded in the patient's productions, . . . precisely what psychoanalytic investigation should seek to illuminate." (Stolorow et al., 1987, p. 5)

The opposing positions are clearly drawn. The reader can only be referred to the works of the respective authors, those of others cited in related sections of this introduction, and papers included in this volume.

[7]Personal discussion and correspondence that both participants kindly shared with me.

Two further topics deserve notice before I comment on the papers in this volume.

INTERSUBJECTIVITY

The *intersubjective approach* evolved over the past 15 or so years in the thinking of a small group of clinicians and theoreticians (Atwood, Brandchaft, Lachmann, Stolorow) who applied self-psychological principles to a spectrum of clinical conditions and situations. They have written extensively, with the aim ultimately to reframe psychoanalysis as a "pure psychology." They state that

> the concept of an intersubjective field gradually crystallized . . . as the central explanatory construct for guiding psychoanalytic theory, research, and treatment. . . . Adopting an intersubjective approach can greatly enlarge analysts' capacity for sustained empathic inquiry and . . . enhance the therapeutic effectiveness of psychoanalytic treatment [Stolorow et al., 1988, p. ix]

The scope of their theory is wide, their writing is compelling, and their ideas have attracted wide attention and interest. Whether this approach will ultimately prove more powerful as an explanatory construct for psychoanalysis than those from which it evolved is impossible to judge at this point. Time and trial ultimately will render the verdict.

SCIENTIFIC DOGMATISM

Kohut's ideas shook psychoanalysis to its core. Traditional psychoanalysts objected. Some thought him in error. Others asserted that his theories were not psychoanalytic and his practice not psychoanalysis, an accusation of false doctrine—heresy.

For a period of time, Kohut and his collaborators attempted to explain his views and answer objections in the hope that his ideas would receive the unbiased examination appropriate to scientific theory. Many did examine his ideas in this manner. Some did not, have not, and will not; and in response to that dogmatic attitude many of those convinced of the value of self psychology have abandoned the attempt to influence "infallible" psychoanalytic doctrine by rational argument.[8]

---

[8]One minor exception was a response (Leider, 1988) to a mistaken and particularly polemical criticism (Reed, 1987).

OVERVIEW OF THIS VOLUME

Such a wide range of topics is addressed in this volume, and different approaches represented, that it is likely that readers of catholic taste will find much to engage them, while those with more specific interests will find papers of sufficient relevance to command their attention. The volume is divided into four main sections. Three contain papers directed in their primary focus to dreams, developmental theory, and clinical issues; the fourth contains papers on diverse topics of general psychoanalytic relevance.

The first section, devoted to dreams and dreaming, returns to a topic of historical prominence in psychoanalysis. In the early days of psychoanalysis, dreams were considered the "royal road to the unconscious," pivotal in the evolution of psychoanalytic theory and central to its therapeutic practice. With the accretion of greater psychoanalytic knowledge and greater recognition of the complexities of normal and disordered psychological functioning, interest in dreams diminished. In this regard, the self-psychological literature is typical of current psychoanalytic discussion, as dreams are not frequently a subject of specific inquiry.[9] This section is, therefore, unique in that it contains three papers (Fosshage, Fiss, Greenberg) and two discussions (Stolorow, P. Tolpin), all directed to the subject of dreams and dreaming. It is additionally unique in that two of the papers approach dreams primarily from the environment of the dream research laboratory, rather than from that of the clinical consulting room.

Fosshage's contribution is clinically derived. He observes that the reported dream is a waking memory of an imagistic mental process that occurred during sleep, and that dream mentation varies in clarity, significance, and functional success. A summary of a revised psychoanalytic model of dreams is presented in which a supraordinate integrative and synthetic function is postulated, and in which dream content does not necessarily involve defensive operations. Finally, Fosshage illustrates his technique of dream analysis in a detailed clinical report.

Fiss provides the reader with a comprehensive survey of dream research, scientifically sound and clinically relevant. He describes two major dream research strategies: (1) correlational studies, which yield information on the formation and formal properties of dreaming; and (2) interactional studies, which yield information on the function of

---

[9]Atwood and Stolorow (1984), Tolpin (1983), and Fosshage (1983, 1988) are conspicuous exceptions.

dreaming. The experimental findings, in his view, support the idea that dreams and dreaming serve a self-integrative function and permit construction of an experimentally derived dream psychology strikingly consistent with self psychological formulations.

Greenberg, too, approaches dreams from the perspective of the laboratory research scientist, as well as from that of a clinician. He believes that the results of REM studies may be taken to indicate that dreams are a manifestation of an effort during sleep to integrate information from current experience with past memories. This function, necessary for optimal psychological performance, is directed to construction of schemata which organize complicated behavioral tasks. In his view, the dream shows how this process occurs and how the supraordinate self functions.

Stolorow, in his discussion, criticizes all three authors for diminishing the roles of defense, disguise, and unconscious mental processes in dreams. He presents his own view, giving greater weight to those factors. Tolpin takes a very different tack and begins with a dream of his own. This dream is utilized as a specimen to examine the ideas of the authors (and others) on the multiple functions of dreaming. The section concludes with the responses of Fosshage, Fiss, and Greenberg to the comments of Stolorow and Tolpin.

The next section, devoted to developmental topics, contains two papers (Shane and Shane; Sands) that show to advantage the imbrication of developmental knowledge with clinical theory and practice.

The Shanes observe that the Chicago conference at which they first presented this paper recalled memories of the past and of the paper (Shane and Shane, 1980) they presented a decade ago at the First Annual Conference on the Psychology of the Self. They revisit the past in their choice of topic and provide a new integrative review of recent developmental information. The integration they make is aimed in two directions: (1) the integration of data and developmental schemata derived from infant and child observation, with the data and developmental reconstructions of self psychology; (2) the integration of developmental theory with clinical practice. Their discussion of new developmental observations (particularly those of Daniel Stern), and their sensitive clinical vignettes, can not but edify the reader.

Sands's paper is very different. She begins with concern about an increasingly important clinical syndrome, eating disorders. Noting that such disorders are overwhelmingly (more than 90%) found in women, Sands undertakes an examination of gender differences in the development of the self in order to better understand eating disorder syndromes. She addresses psychological and cultural contributions to the development of the self in girls and women and in the process takes a step towards rectifying the relative inattention to gender issues for which self psychology has been faulted. The reader will reap dual benefits from this paper: a self-psychological perspective on gender differences, and a comprehensive, multifaceted discussion of eating disorders.

The third section contains four papers (Wolf, Ulman and Paul), Muslin, Kay) directed specifically to clinical theory and clinical practice.

Wolf utilizes his long association with self psychology, and his extensive experience in the consulting room, to provide a broad perspective on theoretical and technical aspects of the therapeutic process. Most central is an examination of the continuing conundrum of the curative agent: of the roles of empathic attunement and explanation in the curative process. Wolf addresses the tension between the objective and the subjective, between the intellectual and the emotional, and concludes that "the effect of . . . interpretations rests more on the meaning of the interpretive experience for the analysand . . . than simply its cognitive-verbal content." This paper, the distillation of Wolf's extensive experience with self psychology, will provide the reader with much to contemplate and is sure to stimulate further thought about "How does analysis cure?"

Ulman and Paul examine the now ubiquitous problem of substance abuse. They observe that psychoanalysis is long on theories claiming to explain the etiology and psychodynamics of substance abuse, but short on specifically devised treatment plans. They aim to remedy this and to that end present the reader with an intersubjective absorption hypothesis as an understanding of substance abuse disorders. Two detailed case histories illustrate their thesis "that the selfobject functions of substances may be absorbed within the . . . therapeutic relationship in the form of self object transference fantasies. . . ." The reader interested in the "difficult case" or in substance abuse will be intrigued by their ideas and clinical examples.

Muslin recognizes that advances in knowledge come more by understanding failures than by recounting successes, and he therefore confronts a subject frequently avoided—interminable or failed analyses. He observes that some patients enter into an analytic process, regress, remobilize early wishes, and then progress to a more mature organization of the self; while others do not, but continue to retain the needs and vulnerabilities of archaic levels of organization. Muslin delineates several factors he finds relevant: the intensity of selfobject deprivation, the lack of surrogate selfobjects, the lack of compensatory selfobjects, and unknown biological factors.

Case illustrations highlight two seemingly similar patients who have very different responses to the psychoanalytic process. Muslin, like Freud, is unable to solve this perplexing problem, yet his discussions will be useful to those who struggle with this taxing therapeutic impasse.

Kay's paper is titled "Self Psychological Perspectives on Suicide," but the title does not do justice to the comprehensive scope of this article. Kay provides a review of epidemiological, biological, sociological, and psychoanalytic knowledge about suicide, attempted suicide, and suicidal feelings. He then examines these phenomena from the vantage point of self psychology, which, in his opinion, is a superior perspective for understanding these events, and for helping those afflicted with such desperate feelings and impulses. Of particular importance is traumatic deidealization, which he examines in detail. Two clinical vignettes illustrate the significance of the factors he discusses.

The final section contains three papers united by the application of self-psychological understanding to subjects of general interest and concern, or, correspondingly, directed to the potential enrichment of self-psychological concepts through the application and integration of knowledge derived from other sources and different methodologies.

Corbett and Kugler provide a scholarly comparison of Jung's concept of the self with that of Kohut. They find the theories to some degree complementary and believe that Jung's concepts provide a useful backdrop against which to understand the later formulations of Kohut. A summary of Kohut's major contributions to the psychology of the self is presented, followed by a detailed review of Jung's concept of the self. The interface between Jung and Kohut is explored, with particular attention to their differing views on the origin and evolution of the self. This erudite essay presents a view of the self from a different perspective and therefore has much to recommend it.

Kriegman and Slavin address the same problem as did Muslin— the powerful sources of resistance to change and the tendency to repeat apparently maladaptive patterns of behavior. Their approach is quite different from Muslin's, as they consider biological factors and evolutionary theory, as well as psychoanalytic explanations (Freud's death instinct, Fenichel's return to the pleasure principle, Kohut's self psychological formulations). They conclude that such concepts as the death instinct, blind repetition, and primary masochism cannot refer to characteristics of adaptive evolutionary value and are unlikely to have become universal parts of our inborn species equipment. Rather, they argue, these persistent repetitions can be better understood as an adaptive search for selfobjects required for the development and cohesion of the self. Kriegman and Slavin cite the clinical approaches of Brandchaft and A. Ornstein, with which they are in general agreement, and add their own recommendations for addressing these repetitions and negative therapeutic reactions.

The final paper, "The Search for the Self of the Future Analyst," is timely, directed to the future, yet rooted firmly in the past. Kligerman addresses many topics: (1) the selection of candidates for analytic training, the essential personal qualities of the analyst, the effects of analytic work on the analyst; (2) the curative factors in the psychoanalytic and psychotherapeutic processes; (3) his understanding of Kohut's creative genius. This paper is truly original, as it is derived from Kligerman's intimate personal knowledge of Kohut, as well as from his own clinical insight and theoretical thought. It can not fail to be of interest to anyone who knew Kohut or is interested in him and his contributions to psychoanalysis.

Self psychology is now firmly established as an important perspective on human development and human suffering. Few in the mental health fields are unaware of self psychology. Some accept none of its ideas. More accept some of its ideas. A few accept too many. Most labor to improve them.

This introduction, and this volume, are directed to all, in the hope they will benefit from greater understanding and their thinking will be stimulated by the ideas contained herein and that they, in turn, will be able to add their own ideas to our expanding theory.

REFERENCES

Atwood, G. & Stolorow, R. (1984), *Structures of Subjectivity*. Hillsdale, NJ: The Analytic Press.

Bacal, H. (1985), Optimal responsiveness and the therapeutic process. In: *Progress in Self Psychology*, Vol. 1, ed. A. Goldberg. New York: Guilford Press, pp. 202–227.

———— (1988), Reflections on "Optimum Frustration." In: *Learning from Kohut*, ed. A. Goldberg. Hillsdale, NJ: The Analytic Press, pp. 127–131.

Basch, M. F. (1976), The concept of affect: A re-examination. *J. Amer. Psychoanal. Assn.*, 24:759–777.

———— (1981), Selfobject disorders and psychoanalytic theory: A historical perspective. *J. Amer. Psychoanal. Assn.*, 29:337–351.

———— (1983a), Empathic understanding: A review of the concept and some theoretical considerations. *J. Amer. Psychoanal. Assn.*, 31:101–126.

———— (1983b), Affect and the analyst. *Psychoanal. Inq.*, 3:691–703.

———— (1984a), The selfobject theory of motivation and the history of psychoanalysis.

In: *Kohut's Legacy*, ed. P. E. Stepansky & A. Goldberg. Hillsdale, NJ: The Analytic Press, pp. 3–17.

—— (1984b), Selfobjects and selfobject transference: Theoretical implications. In: *Kohut's Legacy*, ed. P. E. Stepansky & A. Goldberg. Hillsdale, NJ: The Analytic Press, pp. 21–41.

—— (1986), Clinical theory and metapsychology: Incompatible or complementary? *Psychoanal. Rev.*, 73:261–271.

Beebe, B. & Lachmann, F. M. (1988), Mother-infant mutual influence and precursors of psychic structure. In: *Progress in Self Psychology*, Vol. 3, ed. A. Goldberg. New York: Guilford Press, pp. 3–25.

Bowlby, J. (1969), *Attachment and Loss*, Vol. 1. New York: Basic Books.

Cooper, A. (1988), Changes in psychoanalytic ideas: Transference interpretation. *J. Amer. Psychoanal. Assn.*, 35:77–98.

Demos, E. V. (1988), Affect and the development of the self: A new frontier. In: *The Future of Psychoanalysis*, ed. A. Goldberg. New York: International Universities Press, pp. 27–53.

Fosshage, J. (1983), The psychological function of dreams: a revised psychoanalytic perspective. *Psychoanal. & Contemp. Thought*, 6:641–669.

—— (1988), Dream interpretation revisited. In: *Progress in Self Psychology*, Vol. 3, ed. A. Goldberg. New York: Guilford Press, pp. 161–175.

Freud, S. (1912), Recommendations to physicians practicing psycho-analysis. *Standard Edition*, 12:109–120. London: Hogarth Press, 1958.

—— (1914), On narcissism: An introduction. *Standard Edition*, 14:67–102. London: Hogarth Press, 1957.

—— (1915), Observations on transference-love. *Standard Edition*, 12:157–171. London: Hogarth Press, 1958.

—— (1917), Mourning and melancholia. *Standard Edition*, 14:237–238. London: Hogarth Press, 1957.

—— (1921), Group psychology and the analysis of the ego. *Standard Edition*, 18:69–143.

Goldberg, A. (1988), *A Fresh Look at Psychoanalysis*. Hillsdale, NJ: The Analytic Press.

Kohut, H. (1959), Introspection, empathy and psychoanalysis. In: *The Search for the Self*, Vol. 1, ed. P. Ornstein. New York: International Universities Press, 1978, pp. 205–232.

—— (1966), Forms and transformations of narcissism. *J. Amer. Psychoanal. Assn.*, 14:243–272.

—— (1971), *The Analysis of the Self*. New York: International Universities Press.

—— (1977), *The Restoration of the Self*. New York: International Universities Press.

—— (1984), *How Does Analysis Cure?* ed. A. Goldberg & P. E. Stepansky. Chicago: University of Chicago Press.

Leider, R. J. (1983), Analytic neutrality—a historical review. *Psychoanal. Inq.*, 3:665–674.

—— (1988), Letter to the editor. *J. Amer. Psychoanal. Assn.*, 36:560–564.

Lichtenberg, J. (1983), *Psychoanalysis and Infant Research*. Hillsdale, NJ: The Analytic Press.

—— (1985), Mirrors and mirroring: Developmental experiences. *Psychoanal. Inq.*, 5:199–231.

—— (1989), *Psychoanalysis and Motivation*. Hillsdale, NJ: The Analytic Press.

Ornstein, A. (1981), Self pathology in childhood: Developmental and clinical considerations. *Psychiat. Clin. N. Amer.*, 4:435–453.

—— (1983), Fantasy or reality? The unsettled question in pathogenesis and reconstruction in psychoanalysis. In: *The Future of Psychoanalysis*, ed. A. Goldberg. New York: International Universities Press, pp. 381–396.

—— (1984), Psychoanalytic psychotherapy: A contemporary perspective. In: *Kohut's Legacy*, ed. P. E. Stepansky & A. Goldberg. Hillsdale, NJ: The Analytic Press, pp. 171–181.

Ornstein, P. & Ornstein, A. (1980), Formulating interpretations in clinical psychoanalysis. *Internat. J. Psycho-Anal.*, 63:395–408.

Papousek, H. & Papousek, M. (1979), The infant's fundamental adaptive response system in social interaction. In: *Origins of the Infant's Social Responsiveness*, ed. E. Thoman. Hillsdale, NJ: Lawrence Erlbaum Associates, pp. 175–208.

Reed, G. (1987), Rules of clinical understanding in classical psychoanalysis and in self psychology: A comparison. *J. Amer. Psychoanal. Assn.*, 35:421–446.

Shane, M. & Shane, E. (1980), Psychoanalytic developmental theories of the self: An integration. In: *Advances in Self Psychology*, ed. A. Goldberg. New York: International Universities Press, pp. 19–46.

—— (1986), Self change and development in the analysis of an adolescent patient. In: *Progress in Self Psychology*, Vol. 2, ed. A. Goldberg. New York: Guilford Press, pp. 142–160.

—— (1988), Pathways to integration: Adding to the self psychology model. In: *Learning from Kohut*, ed. A. Goldberg. Hillsdale, NJ: The Analytic Press, pp. 71–78.

Stern, D. (1985), *The Interpersonal World of the Infant*. New York: Basic Books.

Stolorow, R. (1988), Integrating self psychology and classical psychoanalysis: An experience-near approach. In: *Learning from Kohut*, ed. A. Goldberg. Hillsdale, NJ: The Analytic Press, pp. 63–70.

—— Brandchaft, B. & Atwood, G. (1987), *Psychoanalytic Treatment*. Hillsdale, NJ: The Analytic Press.

Terman, D. (1988), Optimal frustration: Structuralization and the therapeutic process. In: *Learning from Kohut*, ed. A. Goldberg. Hillsdale, NJ: The Analytic Press, pp. 113–125.

Tolpin, M. (1971), On the beginnings of a cohesive self. *The Psychoanlytic Study of the Child*, 25:273–305. New York: International Universities Press.

—— (1978), Selfobjects and oedipal objects: A crucial developmental distinction. *The Psychoanalytic Study of the Child*, 33:167–184. New Haven: Yale University Press.

—— (1986), The self and its selfobject: A different baby. In: *Progress in Self Psychology*, Vol. 2, ed. A. Goldberg. New York: Guilford Press, pp. 202–227.

—— & Kohut, H. (1979), The psychopathology of the first years of life: Disorders of the self. In: *The Course of Life*, ed. S. Greenspan & G. Pollock. Washington, DC: US Gov. Printing Off.

Tolpin, P. (1983), Self psychology and the interpretation of dreams. In: *The Future of Psychoanalysis*, ed. A. Goldberg. New York: International Universities Press, pp. 255–271.

Wolf, E. S. (1976), Ambience and abstinence. In: *The Annual of Psychoanalysis*, 4:101–115. New York: International Universities Press.

—— (1983). Aspects of neutrality. *Psychoanal. Inq.*, 3:675–690.

—— (1986), Discrepancies between analysand and analyst in experiencing the analysis. In: *Progress in Self Psychology*, Vol. 2, ed. A. Goldberg. New York: Guilford Press, pp. 84–94.

DIMENSIONS OF SELF EXPERIENCE

Progress in Self Psychology
Volume 5

Dreams

Chapter 1

The Developmental Function of Dreaming Mentation: Clinical Implications

James L. Fosshage

All too typically, the dream has been viewed as a product, an object to be examined from a waking perspective. Thus, from the vantage point of the classical model, dreaming deviations from the waking state are typically not viewed as directly revelatory of the subjective state, but as defensive phenomena or as intricate, complex, disguised wish-fulfillments and conflicts pertaining to those wishes. Consequently, Greenson, as I have discussed in detail elsewhere (Fosshage, 1987a), viewed the progressive elements in Mr. M's dream that contributed to his emergence from a depressed state as solely defensive wish-fulfillments because they did not correspond with the patient's prevailing waking state of depression. Within the classical model the posited ubiquity of defensive operations in the formation of dreams and the correspondent manifest-latent content distinction has, through endless translations of dream imagery, cast upon dreams a waking bias that often precludes an in-depth understanding of the dreaming experience itself.

A reported dream is a waking memory of a mentational process that occurred during sleep. Just as Kohut (1959) more clearly formulated for us the importance of perceiving from within the patient's subjective frame of reference, we also need to understand the dream from within the dreamer's experiential frame of reference. Viewing dreaming as a mentational process positions us more empathically to appreciate the multiple functions and complexity of the dreamer's efforts. From this vantage point, I have proposed a revised psycho-

3

analytic model of the psychological function of dreams. Essential features of this model are as follows (for a detailed presentation see Fosshage, 1983, 1987a; Fosshage and Loew, 1987): 1) Primary process is redefined as imagistic mentation that serves "an over-all integrative and synthetic function" (Fosshage, 1983, p. 689). 2) The supraordinate function of dreaming mentation is the development, maintenance (regulation), and restoration of psychic processes and organization. More specifically, dreaming mentation may function to envision and, therefore, develop and consolidate emergent psychological configurations, such as changes in self and object images. Dreaming may contribute to the momentary resolution of intrapsychic conflict either through the restoration of primary organizational patterns or through a creative and newly emergent reorganization. And dreaming may contribute to the regulation of self-esteem, as well as sexual, aggressive, and other processes wherein wish-fulfillment (instead of a discharge or defensive operation) is viewed as a regulatory process. 3) The manifest-latent content distinction that posits the ubiquitous operation of defensive functioning in dream formation is eschewed and, in turn, the reported dream is referred to as the *dream content that may or may not involve defensive operations;* 4) Dreaming mentation, like waking mentation, *varies in clarity, significance, and functional success.*

Some of the technical implications of this revised model are summarized as follows (for a more complete explication, see Fosshage, 1983, 1987a, b; Fosshage and Loew, 1987): 1) The foremost task is to illuminate as fully as possible the *experience* of the dreamer within the dream, not just the reporter's waking reaction to the dream, and to be particularly alert to similarities and differences between dreaming and waking organizations. 2) "Dream figures and images are typically seen not as the product of disguise, but rather as poignant organizational nodal points for particular affective reactions or thematic experiences " (Fosshage, 1987b, p. 31). Accordingly, rather than translating these images to overcome their disguise, we need to elucidate their specific meanings and use within the dream language. 3) ". . . in contrast to the common assumption that the analyst is always, at least latently, in the dream; with the revised model the analyst is never *assumed* to be present in the dream unless he or she actually appears (or unless the dreamer, of course, directly connects the dream image to the analyst). However, because the primary organizational patterns structure both dreams as well as the transferential relationship, the analytic discussion, *without requiring* translation of dream images, can focus in accordance with the patient's associations on the particular organizational pattern as it emerges in the dream as well as in the transference" (Fosshage, 1987a, p. 165; see Hoffman, 1983, and Stolorow and Lachmann, 1984/85, for a reconceptualization of transference). 4) Rather than repeatedly requesting the patient to associate to single elements of the dream, isolated from the context of the dream, which tends to disrupt and fragment the dreamer's experience of the dream, we need generally to comprehend the series of images, as if they were words constituting a sentence, and the overall dream drama, like sentences forming a story. And 5) because dreaming mentation provides an overall organizing function, it is crucially important to make use of these mentational processes with all our patients regardless of the severity of disturbance.

Because dreaming occurs when stimuli from, and immediate reactions (including correspondent defensive maneuvers) to, the external world are minimized, developmental strivings and correspondent incremental developmental steps are frequently operative and apparent in the dreaming experience. The conceptualization of the developmental function of dreaming within the revised psychoanalytic model enables us to recognize and utilize the dream's developmental increments to further their consolidation.

The following clinical example illustrates the developmental function of dreaming.

CASE ILLUSTRATION

At the time the following dream was reported, the patient, whom I will call Tamara, had been in psychoanalysis for almost two years.

At the beginning of treatment, Tamara was 28 years old, married for several years, and the mother of a young son. She complained of prolonged periods of intense depression, hopelessness, and despair, which reportedly had been exacerbated in a recent previous three-year analysis. She struck me as highly intelligent and articulate, naturally attractive, and, in spite of her depression and wariness, emotionally available and desperately searching for help.

Tamara had been raised in a large family with, reportedly, a very successful, powerful, explosively tyrannical, and vulnerable father and a religiously intense mother, who had developed a severe paranoid disturbance during the middle parts of Tamara's childhood. Tamara's feeling of emotional abandonment by her mother was telescoped in an early memory from the age of three, when she was hospitalized for an unknown physical illness and was not visited by mother for three days, engendering a deep distrust. Tamara's father had selected her as his special one, turning to her for responsiveness to his particular needs in what Tamara now termed a "self-interested love." She came from a deeply religious background and at times experienced intense visions of God, envisioning, particularly during stressful times, an idealized figure to whom she could turn for guidance.

An intense connection was quickly formed in the analytic relationship with marked idealizing and mirroring components. It was on the basis of these components, as well as the management of the subsequent inevitable, and at times severe, ruptures that new hope emerged, and the depression gradually lifted as Tamara began to consolidate a more positive and cohesive sense of self in conjunction with a sense of the other as a reliably caring person. Synchronous with this development was a gradual reemergence, and a more direct expression, of her needs and desires that resulted both in her return to graduate school and a growing awareness of and objection to, from her vantage point, her husband's lack of responsiveness, depression, and negativity. Whereas previously she had often submitted to his angry scapegoating of her, which resulted in a self-depletion as well as a self-protective withdrawal and which, in turn, exacerbated the problematic marital interaction (for example, her withdrawal would further irritate her husband), she now began, often quite angrily, to assert herself. She started painfully to question the basis of her marriage; she realized that she had married her husband partially to accommodate her mother's wishes. For three or four months prior to the following dream, Tamara more directly confronted her husband, mobilizing him to seek treatment. Intense marital conflict persisted and culminated, just prior to the dream, in a brief physical separation, which she initiated to give herself time "to think."

The session began with Tamara relating the dream. The dream reveals the structural changes occurring through the employment of an idealized transference. As will become evident, I viewed this as an idealized selfobject transference, primarily motivated by developmental need and striving, because of its self-enhancing quality (in contrast to an idealized transference either serving a defensive function or emerging as a repetitive relational pattern, both of which ultimately would be self-limiting or self-depleting).

I will first present the dream and some of the detailed notes from this and the next day's session, and then I will summarize the dream's primary meaning, function, and linkage to her waking life. My discussion will be limited to the major themes. The dream was as follows:

I was driving in a car with Bryan [her husband] and mother. The car had broken down. Bryan was trying to repair it, but without success. I wasn't sure where we were going, but I had to be somewhere. I got out of the car and left them with the car. I found a horse stable and I went inside and there was this wonderful stallion, strong and intelligent, but it belonged to someone else. But I decided that I would borrow it and it was okay to do that. I got on this horse and continued on my way. A lot of the riding was on the freeway with lots of traffic, and the cars were at a standstill. But with this horse, it didn't make any difference. I rode very quickly through this traffic—galloping the whole way and the horse knew the way. I didn't have to control the horse and we arrived within two hours. And when I got there, I got off the horse.

And then this strange thing occurred to me—I would have to return the horse and I would lose all the ground I had made. It was a strange moment to have these two things occurring at the same time. But some man who was there said, "Don't worry about it. The horse can go back on his own; he knows his way back." So I just let the horse go. I knew it was a smart horse and it would be okay.

I was at a ballet audition—that was my destination. It was an audition to join a ballet company. And I was in the building and in a room next to a room where the auditions were being held. I could hear people on the other side of the wall warming up. I felt very confident that I was going to audition well and be accepted into the company. But then I had a wave of doubt that swept across me and said, "How can I think I'll be accepted when I haven't danced in 10 or 11 years?" I said it to a man who was with me. He said to me or I said to him, "That's okay. I'm sure I can do it still," and a feeling of total confidence came back.

Tamara expressed her good feelings about the dream. She then referred to the first part, in which "some sense of responsibility undoes my going forward; and, if I can trust that everything will be all right, then I can keep going forward." She then continued, "The last thing [referring to ballet dancing] I knew I wanted to do, not because of Mother and not because of God." Tamara had previously described a traumatic occurrence when she was eleven. She had felt utterly humiliated when her mother failed to provide her with the appropriate ballet clothes and she had to dance in old socks at an audition for a well-known ballet school in a foreign country. She now added, "I didn't tell you about the incident when I was humiliated, but I was accepted. The reason I didn't go was that during the previous year, the [foreign] teacher didn't accept the fact that I couldn't speak the language and gave me assignments I just couldn't do. I felt terribly humiliated. When I was accepted at the conservatory, I had to study in [the foreign language] and dance there, but I didn't want to repeat the experience—the choice was that or the American school. I wanted to dance, but it was connected to something so horrible." She reiterated emphatically, "It was the last time I knew what I wanted to do." I noted to myself that Tamara was experiencing herself more as an active agent and less victimized in the ballet story.

Tamara continued, "In the second part of the dream, I know I can do what I needed to do." I reflected, "You're finding your direction and confidence; you can do what you want to do." We were primarily focusing on the experience of the dreamer with which Tamara was affectively resonating in her waking state; and, although we would want further amplification of this theme in her current waking life, I, at this juncture, inquired about her experience of the stallion in the dream. She replied, "Either you or God or some combination. He was very male. I had some responsibility to the horse and its owner. It wasn't mine, but I had to take care of the horse and its owner." I inquired if she could relate to this in her waking life. She responded, "I feel very responsible to Bryan. I'm anxious about coming here [i.e., to the place where she was now living]. I feel I'll have to go back to Bryan. I don't want to sell the house, and for Matthew [her son]. I want to stay here until I know what I want, but it will be undone. Bryan is not the stallion—I don't feel that he can take care of himself." Tamara was experiencing a responsibility to Bryan, who, like the significant persons of her past, she felt could not take care of himself. However, she was realizing in her dreaming mentation that the other person, in this case the stallion, could take care of himself, enabling her to pursue her own direction. As she proceeded to discuss her relationship to Bryan and the frightening ramifications of a possible marital separation, she recounted how during this painfully conflictual time she had initially turned to God for aid but then had rejected his counsel, desiring to take control of her destiny—a waking reflection that corresponded with her increasing sense of control in the dream.

Tamara opened the next session by saying, "I was afraid that you were angry with me. The stallion in the dream is definitely you. Like I have a responsibility to you—like I can't stay where you brought me." I reflected, "You seem to feel that I have an agenda for you for which you have to be responsible." She responded affirmatively, "At times I feel I have to leave everything." Now in the analytic relationship Tamara was reexperiencing that I, too, had an agenda that she must accommodate in order to maintain the necessary selfobject tie. To facilitate the integration of the change in the organizational pattern that had occurred in her dream, I pointed out the difference between her waking and dreaming states: "So you begin to feel that I, too, have an agenda and to worry about doing enough for me; but in the dream you realize that you don't have to worry about the stallion, that the stallion can take care of himself. Free of that responsibility, you could then proceed to the ballet audition and to your destination." Tamara acknowledged this new development but then replied, at first with a smile implying some perspective, "I feel you do have an agenda. You're still secretly in love with me and you want me to get on with it. . . . But I know this [the separation from her husband] is what I want. I want to leave 'cause I don't want to be where I am—I'd rather find a better relationship. I don't believe I should have what I want. It's not right at the expense of someone else. To want for yourself is wrong and at Bryan's expense is wrong."

Tamara first expressed that my "secret love" for her required her accommodation to *my* agenda, which, in this case, she momentarily felt was to leave her husband—a repetition of the problematic relational pattern. In the fluidity of the moment, however, she quickly moved from this position to one of self-assertion and to *her* agenda, "But I know this is what I want."[1] But then she reexperienced this assertion to be at the other's, namely Bryan's, expense. I felt that Tamara was struggling to determine her direction; but within an intense and needed relationship, particularly needed at this time, she was prone to experience the primary focus as shifting to the other and the other's agenda even though it would be at her expense. This was a pattern that was occurring in both the marital and analytic relationships. At one point in our discussion, we again connected this pattern historically to her relationships with her mother and father wherein she deeply felt a responsibility for them and for their agendas, experiencing that any self-focus detracted from them, was at their expense, and was wrong. The intense conflictual pain and guilt evoked by her contemplation of a marital separation appeared to precipitate a more forceful emergence of this older configuration of accommodation within the transference because of the heightened need for the selfobject tie, the content of which, in this instance, was for her to feel secretly loved by me. All of this understandably impeded the integration of the new developments in the dream. Her dream vision, however, provided a potently imaged nucleus of change that would serve as a foundation for future work and structural change.

[1]These were viewed as shifting self-states, namely, from a state of accommodation to one of self-assertion, each in need of recognition, rather than either serving as a defense against the other, a formulation that would implicitly credit one state as more "basic" at the expense of the other.

To summarize the dream: Tamara was in a car with her husband and mother and the car had broken down. Tamara was unsure where they were going, but, feeling an internal impetus to be somewhere, she left the car and her husband and mother to seek another way. She found a stallion[2] and, even though ". . . it belonged to someone else . . . I decided that I would borrow it and it was okay to do that . . . , possibly relating to her initial disappointment in finding out that her analyst was married (which she had learned from the referral source). Nevertheless, "I got on this horse and continued on my way." She was able to use the analyst and the analysis to move through the impasse in her life ("the cars were at a standstill").

Upon arrival, the dreamer became concerned about returning the horse and thus reverse her progress—a prominent sense of the other's requiring caretaking at her expense, which had been a dominant theme in her life. A man reassures her that the stallion "knows his way back and can go back on his own," *a new experience* that enables her to proceed to her destination. This new recognition that the stallion can take care of himself enables her to move from a responsible and caretaking position at the expense of herself to a rediscovery of her vital internal direction. Tamara arrives at her destination. Gaining strength and confidence with the aid of a supportive and less idealized man (whom she also associated to the analyst, although "he was younger and more peerlike"), she prepares to audition again (a return to a poignant time in memory when development was derailed) and to rectify imagistically what had been in the past, at a time when she was too fragile, a humiliating defeat resulting in the loss of her direction. *This new (momentary) realization that the stallion can take care of himself, the rediscovery of her internal direction, and the consolidation of her confidence are the developmental movements furthered through the dreaming mentational process.*[3]

The dream is remarkable in its clarity and in its sweeping imagistic portrayal of the emergent and ongoing changes in her experience of herself, the analyst, and the analytic relationship. Utilizing her analytic experience, she is now able to envision, at least momentarily, an idealized stallion to transport her through a congested impasse, a resolution of the transferential theme of accommodation, a rediscov-

[2]I later learned that horses had been an important part of Tamara's childhood, illuminating further the selection and meaning of the stallion image.

[3]Note also that these themes and developments are apparent in the dream content itself and do not require invoking the concept of disguise or the translation of dream images. Accordingly, the meanings and affective potency of the particular images, for example, a stallion, can be more fully appreciated and elucidated. The transference is easily addressed in this instance through the patient's direct associations.

ery of her internal direction, and an increasing capacity, aided by the image of a supportive man, for regulating her confidence. At the end of the dream she begins to take over this latter function as she says, "He said to me or I said to him, 'That's okay. I'm sure I can do it still,' and a feeling of total confidence came back."[4]

Tamara's initial clarity about the new realization in the dream—"some sense of responsibility undoes my going forward; and, if I can trust that everything will be all right, then I can keep going forward"—was confounded and difficult to integrate in the wake of her most conflictual immediate life situation and her more familiar waking patterns of organization. Our task, however, is not to abnegate those important momentary developments emergent in the dream, which do not necessarily correspond with the waking state, by rendering them merely a defensive disguise of waking "reality," but to use these developmental movements, which dreaming mentation is so well positioned to promote, to further within the psychoanalytic arena the person's developmental course.

REFERENCES

Fosshage, J. (1983), The psychological function of dreams: A revised psychoanalytic perspective. *Psychoanal. Contemp. Thought*, 6:641–669.
———— (1987a), Dream interpretation revisited. In: *Frontiers in Self Psychology*, ed. A. Goldberg. Hillsdale, NJ: The Analytic Press, pp. 161–175
———— (1987b), New vistas in dream interpretation. In: *Dreams in New Perspective*, ed. M. Glucksman & S. Warner. New York: Human Sciences Press, pp. 23–43.
———— Loew, C. ed. (1987), *Dream Interpretation*. Great Neck, NY: PMA.
Hoffman, I. (1983), The patient as interpretor of the analyst's experience. *Contemp. Psychoanal.*, 19:389–422
Kohut, H. (1959), Introspection, empathy and psychoanalysis. In: *The Search for the Self*, Vol. 1, ed. P. Ornstein. New York: International Universities Press, 1978, pp. 205–232.
———— (1984), *How Does Analysis Cure?* ed. A. Goldberg & P. E. Stepansky. Chicago: University of Chicago Press.
Stolorow, R. & Lachmann, F. (1984/85), Transference: The future of an illusion. In: *The Annual of Psychoanalysis*. New York: International Universities Press, pp. 19–38.

---

[4]The shift in pronouns is a graphic illustration of the shift from the use of the idealized other to an increased reliance on oneself to provide these regulatory functions.

Chapter 2

An Experimental Self Psychology of Dreaming: Clinical and Theoretical Applications

Harry Fiss

In this paper I will describe a number of experimental strategies that my colleagues and I have been using over the years for the study of dreaming. I will describe them from the point of view of self psychology.

What appeals to me about self psychology is, among other things, that its formulations do not depend on physiological models of the nervous system. They are purely psychological in nature and are applicable to a wide spectrum of clinical phenomena. In fact, I am convinced that a marriage between dream research and self psychology will produce a healthy offspring.

It is a peculiar historical anomaly that even though sleep research has made a profound impact on clinical practice, dream research has had remarkably little influence on clinical activity. This is partly because the dream researcher has been so obsessed with reducing everything to biological processes that he has come to look at the dream pretty much as a marginal, even discardable, epiphenomenon. Thus, a huge gap separates the dream researcher from the clinician (Fiss, 1984, 1986). It is as though we have lost sight of the fact that it is not brains that dream but people.

However, the gap is not unbridgeable. It *is* possible to do dream research that is both scientifically sound and clinically relevant. But it has to be research that uses psychological constructs for theorizing and that studies dreaming as a psychological event in its own right, independent of its underlying neurophysiology. A scientist looking

13

into the brain of a dreaming man will never be able to tell from these neural events what the man is dreaming about.

THE SELF-COHESIVE FUNCTION OF DREAMING

Once such an experimental psychology of dreaming is developed, a curious thing happens: the data that emerge are strikingly consistent with self psychology, that is, they easily lend themselves to interpretation in self-psychological terms and at the same time also support self-psychological conceptions. This possibility of linking dream research to self psychology, of laying the groundwork for an experimental self psychology of dreaming, is a prospect that strikes me as extremely exciting.

Before proceeding any further, let me make an important distinction between two principal research strategies that have produced the data base for this new psychology of dreaming. On one hand, we have a whole group of *correlational studies* seeking to explore mind-body correspondences, for example, studies of the relationship between eye movement activity and dream content; on the other hand, there is a large group of investigations of cause-and-effect relationships that I call *interactional*. Now, the correlational studies have by and large yielded information on the nature, origin, and formal properties of dreaming, in other words, on the *formation* of dreaming. They have demonstrated, for instance, that mental activity occurs in all stages of sleep, not only in REM, and that dreams do in fact occur and are not just fabricated in the process of awakening. On the other hand, studies of causal relationships have been useful in illuminating the *function* of dreaming. It is this second group of studies that I find particularly relevant to self psychology. Within this group we must also make an important distinction: we must distinguish between those interactional studies which have yielded *indirect* evidence and those which have provided us with *direct* evidence that dreaming serves a self-integrating function. By indirect evidence I mean evidence that focuses on REM sleep rather than on dream content and therefore depends on the assumed, but imperfect, correlation between REM and dreaming; direct evidence focuses exclusively on dream content and does not depend on this association (Fiss, 1986).

Indirect Evidence

Indirect evidence for the self-cohesive function of dreaming comes from two types of research strategies: (1) REM-deprivation studies and

(2) studies of the effects of certain presleep manipulations on REM characteristics. Let me briefly review the REM-deprivation studies first.

When subjects are awakened at the onset of every REM period over the course of several nights, a by now well-known compensatory increase in REM activity occurs during a subsequent recovery period when subjects are permitted to sleep without interruption (Dement, 1960). This so-called rebound effect has generally been considered to be evidence of a biological need for REM sleep and, indirectly, for dreaming. Of interest to self psychology, however, and I will explain why later, are the effects of REM deprivation on *waking* behavior. REM-deprived subjects, both human and animal, have repeatedly been shown to exhibit behavior that is best described as drive dominated or driven; they show increased anxiety and irritability, voracious appetite, and heightened sexual and aggressive behavior (Dement and Fisher, 1963; Dement et al., 1967; Morden et al., 1968). Concomitant with these manifestations of drive intensification, REM deprivation has also been noted to result in impaired adaptation. Thus, REM-deprived subjects show confusion, memory loss, learning decrements, and difficulty in concentrating (Fishbein, McGaugh, and Swarz, 1971; Pearlman, 1971; Grieser, Greenberg and Harrison, 1972). REM deprivation has also been shown to interfere with the ability to cope with stressful stimuli (Greenberg, Pillard, and Pearlman, 1972). Thus, when we look at the effects of REM deprivation on waking behavior, we can see why REM sleep is so important that Ss need to make up for it when it is taken away: REM sleep, and presumably dreaming, appears to play a critical role in drive regulation, memory consolidation, learning, information processing, and adaptation to stress.

The second experimental strategy that has provided indirect evidence of the dream's adaptive value involves alterations in the presleep environment that present the subject with a challenging or stressful task to be mastered and the assessment of the effects of this manipulation on sleep. For example, when subjects wear prismatic glasses that reverse the visual field—a formidable task—they manifest a marked increase in the amount of time they spend in REM sleep, but only during the difficult initial adjustment period; once the subjects are used to wearing the prisms and their surroundings look normal again, their REM time drops back to normal (Zimmerman, Stoyva, and Metcalf, 1970). REM time has also been found to increase when aphasic patients begin to regain their language function following rehabilitation training (Greenberg and Dewan, 1969). More recently, English-speaking Canadian students who took an intensive crash course in French showed marked elevations in REM sleep during the duration of the course, but only when their learning activity was effective (DeKonnick et al., 1978). Animal studies also indicate that REM time increases as a function of new learning, including maze learning and the learning of discriminatory and avoidance responses (McGinty, 1969; Lucero, 1970; Fishbein, Kastaniotis, and Chattman, 1974; Lecas, 1976).

Direct Evidence

Dream research that offers more direct evidence of the dream's self-integrative function comes from studies of dream content. They too involve some kind of presleep manipulation or specifiable antecedent condition. And again there are two basic paradigms: one I call "dream enhancement" (DE), the other "dream incorporation." Both, incidentally, strongly suggest that dreams do not merely reflect what is already going on in us, but that they actively transform or change a person in a predictable fashion, an assumption that is still being hotly contested.

In the "enhancement" design, subjects are not deprived of their REM periods or dreams but are asked to *focus their attention* on their dreams and their dream content. Thus, rather than being eliminated, dreams are being highlighted. For example, Cartwright, Tipton, and Wicklund (1980) demonstrated that patients trained to attend to their REM dreams remained in treatment longer and made better progress than did patients trained to attend to their non-REM dreams. Similar findings are reported by Fiss and Litchman (1976), whose experiment was like a crash program, designed to "immerse" subjects in their dreams. It maximized dream recall and minimized dream forgetting by having the subjects, who were all psychiatric outpatients, listen attentively to a playback of their own dreams recorded in the laboratory the night before and by encouraging them to reflect on their dreams as much as possible during waking hours. (No dreams were interpreted). Analysis of the data revealed that all subjects showed greater symptom reduction and higher levels of self-awareness after REM-DE than after non-REM-DE. It appears, therefore, that REM dreams, in contrast to other types of fantasy activity, play a unique role in the regulation and integration of the self. Thus, the ancient notion that dreams have curative value does indeed have empirical validity. However, given the complexity and difficulty of the task of proving this, it is hardly surprising that such attempts have been few in number and late in coming.

I would now like to conclude this brief review of dream research by saying a few words about studies using the dream *incorporation* paradigm. In this paradigm, the function of dreaming is investigated not by highlighting dream content but by influencing it and then measuring the effect of this influence on postsleep behavior, using dream content as an independent variable, so to say.

A classic example of this type of investigation is a study by Cohen and Cox (1975), whose subjects were exposed to a stressful failure experience just prior to going to sleep. Those subjects who incorporated the failure experience into their dream content felt better about the experience the next day and were more willing to give it another try than subjects who did not incorporate it.

In an attempt to demonstrate that the dream serves a memory-consolidating function (Fiss, Kremer, and Litchman, 1977), I posed the question some time ago whether incorporating a presleep stimulus would facilitate its subsequent recall. The stimulus in this case was a vivid story about a sea monster attacking a sinking ship. The subjects read the story before going to bed and were instructed to visualize it while falling asleep. Their dream reports were collected by means of the standard REM-awakening technique. As predicted, the story not only influenced the subjects' dreams, but, more important, dreaming about the story actually facilitated its recall the next morning, quite independently of REM physiology. Thus, the hypothesis that dreaming serves a mnemonic function of its own was clearly confirmed.

This completes my unavoidably sketchy review of the relevant dream literature. I have indicated that dream deprivation is causally related to drive intensification and maladaptive behavior and, conversely, that increased dreaming seems to facilitate adaptive and self-preserving behavior. Finally, evidence based only on dream-content analysis has shown that focusing on REM dreams is therapeutically more beneficial than focusing on non-REM dreams; that dreaming about a failure experience helps us cope with it more effectively; and that dreaming about a presleep stimulus facilitates its recall.

DREAMS AND SELF PSYCHOLOGY

Although Kohut makes extensive use of dream *interpretation*, he was not, like Freud, a systematizer in the sense of studying dreams to advance our knowledge of the dream *process*. Thus, we find precious little in Kohut's writings that lends itself to a construction of a dream theory. It is not Kohut himself but his followers who have begun to formulate new and testable propositions about the dream process.

The closest Kohut comes to theorizing about dreaming is his concept of the "self-state" dream, which, according to Kohut (1977), portrays the dreamer's "dread" of the dissolution of the self (p. 109). This conceptualization seems far too narrow to me. Why not consider *all* dreams to be "self-state" dreams, some portending self-dissolution perhaps, others self-integration, some merely reflecting the state of the self, others influencing the state of the self?

In line with this thinking, Atwood and Stolorow (1984) have extended Kohut's formulation and proposed that dream images not only maintain the organization of the self in the face of the threat of self-dissolution, but also consolidate new, emerging structures. Thus, according to Atwood and Stolorow, dream imagery serves not one but two functions: (1) to maintain the organization of a person's subjective world in situations in which already existing structures are beginning to break down, and (2) to stabilize relatively weak or unformed structures that are still in the process of coming into being (p. 114).

Fosshage (1983) has expanded this model to include, in addition to the self-maintenance function of dreaming, a developmental function. From his perspective, dreaming not only maintains psychic structures but also contributes to the development of new organizations.

We also need to attribute a third major function to the process of dreaming: self-restoration. When structures have disintegrated or become fragmented, dreaming serves to restore these organizations so that they can become viable once again.

In summary, it is useful, as Fosshage (1988) suggests, to discuss dreaming from a self-psychological perspective in terms of its contribution to the *development, maintenance,* and *restoration* of the self. This point of view provides us with a convenient schema for evaluating and interpreting dream laboratory data.

The Developmental Function of Dreaming

Newborns spend approximately 50% of their total sleep time in REM. This is more than twice the amount of REM sleep the adult averages. This observation has led to the still very popular speculation that REM sleep is a vitally needed source of internal stimulation during the early growth stages of the organism, facilitating the structural differentiation and maturation of the central nervous system (Roffwarg, Muzio, and Dement, 1966).

But what about dreaming? Until recently, the neonate was thought not to have the cognitive structures necessary for dreaming to occur.

Consequently, the high percentage of REM sleep observed in the infant was thought not to have any psychological significance. However, recent infant research has proven otherwise. A new picture of the infant has emerged, showing that there are in fact prerepresentational and presymbolic experiences in the first year of life, even in the first few months of life. We now know that these experiences form the basis for the emergence of the self and of psychic structure. As the work of Sander (1983), Stern (1983), Beebe and Lachmann (1988) and others has shown, the infant is a highly complex creature from birth on, one who can discriminate his mother's voice from a stranger's, perceive temporal sequences, develop expectations of future events, and *remember*. If that is the case—and the evidence for it is compelling—then it is highly likely that the infant's high rate of REM activity reflects an unusually high level of dream activity, presumably serving the purpose of forming new psychic structures at an early stage in development when such activity would be most urgently needed.

Later in life, too, dreaming probably facilitates growth and development through new structure formation, as shown in studies I have mentioned in which learning new and difficult skills resulted in increased REM and presumably dream activity (Zimmerman, Stoyva, and Metcalf, 1970; Greenberg and Dewan, 1969; DeKonnick et al., 1978).

The Self-Maintenance Function of Dreaming

First, a few words about the role of drive theory in Kohut's self psychology: According to Kohut, it is the self and not drives that occupies a position of primacy. Drives, according to Kohut, should be conceptualized as secondary rather than primary phenomena (Kohut, 1984, p. 109), as breakdown or disintegration products of a fragmented self (Kohut, 1977, p. 128). Whatever the drivenness in question—be it oral, anal, oedipal, rageful, or sadomasochistic—it is invariably a consequence and not a cause of self-depletion.

What I find intriguing is that this drive model of Kohut's fits in beautifully with the results of research on the effects of REM deprivation. If the assumption that dreaming maintains self-cohesiveness is valid, then any interference with the dream process, such as dream deprivation, should lead to self-fragmentation and bring about an intensification of drive and an increase in psychopathological behavior. This is precisely what REM deprivation experiments have shown. You will recall that REM deprivation, and presumably dream deprivation, results in behavior dominated by excessive aggressiveness, sexuality, orality, anxiety, confusion, and reduced ability to cope.

The maintenance of stable self-structures, however, does not require that we consider the issue of drive regulation. When dreaming helps us cope with a stressful experience, or, as I have shown, facilitates recall, then we are also talking about the maintenance of psychic structure, but without reference to drive theory.

The Self-Restorative Function of Dreaming

If psychopathology is the product of a crumbling or fragmented self, then effective dreaming, like effective psychotherapy, may be viewed as a process whose goal is the restoration of the self. The "dream enhancement" technique is as much a therapeutic technique as it is an experimental manipulation. One may assume, therefore, that just as dream deprivation leads to self-fragmentation, a procedure that, like "dream enhancement," highlights or accentuates dreaming would have the opposite effect; that is, it would help restore the self. This in fact is what the research I have described has shown.

IMPLICATIONS FOR RESEARCH AND CLINICAL APPLICATIONS

As far as research is concerned, the value of a new idea depends on its generating original experiments specifically designed to validate or invalidate it. Still awaiting study, for example, is the relationship between dream content and self-esteem. Thus, it would be interesting to study subjects who have recently suffered a narcissistic injury and to see whether, how, and to what extent dreaming about the injury would restore their self-esteem. Such a study is in fact in progress now. Another promising direction concerns the role of the dream in the formation of new psychic structures. To test this idea, we are planning to study the dreams of creative artists. The very act of creation requires a restructuring and reorganization of experience. The literature abounds with suggestions that dreams facilitate creative thinking, that creative people tend to be more active dreamers, and that vivid dreamers and nightmare sufferers tend to be creative people—poets, painters, and writers (Hartmann, 1984). In the light of this background, it would be fascinating to record the dreams of artists over a period of several nights while at the same time keeping track of their artistic productions during the day. Would frequency of dreaming predict creative productivity? What would be the qualitative dream determinants of daytime productivity? For instance, would dreams containing a great deal of primary process, imagery, and concrete symbolization be associated with greater artistic productivity than would be dreams lacking these qualities? This is one study that would surely test the limits of the dream's contribution to the fullest development of a person's potential.

In terms of its clinical applications, the work I have reviewed clearly indicates that we should pay particular attention to our own and our patients' REM dreams. It is extremely easy to discriminate REM from non-REM dream reports. Studies have shown that people can learn to discriminate between REM and non-REM dreams even while they are asleep (Antrobus, 1967; Antrobus and Fisher, 1965).

As clinicians, we should also focus more on themes in the manifest content that parallel the preoccupations of waking life. There is far more continuity between waking and dreaming than people realize. Dreams reveal far more than they conceal and may actually affect our lives. One of the subjects in our dream enhancement study, an extremely passive and unassertive man, dreamed one night that he had killed a lion during a lion hunt. The next day he asserted himself in a most uncharacteristic fashion.

An intriguing question arises: was the dream merely an indicator of things that were already brewing, or was the dream actually instrumental in bringing the event about? Whatever the explanation, we certainly should be on the alert for major psychological changes making their first appearance in the dream.

Does the dream contain any creative solutions to a long-standing problem? Some time ago, a patient of mine with a 10-year history of impotence dreamed that he was performing cartwheels over roof tops. Analysis of the dream revealed that this extraordinary feat symbolized the effort he felt was required to satisfy his wife sexually, just as years ago, as a young boy, he had felt that nothing short of a miracle would keep his mother from abandoning him. His symptom disappeared the day after he had this dream.

Note that in both instances, the lion dream and the cartwheel dream, it was not some obscure, repressed, latent content that was brought to light. The focal problem was right there in the manifest content. Insight was achieved not by translating the ucs into the cs, but by translating from a sensory mode of expression to a verbal mode. I believe this is a difference worth pointing out.

One final point: the manner in which our patients' daily preoccupations are represented in their manifest dreams is probably more significant than the extent to which these preoccupations become incorporated. For instance, in a recent study of recovering alcoholics, undertaken to show that dreaming serves a drive regulatory function, Fiss (1980) found that patients who experienced a strong craving for alcohol tended to have dreamed about drinking in a conflicted way, whereas those whose craving was relatively weak tended to have dreamed about drinking in a gratifying way. Thus, the way in which a drive state is represented in a dream may well determine how "driven" the dreamer feels afterwards. As Atwood and Stolorow (1984) so well put it, dreams are indeed the "guardians of psychological structure" (p. 103).

The gap between researcher and clinician can be substantially narrowed only if, in studies of dreaming, we employ experimental strategies that are experience-*near*. Only by doing so will we arrive at the best possible explanation of why we dream. And a self-psychological framework can go a long way toward helping us achieve this goal.

REFERENCES

Antrobus, J. S. (1967), Discrimination of two sleep stages by human subjects. *Psychophysiol.*, 4:8–55.
——— Fisher, C. (1965), Discrimination of dreaming and nondreaming sleep. *Arch. Gen. Psychiat.*, 12:395–401.
Atwood, G. E. & Stolorow, R. (1984), *Structures of Subjectivity*. Hillsdale, NJ: The Analytic Press.
Beebe, B. & Lachmann, F. (1988), Mother-infant mutual influence and precursors of psychic structure. In: *Frontiers in Self Psychology*, ed. A. Goldberg. Hillsdale, NJ: The Analytic Press, pp. 3–25.
Cartwright, R., Tipton, L., & Wicklund, J. (1980), Focusing on dreams. *Arch. Gen. Psychiat.*, 37:275–277.
Cohen, D. & Cox, C. (1975), Neuroticism in the sleep laboratory: Implications for representational and adaptive properties of dreaming. *J. Abn. Psychol.*, 84:91–108.
DeKonninck, J., Proulx, G., King, W. & Poitras, L. (1978), Intensive language learning and REM sleep. *Sleep Res.*, 7:146.
Dement, W. (1960), The effect of dream deprivation. *Science*, 131:1705–1707.
——— Fisher, C. (1963), Experimental interference with the sleep cycle. *J. Canadian Psychiat. Assn.*, 8:400–405.
——— Henry, F., Cohen, H. & Ferguson, J. (1967), Studies on the effect of REM deprivation in humans and animals. In: *Sleep and Altered States of Consciousness*, ed. S. Kety & E. Evarts. Baltimore, MD: Williams & Wilkins, p. 456.
Fishbein, W., Kastaniotis, C. & Chattman, D. (1974), Paradoxical sleep: Prolonged augmentation following learning. *Brain Res.*, 79:61–75.
——— McGaugh, J. & Swarz, J. (1971), Retrograde amnesia: Electroconvulsive shock effects after termination of REM sleep deprivation. *Science*, 172:80–82.
Fiss, H. (1980), Dream content and response to withdrawal from alcohol. *Sleep Res.*, 9:152.
——— (1984), Toward a clinically relevant experimental psychology of dreaming. *Hillside J. Clin. Psychiat.*, 5:147–159.

—— (1986), An empirical foundation for a self psychology of dreaming. *J. Mind & Beh.*, 7:161–192.

—— Kremer, E. & Litchman, J. (1977), The mnemonic function of dreaming. Presented at meeting of Association for the Psychophysiological Study of Sleep, Houston, TX.

—— Litchman, J. (1976), "Dream enhancement": An experimental approach to the adaptive function of dreams. Presented at meeting of Association for the Psychophysiological Study of Sleep, Cincinnati, OH.

Fosshage, J. (1983), The psychological function of dreams: A revised psychoanalytic perspective. *Psychoanal. Contemp. Thought*, 6:641–669.

—— (1988), Dream interpretation revisited. In: *Frontiers in Self Psychology*, ed. A. Goldberg. Hillsdale, NJ: The Analytic Press, pp. 161–175.

Greenberg, R. & Dewan, E. (1969), Aphasia and REM sleep. *Nature*, 223:183–184.

—— Pillard, R. & Pearlman, C. (1972), The effect of REM deprivation on adaptation to stress. *Psychosom. Med.*, 34:257–262.

Grieser, E., Greenberg, R. & Harrison, R. (1972), The adaptive function of sleep: The differential effects of sleep and dreaming on recall. *J. Abn. Psychol.*, 80:280–286.

Hartmann, E. (1984), *The Nightmare*. New York: Basic Books.

Kohut, H. (1977), *The Restoration of the Self*. New York: International Universities Press.

—— (1984), *How Does Analysis Cure?* ed. A. Goldberg & P. E. Stepansky. Chicago: University of Chicago Press.

Lecas, J. (1976), Changes in paradoxical sleep accompanying instrumental learning in the cat. *Neurosci. Letters*, 3:349–355.

Lucero, M. (1970), Lengthening of REM sleep duration consecutive to learning in the rat. *Brain Res.*, 20:319–322.

McGinty, D. (1969), Effects of prolonged isolation and subsequent enrichment on sleep patterns in kittens. *Electroenceph. Clin. Neorophysiol.*, 26:322–337.

Morden, B., Mitchell, G., Conner, R., Dement, W. & Levine, S. (1968), Effects of rapid eye movement sleep deprivation on shock-induced fighting. *Physiol. & Beh.*, 3:425–432.

Pearlman, C. (1971), Latent learning impaired by REM sleep deprivation. *Psychonom. Sci.*, 25:135–136.

Roffwarg, H., Muzio, J. & Dement, W. (1966), Ontogenetic development of the human sleep-dream cycle. *Science*, 152:604–619.

Sander, L. (1983), Polarity paradox and the organizing process in development. In: *Frontiers of Infant Psychology*, ed. J. D. Coll, E. Galenson & R. Tyson. New York: Basic Books, pp. 333–346.

Stern, D. (1983), The early development of schemas of self, of other, and of "self with other." In: *Reflections on Self Psychology*, ed. J. Lichtenberg & S. Kaplan. Hillsdale, NJ: The Analytic Press, pp. 49–84.

Zimmerman, J., Stoyva, J. & Metcalf, D. (1970), Distorted visual feedback and augmented REM sleep. *Psychophysiol.*, 7:298.

Chapter 3

The Concept of the Self-State Dream, Revisited: Contributions from Sleep Research

Ramon Greenberg

Kohut's (1977) major contribution to our understanding of dreams consists of the idea of the self-state dream. He considered this to be a special type of dream in which the images portrayed the self as under threat and for which no associations that might increase understanding of underlying latent content could be evoked. He likened these dreams to the posttraumatic dreams with which we are all familiar. I find it interesting that, like Freud, Kohut wished to separate off this special group of dreams from other dreams, for, as is well known, Freud (1920) discussed posttraumatic nightmares as "Beyond the Pleasure Principle" and not subject to the same theoretical understanding as "ordinary dreams." I would like to show that the results of recent sleep research and the formulations of other psychoanalytic thinkers point to a more unified understanding of dreams in which these apparently special cases are part of a spectrum of dreams rather than exceptions to the rule.

The observations of sleep researchers have raised questions about classical psychoanalytic dream theory and lead to a view of dreaming that can also be applied to Kohut's definition of the self-state dream. These questions also fit with revisions that self psychology itself has suggested about psychoanalytic theory in general. In the late 1960s several investigators (Newman and Evans, 1965; Breger, 1967; Dewan, 1970; Greenberg, 1970), inspired by the newly emerging findings from the EEG study of sleep, suggested that REM sleep, that phase of sleep associated with dreaming, might play a role in the processing of 'new information. While these authors had similar ideas, there was, at that time, little experimental evidence bearing directly on their hypotheses. They were reasoning from basic sleep research findings and from information gathered from earlier clinical, psychological, and computer experience. These hypotheses were important, however, because they gave direction to a series of experiments that explored the effects of REM deprivation on learning and adaptation. The findings were quite consistent and were replicated in a number of laboratories around the world. Studies (see Pearlman, 1981, for a review) using rats and mice as subjects examined the effects of REM deprivation on a variety of learning tasks. Some of these were one-way avoidance, the two-way shuttle box, latent learning of mazes, and discrimination tasks. The results of these experiments showed that REM deprivation during training impaired the acquisition of the more complicated tasks while not affecting the simpler ones.

In a parallel fashion, studies (see Greenberg, 1981, for a review) in humans examined the effects of REM deprivation on such tasks as learning word lists, creative thinking, adaptation to the viewing of an anxiety-provoking film, and performance on the Rorshach test. Here again, REM deprivation seemed to affect the more complicated tasks in a manner that could be interpreted as impairment of adaptation. Based on the results of these studies, we suggested that REM sleep is necessary for what Seligman (1970) has called unprepared learning while playing no role in prepared learning. Since prepared learning depends on built-in instinctual or on well-learned patterns of behavior necessary for survival, it makes sense that an animal would not need to sleep on it in order to learn. However, the more complicated, unprepared learning requires some change in behavior involving integration of unfamiliar information, and here REM sleep seems to be necessary.

REM sleep not only is necessary for adaptation to these difficult tasks, but can be responsive to demand. When REM levels were measured during learning, an increase in REM occurred during the learning of those tasks which had been impaired by REM deprivation. Thus, during training for the two-way shuttlebox (Hennevin and Leconte, 1977), rats had higher levels of REM; students who showed improvement during an intensive foreign-language course had increases in REM from baseline levels (DeKonnick et al., 1977); and subjects who were in a state of psychological disequilibrium had earlier onset of REM sleep than when they showed relative quiescence of conflictual activity (Greenberg, Pearlman, and Gampel, 1972; Greenberg and Pearlman, 1975a).

The results of the REM studies can lead to a theory of REM function that can be applied to our understanding of dreams by considering the dream as a manifestation of that function. Put simply, we see dreaming as the integration of information from current experience with past memories in order to produce schemas that are organizers of complicated behavioral tasks. Thus, the dreamer can learn and can modify or adapt behavior to new demands of the environment. This process can lead to a change in behavior, or it can lead to the use of old patterns of behavior to cope with new situations. Furthermore, this process may be successful to a greater or lesser degree. For example, the traumatic dream represents an instance of failure of the hypothesized dream function, because the new experience is not integrated at all. Instead, the traumatic episode is presented without any evidence of connection with other experiences of the dreamer. One could express this idea in another way by saying it is a portrayal of the failure of self-integration or cohesion, what Kohut called the self-state dream.

Applying this hypothesis to dreams leads to the following ideas. The dream shows how this process occurs, that is, how the supraordinate self is functioning. The content of the dream is a reflection of issues with which the dreamer is struggling, which may vary from problems in mastering external issues to problems in the maintenance of internal equilibrium, that is, self-cohesion. It demonstrates, in varying proportions, information from present experiences and from the past, expressed in imagery that is part of the dreamer's own private language (Greenberg and Pearlman, 1980) for representing a particular situation. Usually the dream is dealing with and portraying matters that are problematic in the dreamer's current waking life. The origin of the problems may relate to past experiences, and that is why one sees material from the past in dreams. The dream thus portrays problems and also the dreamer's efforts at coping with these problems. Since this formulation does not include the traditional ideas of disguise and latent content, I should explain why these have been omitted.

First, the evidence for drive discharge in dreams has not been confirmed by studies of REM sleep and REM deprivation. The idea of disguise derives from the notion that it is necessary to hide the meaning of the dream in order to hide the forbidden drives that seek expression. Without the concept of drive discharge, the idea of disguise is no longer necessary. Latent content also assumes a hidden meaning for the dream. We suggest, instead, that the dream requires translation into our waking language rather than requiring the uncovering of a hidden meaning. In line with this thinking, we find that the manifest content is not an inconsequential daily residue that is the carrier of the latent dream wishes but actually represents issues with which the dream is dealing. Understanding of the dream evolves from an understanding of the sources of manifest content. Put another way, we ask what waking concerns the images in the dream are presenting. Thus, we offer an alternative to the traditional approach to the dream, not just a negation of the classical theory and practice. Kohut also raised questions about the role of drive discharge in our understanding of psychologic functions.

Before describing research on dreams that further illuminates these ideas, I would like to mention other psychoanalytic writers who have presented similar points of view. Maeder (1916) in his monograph "The Dream Problem" discussed both the subjective meaning of the dream and the prospective function of dreaming. His idea of the subjective meaning of the dream was that every element in the dream represented a different aspect of the self. This applied to all dreams. He also described the objective meaning of dreams, in which the various elements of the dreams represented people and interactions related to the dreamer's waking life. In both cases the manifest dream presented a picture of what was going on in the dreamer's inner and outer life. With regard to the prospective function of the dream, Maeder suggested that the dream looked not only to the dreamer's past, as Freud had proposed, but also to future actions that might be taken in respect to the issues being dreamed about. Later analytic thinkers such as French and Fromm (1964), Bonime (1982), Hawkins (1970), Fiss (1986), and Fosshage (1983) have presented similar perspectives on dreaming.

Let us now return to the research, this time to that involving the dream itself. Based on the ideas stemming from the REM sleep studies, we began to examine dreams collected in the sleep lab (Greenberg and Pearlman, 1975b), from ourselves (Greenberg and Pearlman, 1980), and from Freud's own Irma dream (Greenberg and Pearlman, 1978). We had available a sample of dreams from a patient in psychoanalysis, for whom we also had transcripts of analytic hours; and also a large sample of our own dreams. We found a marked correspondence between the manifest dreams and important issues in the analytic material, in our own waking life and in Freud's letters to Fliess (Schur, 1966). For example the patient, after an hour in which he had struggled to contain his sadness about his father's death, dreamed of transferring some of his father's effects from one refrigerator to another. We saw this as a portrayal, in images, of the issue rather than of a latent content. In our own dreams, we also found a striking correspondence between the images in the dreams and important waking concerns. Freud's Irma dream showed clear incorporations in the manifest content of the events involving Fliess's operation on Freud's patient Emma. This led us to a reconsideration of the meaning of that dream.

In our current work we have been more specific and focused in the assessments of dream material. We have been using the dreams of the analytic patient previously mentioned and also dreams collected in the laboratory from a student volunteer. Transcripts of extensive pre- and postsleep interviews covering the activities and feelings on the days before and after the collection of the volunteer's dreams were provided by Dr. David Foulkes. The problems portrayed in the dreams were identified, and we found identical problems apparent in the waking material. We have also found evidence of attempts at solution for these problems in the dreams, sometimes more and sometimes less successful.

A full presentation of this recent research is not possible here, but we find the results to be consistent with the earlier work cited. We formulate a dream process in which the manifest dream portrays the self and its struggles to integrate or to master problems. Drive discharge, disguise, and latent content do not seem to play a part in understanding the dream. I will return to the relation of these findings to self psychology and the self-state dream after first presenting a clinical example.

CASE ILLUSTRATION

The patient, a young professional woman in her mid-30s, called for an extra appointment, saying that last Thursday she'd had another dream about a session and did not want to wait a whole week to talk about it. When she came, all she could remember was that she was having another session with me. It wasn't this office. It was a beautiful, wood-panelled office. Two other dreams were mentioned, but she then went on to talk about her current concern regarding plans to fly to a meeting. Her fear of flying is the major problem remaining in her treatment. She is receiving a good deal of pressure from her husband and daughter to make the trip. She also talked to her mother, who is in Florida, having enjoyed the flight down. Her mother said that the patient would be glad to fly if mother would just forbid it. The people at work are also wise to her and her anxiety. The patient then brought up the other two dreams that she found disturbing.

1. She was in her house and went into the "maid's" room, which is off the bedroom. It was all black—burned out. There were some

icons that were undamaged but covered with soot. In front of them was a fret with some candles burning behind it. She was very upset, both in the dream and when she woke up.

2. She was with her husband and daughter driving past the old Globe building with the old printing press. It was an old Victorian building with big cupolas. Then they came to the new Globe building with a press. It was flat and looked like a factory. They were in line either for coffee or to get on a plane. There were two adolescents in front of her. She heard someone say that if they got on the plane they would all die. She left the line and went back to the Globe building. A lot of people were watching something. She looked past them and saw two homosexuals engaged in sadomasochistic sex. She had the feeling that that is all there is in the papers—bad news like plane crashes and sex.

She said that her mother had Greek icons in the house. She was not sure whether there was a perpetual light or just one candle lit sometimes. She talked about her fear of flying and how her mother had gotten over hers but had left her with it. I asked about the icons and whether they were connected with mourning. She said they were not. There was a special wheat dish for mourning that they had when her grandmother died. She became very sad as we talked about her anxiety about flying as the only connection she had left with her childhood and with mother's superstitions. She has had to disown all of that in the other aspects of her life. She envies her daughter and wished she were her. She felt bad about that. Her daughter admires her so much and she never had that feeling with her mother. She never felt mother was pretty, although father said she was. Only recently has she begun to feel that she herself is attractive. She was very sad as she talked about what she has missed and connected this with her feeling that she has no connection with her childhood except superstitions and fear of flying.

A few weeks later she flew with much less anxiety than is usual for her and said she was actually looking forward to another trip.

Space limitations make it necessary to present the evidence for my conclusions concisely, but I hope to demonstrate the relation of these ideas to the research and clinical material. Kohut (1977) suggested that the term self-state be applied only to dreams showing problems in maintaining self-cohesion. If, instead, we consider dreams in relation to the selfobject function, then dreams can be seen as struggles with the vicissitudes of that function, sometimes showing total failure and sometimes showing the efforts to develop or hold on to selfobject functions so as to maintain or improve the state of the self. In the clinical example presented, one can see the connection between what the patient felt was missing and what she was yearning for, expressed in her envy of her own daughter's relationship with her. One might understand her seeing me in a beautiful, wood-paneled office as an indication that she could picture herself in a much better place, corresponding to her statement that she was beginning to see herself as attractive. I might mention that early in her treatment she indicated her wish for me to admire her and to view her as my favorite patient. The wood-paneled office dream had no associations to it; and although it was not unpleasant, as in Kohut's self-state dream, it can nevertheless be seen as a picture of a self-state. The later dreams show more selfobject issues. Understanding the dreams in this manner is consistent with the hypotheses about dream function that have been developed from the sleep research. They suggest efforts at integration and struggles with problems, which are portrayed in the imagery of the dreams. Ideas about drive discharge, disguise, or latent content are not necessary for the understanding of dreams. There is no need to propose that a dream showing a fragmenting self is a different species, any more than the traumatic dream, as described by Freud (must) be seen as an exception to the ordinary dream. All dreams can be understood as portraying and serving the function of dreaming sleep, that is, the effort to deal with problems in order to establish, maintain, and improve self-integration, equilibrium, or cohesion.

REFERENCES

Bonime, W. (1982), *The Clinical Use of Dreams*. New York: DaCapo Press.

Breger, L. (1967), Function of dreams. *J. Abn. Psychol.*, 72(5):1–28.

DeKonnick, J., Proulx, G., King, W. & Poitras, L. (1977), Intensive language learning and REM sleep. *Sleep Res.*, 7:146.

Dewan, E. (1970), The programming (P) hypothesis for REMS. *Internat. Psychiat. Clin.*, 7:295–307.

Fiss, H. (1986), An empirical foundation for a self psychology of dreaming. *J. Mind Beh.*, 7:161–192.

Fosshage, J. (1983), The psychologic function of dreams: A revised psychoanalytic perspective. *Psychoanal. Contemp. Thought*, 6:641–669.

French, R. & Fromm, E. (1964), *Dream Interpretation*. New York: Basic Books.

Freud, S. (1920), Beyond the pleasure principle. *Standard Edition*, 18:7–64, London: Hogarth Press, 1955.

Greenberg, R. (1970), Dreaming and memory. *Internat. Psychiat. Clin.*, 7:258–267.

————— (1981), Dreams and REM sleep—An integrative approach. In: *Sleep, Dreams, and Memory*, ed. W. Fishbein. New York: Spectrum, pp. 125–133.

————— Pearlman, C. (1975a), REM sleep and the analytic process: A psychophysiologic bridge. *Psychoanal. Quart.*, 44:392–402.

———— ———— (1975b), A psychoanalytic dream continuum: The source and function of dreams. *Internat. Rev. Psycho-Anal.*, 2:441–448.

———— ———— (1978), If Freud only knew: A reconsideration of psychoanalytic dream theory. *Internat. Rev. Psycho-Anal.*, 5:71–75.

———— ———— (1980), The private language of the dream. In: *The Dream in Clinical Practice*, ed. J. Natterson. New York: Aronson, pp. 85–98.

———— ———— Gampel, D. (1972), War neuroses and the adaptive function of sleep. *Brit. J. Med. Psychol.*, 45:27–33.

Hawkins, D. (1970), Implications for psychoanalytic theory of psychophysiologic sleep research. In: *Psicofisiologia del Sonno E del Sogno. Proceedings of an International Symposium. Rome 1967*, ed. M. Bertini. Milan: Editrice Vita E Pensiero, pp. 136–143.

Hennevin, E. & Leconte, P. (1977), Etudes des relations entre le sommeil paradoxal et le process d'acquisition. *Physiol. Behav.*, 18:307–319.

Kohut, H. (1977), *The Restoration of the Self*. New York: International Universities Press.

Maeder, A. (1916), The dream problem. *Nervous and Mental Disease Monog. No. 22*. New York: New York Pub.

Newman, E. A. & Evans, C. R. (1965), Human dream processes as analagous to computor programme clearance. *Nature*, 206:534.

Pearlman, C. (1981), Rat models of the adaptive function of REM sleep. In: *Sleep, Dreams, and Memory*, ed. W. Fishbein. New York: Spectrum, pp. 37–45.

Schur, M. (1966), Some additional "day residues" of "the specimen dream of psychoanalysis." In: *Psychoanalysis*, ed. R. Lowenstein, L. Newman, M. Schur & A. J. Solnit. New York: International Universities Press, pp. 45–85.

Seligman, M. (1970), On the generality of the laws of learning. *Psychol. Rev.*, 77:406–418.

Chapter 4

Commentaries

THE DREAM IN CONTEXT
Robert D. Stolorow

Psychoanalysis, in its essence, is a hermeneutic and historical science whose principal research method is and always has been the in-depth case study. Psychoanalytic propositions do not readily lend themselves to experimental procedures, and it is a rare and unexpected yield when data culled from the laboratory are found to bear meaningfully on psychoanalytic theory and practice. Greenberg and Fiss present two such welcome harvests, summarizing a variety of data from sleep and dream research that they believe offer support for a self-psychological understanding of dream function. Fosshage also offers important ideas about dream function, his data coming not from the laboratory but from the consulting room, where, I must confess, I also feel more comfortable.

Greenberg's contribution gave me some difficulty. According to him, the results of REM studies lead to a view of dreaming as "integrating information from current experience with past memories to produce schemas that are organizers of complicated behavioral tasks. Thus, the dreamer can learn and can modify or adapt behavior to new demands of the environment." "The dream," he continues, "portrays problems and also the dreamer's efforts at coping with these problems." Thus, if I understand Greenberg's argument correctly, he believes that the REM data show that the function of

33

dreaming is to aid adaptation and mastery. While this is a useful idea, illuminating *one* of the multiple purposes of dreams, it does not seem to me to be directly applicable to the principal domain of self-psychological inquiry—namely, *the organization of self-experience* and its vicissitudes in relation to the subjectively experienced surround. I agree with Greenberg that the theory of the self-state dream should be broadened and that all dreams can be seen to depict the organization of self-experience along a continuum of varying degrees of integration or cohesion, but I do not see clearly that his analysis of the sleep research data can provide the basis for this theoretical expansion.

Fiss, too, proposes that all dreams can be seen as indicators of varying self-states. However, the conclusions that he draws from dream research data pertain more directly to the realm of self-experience. This is consistent with his advocacy of "experimental strategies that are experience-near," an important methodological suggestion if such research is to be relevant to a depth psychology of human experience. Fiss extends the methodology of empathic inquiry to experimental data; that is, he uses the data to make inferences about the organization of subjects' self-experience and about the function of dreaming in contributing to "the development, maintenance, and restoration" of self-experience. I found his arguments persuasive and heartening.

Fiss cites Atwood's and my (1984) work on dream function approvingly, indicating that our theoretical ideas are supported by dream research findings. I would like to summarize these ideas in somewhat greater detail. Our aim was to shed light on what we regarded as the most distinctive and central feature of the dream experience—the use of concrete perceptual images endowed with hallucinatory vividness to symbolize abstract thoughts, feelings, and subjective states. We proposed that concrete symbolization in dreams serves a vital psychological purpose for the dreamer, and that an understanding of this purpose illuminates the importance and necessity of dreaming. We wrote:

> It is in the need to maintain the organization of experience . . . that we can discover the fundamental purpose of concrete symbolization in dreams. When configurations of experience of self and other find symbolization in concrete perceptual images and are thereby articulated with hallucinatory vividness, the dreamer's feeling of conviction about the validity and reality of these configurations receives a powerful reinforcement. Perceiving, after all, is believing. By reviving during sleep the most basic and emotionally compelling form of knowing—

through sensory perception—the dream affirms and solidifies the nuclear organizing structures of the dreamer's subjective life. Dreams, we are contending, are the *guardians of psychological structure,* and they fulfill this vital purpose by means of concrete symbolization [pp. 102–103].

We proposed further that dream symbolization serves to maintain the organization of experience in two different senses. On one hand, dream symbols may actualize a *particular* organization of experience in which specific configurations of self and other, required for multiple reasons, are dramatized and affirmed. In emphasizing that the aims of defense and disguise contribute to the construction of such symbols, and that therefore the distinction between manifest imagery and latent meaning continues to be applicable, our views differ from those of Greenberg, Fiss, and Fosshage.

On the other hand, dream symbols may serve not so much to actualize particular configurations of experience as to maintain psychological organization per se. With *these* dream images, the distinction between manifest and latent content is less germane, because the aim of disguise has not been prominent. Instead, the vivid perceptual images of the dream serve directly to restore or sustain the structural integrity and stability of a subjective world menaced with disintegration. This function of dream symbols is clearly illustrated by the self-state dreams discussed by Kohut (1977). By vividly reifying the experience of self-endangerment, the dream images bring the state of the self into focal awareness with a feeling of conviction and reality that can only accompany sensory perceptions. The dream imagery thereby both encapsulates the danger to the self and reflects a concretizing effort at self-restoration. Finally, we noted that the organization-maintaining function of dream symbolization can be observed not only when existing structures are threatened, but also when *new* organizations of experience are coming into being and are in need of consolidation—the developmental function of dreaming accented by Fosshage.

Following Kohut's emphasis on empathic-introspective investigation, Fosshage enjoins the analyst to explore the dream from within the dreamer's subjective frame of reference, "to illuminate as fully as possible the *experience* of the dreamer within the dream." Such an approach, he claims, unveils and furthers the emergent developmental movements envisioned in, and promoted by, the dreaming mentation. His clinical material elegantly and convincingly illustrates his thesis.

Like Greenberg and Fiss, Fosshage downplays the role of unconscious processes and of the aims of defense and disguise in the formation of dreams, and correspondingly his clinical approach eschews the technique of eliciting associations to dream elements. Here I fear that Fosshage, Greenberg, and Fiss are all in danger of throwing out Freud's clinical dream baby with its metapsychological bathwater. What we need is not an approach to dreams that deemphasizes the unconscious, but a *revised theory of the unconscious* that is consistent with current clinical knowledge. The concepts of unconscious mental processes and unconscious motivation do *not* have to be conflated with the doctrine of instinctual drive.

Atwood and I (1984) distinguished two realms of unconsciousness that are important for psychoanalysis—the prereflective unconscious and the more familiar dynamic unconscious. The term "prereflective unconscious" refers to the shaping of experience by invariant organizing principles that operate outside a person's conscious awareness:

> In the absence of reflection, a person is unaware of his role as a constitutive subject in elaborating his personal reality. The world in which he lives and moves presents itself as though it were something independently and objectively real. The patterning and thematizing of events that uniquely characterize his personal reality are thus seen as if they were properties of those events rather than products of his own subjective interpretations and constructions [p. 36].

We contended that an understanding of this form of unconsciousness sheds new light on the unique importance of dreams for psychoanalytic theory and practice:

> The prereflective structures of a person's subjective world are most readily discernible in his relatively unfettered, spontaneous productions, and there is probably no psychological product that is less fettered or more spontaneous than the dream. As human subjectivity in purest culture, the dream constitutes a "royal road" to the prereflective unconscious—to the organizing principles and dominant leitmotivs that unconsciously pattern and thematize a person's psychological life [p. 98].

It is precisely this unconscious patterning of experience that Fosshage elucidates so beautifully in his work with his patient's dream. His analysis moves well beyond the dream's manifest imagistic content to the thematic *structure* of that content, from which he can then make inferences about the principles unconsciously organizing his patient's experience.

Stripped of metapsychological encumbrances, the term "dynamic unconscious" refers to that set of configurations that conscious experience is not permitted to assume, because of their association with emotional conflict and subjective danger (Atwood and Stolorow, 1984). From a perspective informed by self psychology, the dynamic unconscious is seen to consist not of instinctual drive derivatives, but of disavowed central affect states and repressed developmental longings, defensively walled off because they failed to evoke the requisite attuned responsiveness from the early caregiving surround (Stolorow, Brandchaft, and Atwood, 1987). This defensive sequestering of central emotional states and developmental needs, which attempts to protect against retraumatization, is the principal source of resistance in psychoanalytic treatment and also of the necessity for disguise when such states and needs are represented in dreams. Where disguise is prominent, associations to elements can assist in the illumination of the dream's intersubjective context of origin.

Let me illustrate with an episode that occurred some 17 years ago, when I was still a psychoanalytic candidate in training and just becoming familiar with Kohut's early papers on narcissism. The episode made a lasting impression on me, and I learned a great deal from it. I had been working psychotherapeutically with a young woman for about a year, during which we seemed to make little progress in establishing a therapeutic bond. At this juncture she suffered what was for her a severe trauma—she was mugged and robbed while trying to enter her apartment house after returning home from a therapy session. Shortly thereafter she told me she had decided to leave treatment. During what was to be our last session, she reported a dream.

In the dream, she was in a session with her therapist, a black woman. A robber broke into the consulting room as the therapist sat helplessly and did nothing. The patient's feeling in the dream was one of disparagement of the therapist. Her only associations were to the mugging and to a joke she had recently heard, the punch line of which described God as a black woman. Putting together the trauma of the mugging and the patient's manifestly disparaging feelings in the dream, I commented that perhaps she felt disappointed that I had not been able to protect her from the assault. The patient was untouched by my interpretation and terminated, with no apparent understanding of her reason for doing so.

With hindsight it seems clear that the patient's association to the joke about God pointed to a powerful, walled off, archaic idealizing longing, mobilized in the transference by the trauma of the mugging. My interpretation of her disappointment failed to take into account that this longing was *highly disguised* in the dream's manifest content, because it was being deeply resisted, as it had been from the outset of treatment. What the patient needed was for me to investigate her *fears* of reexposing her idealizing yearnings to a transference repetition of crushing childhood disappointments and to extend empathic inquiry to her perceptions of qualities in me that lent themselves to her expectations of retraumatization. Only by fully exploring this intersubjective situation could her dream, and the resistance it encoded, have been comprehended.

Let us now consider the intersubjective field in which Fosshage's patient's dream crystallized. The patient's transference relationship with Fosshage can be seen as having two essential poles or dimensions (Stolorow, Brandchaft, and Atwood, 1987). At one pole is her yearning for requisite selfobject experiences that were missing or insufficient during her formative years. In this dimension she experiences Fosshage as a longed-for new object who aligns himself with her strivings for differentiated selfhood, her search for a distinctive inner direction of her own. At the other pole are her expectations and fears of a transference repetition of early pathogenic experiences. In this dimension she believes that she must accommodate to Fosshage's requirements in order to maintain the tie with him. Both poles of the transference are clearly represented in the patient's dream: on one hand, the wonderful stallion (Fosshage) liberates her and enables her to pursue her own direction; on the other hand, she feels responsible for the stallion and required to take care of him. Fosshage's interpretive approach to the dream seems well designed to facilitate and strengthen the selfobject dimension of the transference as he seeks to recognize and utilize the dream's developmental movements in order to "further within the psychoanalytic arena the [patient's] developmental course." In my opinion, he achieves this aim masterfully, yet I wonder if something important is being left out.

The patient declares that Fosshage is secretly in love with her and has an agenda of his own for her, clearly replicating her experience of her father's "self-interested love." It seems to me that Fosshage is in love with *development* and that his patient has been responding to, and benefiting enormously from, this passion. What has been the specific impact of this love on the patient's experience in the transference, and how is this impact depicted in her dream?

A stallion is an animal that loves to *move*, and the patient's dream is, above all, saturated with forward movement, both physical and psychological. When the patient insists that Fosshage wants her to "leave everything" and "get on with it," I believe she is communicating her perception of the agenda that he does, in fact, have for her—that she go forward in her quest for a more distinct self-definition.

As with her father, this is an agenda to which she feels she must accommodate if she is to maintain the bond with Fosshage as his "special one."[1] I am suggesting that, alongside the patient's genuine developmental progress, her unconscious compliance with Fosshage's developmental agenda has codetermined the galloping pace of the analysis and that this entire, complex intersubjective system is both represented and disguised in her dream imagery. Dreams, I am contending, cannot be comprehended psychoanalytically apart from the intersubjective contexts in which they take form.

REFERENCES

Atwood, G. & Stolorow, R. (1984), *Structures of Subjectivity*. Hillsdale, NJ: The Analytic Press.

Kohut, H. (1977), *The Restoration of the Self*. New York: International Universities Press.

Stolorow, R., Brandchaft, B. & Atwood, G. (1987), *Psychoanalytic Treatment*. Hillsdale, NJ: The Analytic Press.

ON DREAMING AND OUR INCLINATIONS
Paul H. Tolpin

> *Dreams are faithful interpreters of our inclinations; but there is art required to sort and understand them.*
> —Montaigne, "Of Experience"

For a number of reasons I had a lot of difficulty trying to clarify my thinking about the important and challenging preceeding chapters. For several weeks after I received them I spent considerable time pondering the various ideas presented by the authors. I weighed their arguments in my mind, trying to reformulate their notions in terms more congenial to me. After a while I found that I was becoming increasingly irritated because I was unable to clarify my thinking, to write down what I had to say and have done with it. Then one night I had a disturbing dream. I awoke from it feeling anxious; I thought about it briefly and then fell back to sleep. On the way to the train the next morning I thought about it again. It wasn't all that complicated, but it was still puzzling.

This was the dream. I was having a discussion with someone I thought I knew—perhaps a colleague. He was talking to me about

---

[1] I wish to emphasize that I speak here from the perspective of the patient's psychic reality—that is, her subjective experience in the transference.

ideas he had about something . . . some theory . . . some kind of psychoanalytic theory . . . conceptual issues. It was vague. He had made a statement. When I questioned him about it, he repeated what he'd just said and then said the same thing in another way. It still wasn't clear to me. I was becoming annoyed. "What do you mean?" I asked. Again he answered, but I still couldn't follow him—or I couldn't hear him well enough. By this time I was really angry. Almost shouting, I said, "I don't understand what you're talking about. Will you please say what you mean? Come on, can't you think straight?" or something like that. That's all there was to it.

What had prompted this dream? I began to associate to it. I tried to picture the colleague I was talking to. He was someone I knew from somewhere in the past, or I had seen him recently. The upcoming self psychology meeting and the papers I was to discuss came to mind. Was I arguing with the authors? Could be. I went on musing about various other possibilities, ending up, a bit desperately perhaps, with a competitive oedipal formulation. No, that couldn't be it. But nothing I thought of seemed to hit the mark. I decided not to think about it anymore.

Once at my office I started to get things ready for the day. Deciding I needed a few aspirins for an incipient headache, I went to the closet and opened the medicine cabinet. Suddenly an image of the dream returned, and suddenly I knew who the colleague I had been so angry with was: I had just seen him in the mirror; I had met the enemy—and I was he! Clearly, the tension I had been feeling about the various issues raised by the papers had finally gotten to me that night. The dream was on Thursday night-Friday morning, and I had promised myself to begin writing my commentary on Saturday. There were a few other determinants to the dream—but I don't have to tell all to make my point.

In the next few minutes I recalled again the increasing exasperation I had had with myself in the past week or so. While I was positively impressed with some of what I read, I had considerable discomfort with some of the experimental methodology, the levels of conceptualization, some of the leaps from data to conclusions, the interpretation of a particular dream, and so on. And using my own dream as a dream type, I didn't see that it necessarily or readily or usefully fit any of the three categories of supraordinate functions of dreams (the maintenance, restoration, and development of psychological organization) that the authors had argued for. But there was something else, too, beyond all that, that bothered me and that I was unable to put my finger on. For the time being, my thought research ended there. That weekend I did more thinking. I turned to Freud (1900),

"The Interpretation of Dreams," particularly chapter 2, then to my own 1983 paper, "Self Psychology and the Interpretation of Dreams," and more importantly to my own experience with analyzing the dreams of my patients and of myself as well.

First Freud: Freud described the detailed analysis of a dream of his own, the Irma dream, as it is called. He concluded that the motivating force of that dream was the necessity to exculpate himself from the implicit charge by another doctor that he had bungled Irma's treatment. What makes the investigation of that dream so important in the history of psychoanalytic ideas is not only Freud's demonstration of his piecemeal method of interpreting dreams, which to a considerable extent continues to hold sway over traditional analysis (and which method Dr. Fosshage has rightfully questioned), but, more importantly, that it gave rise to one of the most influential conceptual generalizations in psychoanalysis. Freud said, "When the work of interpretation has been completed, we perceive that a dream is the fulfillment of a wish" (p. 121). Although in one notable footnote (1900, pp. 506–507, *fn2*; see also pp. 503–505),[1] Freud seemed to modify that assertion, his basic conception remained essentially unchanged. (That passing observation certainly did not exclude the wish-fulfillment theory, but it did implicitly place it in the subsidiary role of one of a number of motivating possibilities.) Today it appears that Freud overgeneralized his discovery and that we must include other motivations for dreaming in a broader theory of the function of dreams.

Further theoretical considerations: In my 1983 paper, I argued that Kohut had indicated directions for understanding dreams that had been little recognized before. Extending Kohut's notion of the self-state dream, I suggested that not only could dreams in which the self was in danger of disintegration be designated self-state dreams, but that dreams about the general functioning of the self in relation to itself or in relation to selfobjects could also be considered self-state dreams; or, the better to differentiate them from calamitous states of failing self-cohesion, they could be called state-of-the-self dreams, or dreams understood by way of self-psychological theory, awkward though that locution would be. Or better still I would now say that self-state dreams can be understood to exist along a continuum. There are degrees of self-disruption ranging, for example, from

---

[1]The most crucial sentence of that footnote, added in 1925, is as follows: "The fact that dreams concern themselves with attempts at solving problems by which our mental life is faced is no more strange than that our conscious waking life should do so; beyond this it merely tells us that activity can also be carried on in the preconscious —and this we already knew."

calamitous disintegration to mild distress; and there are qualitative expressions of varieties of moods. The decisive issue is that the primary focus of the dream is the expression of the state of the self, of aspects of its mood, or of its organization.

Armed now with the concepts just mentioned, I understood my dream this way. It portrayed what I had been struggling with during the preceeding days. There it was: an aspect of my self was actively responding to the distress I was feeling about my inability to master a problem I thought I should be able to master without much difficulty. I was dissatisfied with myself, angry at myself and my imperfections. My healthy, and perhaps not so healthy, defensive grandiosity had been mobilized and threatened. (There were also further, deeper issues I was aware of in myself that upset and annoyed me too.) In this instance the dream depicted the experience of the struggle itself, not the content of the struggle. In that sense it was like a self-state dream, but without the threat of self-dissolution. In addition, within a self-psychological framework I could also understand it to be implicitly motivated by the desire to fulfill a wish to master my conceptual block and get on with my work. Further, even though I could not readily place my dream in any of the categories of dream function suggested by the contributors in this volume, I could see how their conceptualizations might be useful for other types of dreams. Perhaps my dream could be included in another, as yet unnamed category. At any rate, aside from that, there were clear similarities between my formulation about the microclinical interpretive approach to understanding dreams and that of this volume's contributors. The function of dreams and dreaming, then, could be understood to include all these and perhaps still other motivations.

But I still felt uneasy. I began to recognize that without consciously being aware of it I was operating under the influence of two broad, basic assumptions about dreams. The first was the old-fashioned general principle that dreams usually operate to attempt to reduce disturbing tensions to an acceptable degree. The second was that dreams were a variety of thought, peculiar to the *sleeping* state, as Freud had said, and that they expressed (in their unique, usually visual, metaphorical form) the various kinds of mentations, conscious or otherwise, that we have during our waking life, and during portions of our sleeping life as well. Carrying these thoughts a few steps further, I finally realized that I was influenced by one more, underlying, basic notion about dreams that at the time of my dream of the dialogue with myself had been quite unclear to me and had probably been the most significant cause of my distress and of my consequent inner dialogue. The notion was this: I realized that, unlike the other contributors to this volume, I did not think that dreams had a "function" in their own right.[2] By that I mean that dreams are night thoughts and feelings that we have become consciously aware of, however "fully" remembered or scarcely recalled they may be. I believe that the other contributors have also been guided by that assumption, but to my way of thinking, dreams have no inherent motivating force, but are, rather, simply windows to the usually unconscious, continual operations of the mental processes that constitute the experiencing self to which REM sleep gives us brief access.

The content of dreams is a vast variety of unconscious feelings and thoughts and the innumerable ways of dealing with those feelings and thoughts that our minds are capable of. Dreams, then, may consist of messages about somatic states, or they may be attempts to reduce internal psychological tensions. They can express conflicts, erotic and aggressive urges, wishes and fears of all kinds. They can express states of the self, moods, defensive tendencies, states of disorganization, states of satisfaction or desire, attempts to solve intellectual problems, visions of creative possibilities, and so on. They combine archaic memories and current experiences. They express loves and hates, hopes and despair. The list clearly is incomplete.

These mentations, whether we are conscious of them or not, are organized and re-organized during the day as the day's events impinge upon us. They are then further shaped and reshaped during the night. Under the right circumstances, some of these become dreams. But since the dreams are not just "still" photographs, the organizing activities of the mind (presumably including those designated by the contributors to this volume as the supraordinate functions of maintenance, restoration, and development) that already are in operation, continue to function in the course of the dream and continue to alter it. Still, it is not the dream itself but the prior and continuing functioning of the mental processes of the self that are primary; what we are illuminating, then, when we investigate dreams is not the function of dreaming but the functioning of unconscious aspects of the experiencing self.

If what I have said is correct, does it detract from what I believe are the clinically most relevant formulations of Fiss, Greenberg, and Fosshage? To some extent it does, and in other ways it does not. What it does, however, is alter the importance of the role of dreams and dreaming in the overall functioning of the mind. It requires that the overarching, supraordinate functions that have been attributed to

[2]I am not questioning the apparently critical importance of the experience of REM sleep for neurophysiological homeostasis.

the dream be repositioned within the domain of some particular guiding sector of the self. If what I have said about the function of dreams is correct, the important and ingenious experimental work with dreams presented in this volume will have to be rethought so that the meaning of the findings can be reassessed.

Now I want to leave the conceptual issue of the function of dreams and turn to several clinical issues I think are importnat to underscore. First, Fiss comments on the value of expanding Kohut's theorizing about the self-state dream, and I certainly concur with him about that. Apparently we were both thinking independently along the same lines. He also points out in the analysis of his patient's cart-wheel dream that "the focal problem was present . . . in the manifest content" and that insight was achieved by "translating from a sensory mode of expression to a verbal mode." He is arguing here for a new look at the issue of manifest and latent dream content and question-ing an across-the-board assumption of the defensive nature of dream language. I think that is a basic insight into the understanding of dreams. Similarly, Greenberg questions the classical notion of dis-guise as defense in a manifest dream. He understands the disguise effect as a type of language or thinking mode that has to be translated into another language and thinking mode and further argues that we must ask "what waking experiences the image in the dream is presenting," not what it is hiding. Finally Fosshage deals similarly with the assumed defense function of the manifest dream and argues, rather, that, properly understood, the manifest dream can be openly revelatory of the subjective experiences of the dreamer.

All three of the authors, then, are urging a new way of looking at the manifest and latent content of dreams. And I strongly agree with them about that. But I hasten to add that *some* manifest content in some dreams may be a "disguise" in the sense that a purposeful attempt is made to conceal feelings and thoughts from observing sectors of one's self, just as presumably is done in undreamt, unob-served mentation. In addition, Fosshage also states a position similar to mine when he says that "the reported dream is the waking memory of a mentational process that has occurred during sleep." (I have already indicated my agreement with his questioning of Freud's piecemeal method of associating isolated images to dreams, and, again, I can only agree. But, of course, at times associations to the details of a dream lead to valuable insights. I don't think Fosshage would disagree with me about that.)

I can only applaud Fosshage's extraordinarily sensitive and insight-ful analysis of Tamara's dream. It does seem to support his contention that "dreaming mentation . . . is positioned to promote . . . the individual's developmental course." However, for reasons already stated, I would partially demur on this, since Fosshage's assumption is that this is the work of the dream rather than the antecedent and on-the-spot work of the experiencing self-mind reflected in the dream. Moreover, while this dream seems clearly to demonstrate a progressive development, it must be considered in the context of continued firmness and reliability of the self that can only be known over time. Finally, I want to underscore what I think is Fosshage's most important summary statement. It is that our method of investigating our patients dreams must attempt "to illuminate as fully as possible the *experience* of the dreamer [as it is expressed] directly *within* the [manifest] dream. . . ." (Of course, both the patient's and the analyst's associations to the dream elements and the overall sense of the dream remain essential to its being understood.) For me that is an injunction we must always struggle to attain. The vastly expanded vistas of the mind's functioning offered by self-psychological theory allow us far greater possibility of success in that undertaking.

Let me end, then, as I began, with Montaigne's words, which I think by now have taken on wider meaning: "Dreams are faithful interpreters of our inclinations; but there is an art required to sort and understand them."

REFERENCES

Freud, S. (1900), The interpretation of dreams, *Standard Edition*, 4 & 5. London: Hogarth Press, 1953.
Tolpin, P. (1983), Self psychology and the interpretation of dreams. In: *The Future of Psychoanalysis*, ed. A. Goldberg. New York: International Universities Press.

REPLY
James L. Fosshage

Tolpin and I concur that dreaming is a complex, image-dominated mentational process that continues and closely corresponds with waking mentational processes. Tolpin's view of all mentational processes as expressions of "the experiencing self-mind" positions us accurately, I believe, to address the overall functions and motivations of a person's waking and dreaming mentation. What I have posited to be the supraordinate functions of dreaming mentation (which include the function of conflict resolution, applicable to Tolpin's dream; see Fosshage, 1983, p. 658) also applies to waking mentation.

However, in contrast to waking mentation, dreaming mentation is an entirely unconscious process, utilizes predominately the imagistic mode, and is uniquely positioned during sleep—a time of solitude when stimuli from and behavioral responses to the external world are minimized—to address internal concerns. The consequences of these unique features of dreaming mentation are exactly what we are attempting to illuminate. For example, in my understanding of Tamara's dream I did not imply, as Tolpin suggests, that developmental steps were occurring *solely* through dreaming, but rather that the movements emerging out of the waking (conscious and unconscious) context of the analytic relationship were furthered through dreaming mentation. Dreaming both reflects and consolidates emergent psychological configurations, specifically views of oneself and others and relational themes. That new developmental thrusts occur in both forms of mentation (waking and dreaming) is to be expected and is clinically validated. Times of solitude (dreaming or waking) and times of togetherness (waking) each contribute to new organizations of experience.

Stolorow states, "Like Greenberg and Fiss, Fosshage downplays the role of unconscious processes and the aims of defense and disguise in the formation of dreams. . . . What we need is not an approach to dreams that deemphasizes the unconscious. . . ." Stolorow maintains the link between unconscious processes with aims of defense and disguise in dream formation and thereby concludes, inaccurately, that my deemphasis of defensive operations in the formation of dreams is equivalent to a deemphasis of the "unconscious."

Dreaming, a mentational mode occurring during sleep, *is an unconscious process,* that is, a process that is outside the field of consciousness. I am suggesting that we need to assess dreaming as a distinct state, distinguished from the waking state; that we need to illuminate this state in the clinical arena as best we can from a waking perspective by empathically entering into the dreaming experience itself. In focusing on the developmental function of dreaming, I am adding an often neglected dimension to dream analysis in the attempt to illuminate unconscious processes. *Clearly Stolorow's and my conceptualizations of unconscious processes, specifically the extent to which defenses operate within dream formation, differ.* The extent to which defenses are functioning in dream formation is ultimately an empirical question, albeit an extremely complex one, that Fiss and Greenberg address through REM research.

In discussing unconscious processes, Stolorow distinguishes "two realms of unconsciousness . . . the prereflective unconscious and the

more familiar, dynamic unconscious." With regard to the prereflective unconscious, he states:

> It is precisely this unconscious patterning of experience that Fosshage
> elucideates so beautifully in his work with his patient's dream. His
> analysis moves well beyond the dream's manifest imagistic content to
> the thematic *structure* of that content, from which he can then make
> inferences about the principles unconsciously organizing his patient's
> experience.

I agree that my analysis focused on the thematic structure of the
"manifest" content. However, in my judgment I did not move "well
beyond" the "manifest" content, but I attempted to illuminate the
thematic structure inherent in the "manifest" content (what I prefer to call
the *dream content*). These differences in the description of the interpretive process importantly reflect the extent to which the dream content
is viewed as directly or indirectly revelatory of the subjective dream
state. I believe that *these thematic structures can be directly illuminated
from the examination of the dream material itself without evidence of disguise
and the corresponding necessity of translation of dream imagery.*

Stolorow's distinction between the prereflective and the dynamic
unconscious, while facilitating recognition of organizational patterns,
unfortunately tends to preserve the latter concept (the dynamic
unconscious), despite its extrication from drive theory, encapsulated
in its classical linkage with ubiquitous defensive processes in dream
formation. Although these two realms may be conceptually distin-
guishable, as revealed in clinical practice the operation of organizational principles or schemata and defensive processes are so
intricately interwoven as to be inseparable. Additionally, my concep-
tuallization of defensive operations focuses not on the employment
of specific mechanisms, but on the recognition of momentary functional aspects of the organization of experience. For example, the
self-protective function of the dreaming experience does not lead to a
disguise of imagery but is illuminated by examining its relationship
to the waking context prior to the dream. This aspect of an organizational pattern is best revealed in clinical practice through *associations
to elements wherein the elements are not taken in isolation but as they are
embedded within the thematic context of the dream.* Space does not permit
exploration of the applicability of the traditional notion of disguise in
the light of our changing formulation of defensive processes.

Interpreting the dream, Stolorow focuses on the delineation of the
intersubjective context of Tamara's dream. He notes, corresponding
to my description, both the selfobject dimension of the transference

("... she experiences Fosshage as a longed-for new object who aligns himself with her strivings for differentiated selfhood, her search for a distinctive inner direction of her own") and the accommodation dimension of the transference ("expectations and fears of a transference repetition of early pathogenic experiences"). He then suggests that my "love with *development*," that is, my organizing principle, affects the analytic arena in two ways. He feels that Tamara has benefited "enormously from this passion" in the facilitation and strengthening of the selfobject dimension of the transference. In addition, he describes the following:

> When the patient insists that Fosshage wants her to "leave everything" and "get on with it," I believe she is communicating her perception of the agenda that he does, in fact, have for her—that she go forward in her quest for more distinct self-definition. As with her father, this is an agenda to which she feels she must accommodate if she is to maintain the bond with Fosshage as his "special one." I am suggesting that, alongside the patient's genuine developmental progress, her unconscious compliance with Fosshage's developmental agenda has codetermined the galloping pace of the analysis and that this entire, complex intersubjective system is both represented and disguised in her dream imagery.

Stolorow is accurate, I believe, in noting that Tamara's experience of my emphasis on development could have been assimilated into her expectation of the need to accommodate to my personal agenda in order to maintain the necessary tie. (Indeed, clear evidence of this emerged at other junctures in the analysis.) Within this momentary waking state, Tamara was clearly struggling within the transferential relationship with the repetitive and conflictual issue of accommodation, a familiar relational pattern that, as I suggested, was precipitated during a particularly stressful time requiring a fortified self-selfobject connection. However, at this particular juncture, rather than speaking of my "developmental agenda," Tamara spoke of my "secret love" (and she was indeed capable of engendering loving feelings in me) as my personal agenda that required her to leave her husband to secure the tie with me, a very complex intersubjective scenario we were addressing and in the process of analyzing.

On a more general level, the extent to which a patient's "progress" may be an accommodation to the analyst, rather than genuine developmental progress, is always a matter of concern in psychoanalysis. Moreover, the interaction of two subjectivities will inevitably result in transferential enactments. What is crucial, however, and perhaps central, is the analysis of these enactments to prevent retraumatization and to free the patient from their compulsive repetition. The degree to which the analyst is dominated by specific organizational patterns will delimit the analyst's ability "to decenter," required in order to understand the subjective experience of the patient, and will determine whether the enactment becomes an analyzable event or a retraumatization for the patient. This act of understanding and explaining is the foundation of the "new" experience in the analytic arena.

Although the patient was struggling with the repetitive accommodation theme during these waking moments, *a new experience* was clearly imaged in the dream in which the dreamer did *not* have to accommodate to the other's agenda. This new experience is depicted in her dream with the realization that the stallion can take care of himself, enabling her to proceed to her destination. And, importantly, in contrast to her transferential expectations and fears, the exercising of her new-found freedom from her role as caretaker did not rob her in her dream of the necessary selfobject tie, subsequently present in the form of a supportive man. Presumably through the persistent analysis of the accommodation theme and corresponding enactments, in combination with the facilitation of the self-selfobject tie, the patient, as evidenced in the dream, was experiencing emergent freedom from the repetitive theme of accommodation and consolidating a positive cohesive sense of self. This new freedom and self-reorganization emerging in her dream was, as I previously stated, confounded by the more familiar and conflictual accommodation theme in the waking state. Thus, the dreaming and waking states each have their particular tone and shape and the degree of correspondence varies from moment to moment. *Although accommodation might have "codetermined the galloping pace of the analysis," the dream portrays, at that moment, that genuine developmental progress is ruling the "night."*

Although the accommodation theme clearly emerges in waking mentation during the ensuing analytic hours, is there evidence of its functioning in this particular dreaming state? Stolorow (personal communication) concluded, on the basis of the considerable movement evident in the dream (taking it, from my vantage point, in isolation from the dream context) combined with the patient's waking reflections about accommodation, that the accommodation theme was present but disguised in the dream. This contention exemplifies my thesis of the subordination of dreaming to waking mentation, that is, if a theme emerges in waking thought but is not directly revealed in the dream, rather than viewing the two states as distinctly different, the theme is assumed to be latently present and, therefore, disguised in the dream. The door is thereby reopened potentially to massive translations of dream imagery that, in turn, "disguise" the dreaming experience or the actual meaning of the dream.

In contrast, I propose that an important developmental thrust was clearly imaged in Tamara's dream. Through her dreaming mentation, she furthers the process, based on her analytic experience, of establishing personal freedom from her repetitive experience of accommodation, facilitating the rediscovery of her internal direction. Clearly, accommodation is an organizational (transferential) mode easily evoked, as was evident in the analytic (waking) work. But to assume on this basis, even though the accommodation theme was not apparent in the dream, that it must be a part of the dreamer's experience at that moment, and therefore is present somewhere in the dream in disguised form, is to assess the dream from a waking perspective, imposing a waking bias on the dream and blurring the dreaming experience. Clinically, this error potentially undermines the patient's developmental thrusts just as they are emerging in her dreaming experience.

REFERENCES

Fosshage, J. (1983), The psychological function of dreams: A revised psychoanalytic perspective. *Psychoanal. Contemp. Thought*, 6:641–669.

REPLY
Harry Fiss

I am heartened by Dr. Stolorow's positive comments about my paper and by the fact that he found my conclusions "persuasive." These are indeed welcome words. I am also greatly indebted to him for his seminal ideas on dreaming and the organization of self-experience (Atwood and Stolorow, 1984, pp. 97–117).

However, I take exception to his implication that I am not paying sufficient attention to latent content or that I am excluding or minimizing the unconscious in my conceptualizations. "In emphasizing that the aims of defense and disguise contribute to the construction of dream symbols and that therefore the distinction between manifest imagery and latent meaning continues to be applicable, our views differ from those of Greenberg, Fiss, and Fosshage," Stolorow writes. "What we need is not an approach to dreams that excludes the unconscious, but a revised theory of the unconscious that is consistent with current clinical knowledge."

It appears to me that Stolorow misunderstands something about my view of the function of the dream process. I am not at all suggesting, as some of my colleagues seem to be doing, that we should disregard latent content, nor am I diminishing the importance of the unconscious. I *am* proposing that we pay more attention to the *manifest* content. Clearly there is a need for both concepts. Nor should the role of wish fulfillment in dream formation be discounted either. A case in point is the study referred to in my paper (Fiss, 1980) in which recovering alcoholics were found to crave alcohol when they dreamed about drinking in a conflicted way; when they had gratifying dreams about drinking, they generally experienced very little craving. Bokert (1968) similarly found that thirsty subjects who incorporated water into their dream content were less thirsty the following morning and drank less water than subjects who did not dream about water. The wish fulfillment hypothesis is strongly supported by these findings. On the other hand, little evidence for a need to disguise or transform the wish (to drink) could be found in either of these studies.

That disguise is unnecessary for wish fulfillment to occur in dreaming is further indicated by the results of a study by Fiss, Klein, and Shollar (1974) in which all REM periods were artificially shortened (that is, interrupted) over a period of four consecutive nights. The study was undertaken to find out whether the dream process would intensify and accelerate as a result of these interruptions. The results showed that this is exactly what happened: the content of the dreams reported by the subjects became progressively more and more elaborate and more and more affect laden; but at the same time the content also became more openly wish fulfilling, less disguised, and less bizarre. Concomitantly, the subjects' polysomnograms (sleep recordings) indicated that the subjects slept most soundly when they were having their most intense, conflictful, and dynamically revealing dreams! It was as though the interruptions had helped bring the subjects' focal conflicts into ever sharper focus, without in the least disturbing their sleep. For example, one of our subjects, a sexually dysfunctional young man conflicted over his homosexuality, initially reported such dream symbols as a bottle top breaking off or the seat of a motorcycle inflating. These images gave way with increasing frequency to transparent, undisguised scenes such as "it ended up in bed with somebody, a man." It was as though these subjects slept in order to dream (and not the other way round) and dreamed in order to concentrate periodically on what was troubling them most—perhaps to work out some kind of solution?

Perhaps this is why dream symbols "dramatize," "affirm," or "reify" our experiences. In fact, Stolorow tells us that dream symbols "actualize" or "solidify" our experiences so that the cohesiveness of the self may be better maintained. I don't see that my inferences differ markedly from his. In fact, his and mine are remarkably consistent. This congruence is all the more noteworthy if we consider that they originate from two entirely different sources: mine from sleep laboratory data, his from clinical observation.

Stolorow also refers to the "intersubjective context" in which dreams take form and without which they cannot be comprehended. This point is well taken. That dreams serve a communicative function has long been postulated (Bergmann, 1966). The results of the study reported by Fiss, Klein, and Shollar (1974) support this idea, as the subjects needed not only to experience or recall a dream, but also to communicate a dream. Thus, the intensification of the dream process that resulted from our interruption procedure can also be understood as increased pressure to talk about the dreams; and the gradual disappearance of symbolic transformation over the course of the four nights may be viewed as reflecting the subjects' increasing willingness to give away their "secrets" behind a protective cloak of seemingly innocent story telling. For instance, it was not until after his participation in the experiment that the aforementioned sexually preoccupied young man was able to admit that he had sexual problems. The importance of the dream's intersubjective context is also underscored by the finding by Whitman, Kramer, and Baldridge (1963) that the same subjects reported different dreams in the laboratory and on the psychoanalytic couch.

That dreaming and dream reporting have distinct psychological functions is also shown by the fact that subjects who are encouraged to report their dreams have significantly longer REM periods than do subjects who are prevented from reporting their dreams (Fiss and Ellman, 1973). The validity of the concept of the intersubjectivity of dreaming can thus hardly be disputed. Once again we find that sleep laboratory data are remarkably consistent with self-psychological formulations about the dream process.

This brings me to a point raised by Dr. Tolpin in his discussion of my paper. He states that "dreams may consist of messages about somatic states, or they may be attempts to reduce a variety of internal psychological tensions. They may express conflicts, erotic and aggressive urges, wishes and fears of all kinds, states of one's self, moods, defensive tendencies, states of disorganization, states of despair, attempts to solve intellectual problems, visions of creative possibilities, and so on. . . . The function of dreams and dreaming . . . can be understood to include all these and perhaps still other motivations."

There is little question that we are moving in the direction of a *multifunctional* model of dreaming. Freud (1905) actually had such a model in mind in his analysis of the case of Dora, in which he advanced the idea that the meaning of a dream could be "of as many different sorts as the process of waking thought; in one case it could be a fulfilled wish, in another a realized fear, or again a reflection persisting on into sleep, or an intention, or a piece of creative thought" (p. 68). Freud never took this idea seriously, however, and continued to favor his concept of wish fulfillment. Even the Irma dream, which so clearly serves a defense function, is portrayed as validating his wish-fulfillment hypothesis. Were he alive today, he would probably concede that, in addition to wish fulfillment, dreams may serve multiple ego-functions (adaptive, defensive, drive-and-mood-regulatory, conflict-solving), communicative-intersubjective functions, identity-preserving functions, and so on. "The list is clearly incomplete," Tolpin correctly states. But this is precisely why an organizing schema centered on the structuring of experience in terms of such broad-based categories as "self-maintenance," "self-development," and "self-restoration" can help us construct a truly comprehensive theory of dreaming. Only higher order constructs such as those focused on the self can lead to clinically relevant and empirically valid propositions about the function of dreaming. I do not agree with Tolpin that "what we are illuminating when we investigate dreams is not the function of dreaming but the function of mind." Dreaming is as much "mind" as any other form of experience. Yet would anyone seriously argue that a drug-induced hallucination is functionally the same as concentrated problem-solving activity? Mind is a many splendored thing, and to do it justice may well require a multifaceted experimental approach. Only by dealing with complex human phenomena can a cognitive psychology offer a meaningful (nonmechanistic) account of meaningful human behavior (Williams, 1987).

REFERENCES

Atwood, G. E. & Stolorow, R. (1984), *Structures of Subjectivity*. Hillsdale, NJ: The Analytic Press.

Bergmann, M. (1966), The intrapsychic and communicative aspects of the dream. *Internat. J. Psycho-Anal.* 47:356–363.

Bokert, E. (1968), The effects of thirst and a related verbal stimulus on dream reports. *Diss. Abs.*, 28:122–131.

Fiss, H. (1980), Dream content and response to withdrawal from alcohol. *Sleep Res.*, 9:152.

———— & Ellman, S. (1973), REM sleep interruption: Experimental shortening of REM period duration. *Psychophysiol.*, 10:510–516.

———— Klein, G. & Shollar, E. (1974), "Dream intensification" as a function of prolonged REM period interruption. In: *Psychoanalysis and Contemporary Science*, ed. L. Goldberger. New York: International Universities Press, pp. 399–424.

Freud, S. (1905), Fragment of an analysis of a case of hysteria. *Standard Edition*, 7:7–122. London: Hogarth Press, 1953.

Whitman, R., Kramer, M. & Baldridge, B. (1963), Which dream does the patient tell? *Arch. Gen. Psychiat.*, 8:277–282.

Williams, R. (1987), Can cognitive psychology offer a meaningful account of meaningful human action? *J. Mind & Beh.*, 8:209–221.

REPLY
Ramon Greenberg

Drs. Tolpin and Stolorow and I share some confusion about each other's comments, but after reflection I think I understand the source of our confusion. My sense of their remarks is that we are all saying essentially the same thing in different languages. If I understand their questions, they had trouble integrating the material from research into a self psychologic perspective and therefore believed that I was saying something different.

Stolorow responds to my hypothesis that dreaming is "integrating information from current experience with past memories in order to produce schemas that are organizers of complicated behavioral tasks. Thus, the dreamer can learn and modify or adapt behavior to new demands of the environment." He feels this is not directly applicable to the domain of self psychological inquiry—"namely, the organization of self-experience and its vicissitudes in relation to the subjectively experienced surround." I think his idea is quite similar to mine but is expressed in purely self-psychologic language. Because I was trying to capture the overall function of dreaming, including the evidence of the role of REM sleep in animals, I tried to phrase my hypothesis in broad, general terms. I find his formulation to be a special case but not a different one. Obviously we cannot use the language of self psychology in referring to animals. The clinical example I provided attempts to illustrate how this view of dream function can be applied in a self psychology mode. While in this presentation I limited the discussion to the concept of the self-state dream, elsewhere (Greenberg, 1987) I have tried to demonstrate how well the ideas derived from sleep research can also fit with those of self psychology.

Stolorow's comments about imagery are true insofar as the dreamer is aware of the dream, especially when the dream becomes the focus in a clinical setting. However, I do not think this is the function of the imagery in dreams. What I have tried to suggest, instead, is that the imagery in the dream is an illustration of the process that is going on in REM sleep. It is the form that the organizational process takes. (This is also relevant to Tolpin's idea that the dream is only a window to the mind's ongoing activity). The research I have cited suggests, rather, that the mental activity in REM sleep is *different* from that during waking and performs a function that cannot occur in the waking state.

Stolorow questions my omitting consideration of the role of defenses in dreams and of the use of associations in their understanding. Of course defenses appear in dreams, but not to disguise dream meaning. Rather they are there because they are one of the means for handling the problems presented the "self in relation to the subjectively experienced surround" (Stolorow's wording). Finally, I would certainly say that associations to the dream are necessary for understanding. How else can one determine the connection with the waking problems with which the dream is dealing or the connections with the past that underlie these problems. The clinical example I have presented clearly demonstrates the importance of the patient's associations for an understanding of her dreams.

Let me now address Tolpin's comments. I find his observations about broadening the concept of the self-state dream to be very much in line with what I have been trying to say. His (Tolpin, 1983) excellent paper "Self Psychology and the Interpretation of Dreams" makes the similarity even more striking. However, our use of different language has created some difficulty in seeing the overlap. Tolpin suggests that his dream is, in effect, outside the categories of dream functions that Fiss and I proposed. On the contrary, it illustrates a point that I apparently did not make sufficiently clear. The functions that we propose for dreaming are not always successfully carried out in the dreams. That is, there are more or less effective dreams. The traumatic dream is an example of the total failure of the integrative process. Tolpin's dream also shows a failure in the process. As he suggests, he continued to have difficulty in integrating the sleep research findings into his view of dreaming.

Despite my disagreement with some of the issues raised by Tolpin and Stolorow, I welcome the opportunity they provide to clarify my ideas. We seem to have arrived at very similar places in our understanding of dreams. Stolorow and Tolpin must certainly be added to the list of analysts who have presented a view of dreaming that differs in some respects from Freud's but that is consistent with the research derived ideas I have presented.

REFERENCES

Greenberg, R. (1987), Self psychology and dreams: The merging of different perspectives. *Psychiat. J. Univ. Ottawa*, 12:98–102.
Tolpin, P. (1983), Self psychology and the interpretation of dreams. In: *The Future of Psychoanalysis*, ed. A. Goldberg. New York: International Universities Press, pp. 255–271.

Development

Chapter 5

Child Analysis and Adult Analysis

Estelle Shane
Morton Shane

At the first Conference on the Psychology of the Self in 1979, we presented a paper (Shane and Shane, 1980) on the development of the self. After reviewing the extant literature on self-development, we chose to focus on Kohut, Mahler, and Piaget as the most original and cogent contributors at that time. In particular, we hoped to find congruencies between the reconstructed view of development put forward by Kohut (1959, 1971, 1977, 1984) based on his self-psychologically informed analyses of adults, and the prospective view of development put forward by Mahler (1968; Mahler, Pine, and Bergman, 1975) based on her classically informed observations on infants and toddlers. We looked to Piaget (1923; 1973; Piaget and Inhelder, 1966) to establish the cognitive limits on theoretical speculation. Our focus at the time was on the interesting tension established in gathering data about psychological phases of development from two different perspectives, the reconstructed and the directly observed. We minimized the differences in theoretical orientation because we wanted to establish a basis for a constructive integration among three creative approaches to understanding development, forming in that way an agreed upon delineation of an integrated psychoanalytic self, not a Kohutian self, nor a Freudian-Mahlerian self, nor a Piagetian self, but a self that might be acknowledged by all developmentally informed psychoanalysts as a beginning format for discussion, debate, and theoretical negotiation.

Since then much has changed. Psychoanalytic infant observation

59

has expanded vigorously (e.g. Greenspan, 1981; Lichtenberg, 1983; Emde and Sorye, 1983; Stern, 1985), definitively undercutting Mahler, Pine, and Bergman's (1975) observations regarding the first year of life. Gone from serious theoretical consideration are the autistic and symbiotic phases; gone, too, is "hatching" at six months; and seriously challenged is the entire separation-individuation process leading to autonomy. While Mahler's descriptions of children interacting with their parents during the second year of life remain valid and continue to germinate original research in such areas as gender identity (Stoller, 1976, 1979), father hunger and triangulation (Herzog, 1980), and reactive aggression (Parens, 1979), the first-year-of-life developmental underpinnings for this research will have to be revised and, in fact, are in the process of such revision (Pine, 1981). By comparison, self psychology has borne the impact of infant research much better and, in fact, has been largely affirmed, although, as we will suggest, some revision of theory was required to remain consistent with the newer contributions. As for Piaget and the use of his theories of cognitive development for setting limits on the notion of what the infant is able to do, think, and fantasy, recent infant research has also brought into some question his timetable of earliest cognition (Stern, 1985).

But what about the task we undertook to integrate Freudian-based Mahlerian and Kohutian-based self-psychological theories of development? It seems to us that Kohut himself has provided a way for this synthesis. In order to accomplish this integrative expansion, this assimilation of the mainstream into self psychology, Kohut (1984) identified classical concepts that required rethinking, reorganizing, and reprioritizing. Some time-honored ideas had to be modified, or adapted, or discarded outright. In this essay, we will undertake to assess the merit of some of Kohut's proposals, not just for self psychology, but for all of analysis, as we feel Kohut intended.

But how does one evaluate the effectiveness of new ideas? As clinicians, we most often ask, does it lead to a broader, or clearer, understanding of the clinical issues? Yet we should also ask, whenever relevant, is the theoretical idea either consistent with infant observational research or, at the least, not invalidated by that research? This is especially important now with the accelerated progress that has been made in the field of infant observation and developmental studies. We propose, therefore, to look at some of the developmental precepts of self psychology advanced by Kohut in *How Does Analysis Cure?* (1984) in the light of adult analysis, child analysis, and infant research.

For several reasons, we have chosen out of the large universe of contributors to turn to Stern (1985) as our source for infant observation. For one thing, he has summarized a great deal of the widely divergent current research in this field. For another, he is a psychoanalyst, so his perspective and his concerns are essentially clinical. Finally, he places the sense of the self at the center of his inquiry and his developmental schema. Putting aside the expectable stages and phases of development prominent in psychoanalytic and cognitive theory, he invents his own developmental progression based on four senses of the self *subjectively* perceived by the infant. These senses of the self, while sequential in emerging, once present, remain throughout life. They are: the sense of the emergent self, beginning at birth to two months; the sense of the core self, beginning at two to six months; the sense of the subjective self, beginning at seven to 15 months, and the sense of the verbal self, beginning from 15 to 36 months.

We will start with a general consideration of self psychology's concept of the selfobject, defined as an object that may be experienced by the subject as without a separate center of intentionality and that functions to sustain, strengthen, and enhance the self.

Stern offers solid support for this concept, the beginnings of which can be observed at the age of two to six months, Stern's period of emergence of the core self, when the infant first develops the capacity to experience an other as a separate, organized, distinct entity. Naming this entity the *self-regulating other*, Stern describes this other as functioning to stabilize the core self and to regulate the infant's own experience. What is important here is that the self-regulating other inferred from direct observations on infants in interaction with their mothers is remarkably close to the selfobject concept derived from adult analysis. Stern captures the essence of what is meant in self psychology by a selfobject function when he describes the infant's subjective experience of a self-regulating other. He says, "The self experience is indeed dependent upon the presence and action of the other, but it still belongs entirely to the self. . . . Thus, the core self is related (but not fused) with the core other and yet is experienced as a functional part of the self experience" (p. 105).

However, Stern seems uncertain about the equivalence of his concept of self-regulating other and self psychology's concept of a selfobject. While he notes that the functions attributed to the two concepts are identical, and while they both refer to a subjectively perceived other, interactions with which are experienced as belonging to the self, he demurs because, for one thing, Stern believes, erroneously, that the selfobject is still defined in self psychology as beginning in archaic fusion with the self. Repeatedly noting that research demonstrates prewired emergent structures of self and other distinct from one another almost from the beginning of life, he maintains that he finds no evidence for the postulate that the infant begins life in a psychological merger with the other. The merger states prominent in psychopathology, and in moments of intense intimacy or intense need during adult life, are not conceptualized in infant observation as a prolonged phase of normal development but, rather, as fleeting experiences of intense affect-sharing that do occur in infancy as well as throughout life.

Of course, it is true that fusion was once hypothesized in self psychology as part of a normal prolonged developmental experience of the infant in the archaic self-selfobject matrix, similar to Mahler's symbiotic phase in normal development. But self psychology, responsive to the findings of infant observation, was able to rethink, and then drop, the normal merger aspect. This rethinking permitted the selfobject concept to maintain its primary functions of sustaining, supporting, and strengthening the self, with these functions being experienced as part of the self but not represented as fused with it. A second reason that Stern may hesitate to make a simple equation between the self-regulating other and the selfobject function is the laudable respect he maintains for the unbridgeable gap between the reconstructed clinical infant and the observed actual infant, a position we can only strongly agree with, but which we feel should not unduly impede one from seeking roots in the preverbal infant experience that correspond to transference manifestations.

Confirmation of a new selfobject transference introduced by Kohut (1984) in *How Does Analysis Cure?* can also be found in infant research. Kohut had provided an enlarged repertoire of potential transference categories, namely, the mirroring and idealizing transferences, facilitating analytic purchase on heretofore unreachable pathology and instituting a developmental line of narcissism progressing in normal development and in analysis from archaic to mature forms. In *How Does Analysis Cure?*, he elaborates on and more sharply distinguishes a third selfobject transference, the alter-ego or twinship transference, viewing it as representing one of the three basic self-affirming and self-maintaining experiences in early childhood that have been clearly recognized to date and leaving the way open for the delineation of other selfobject transferences in the future. Kohut postulates that the alter-ego relationship reflects experiences that cannot be classified as either mirroring or idealizing but instead repeat in the transference a distinctly different category of experience, essential human relatedness and alikeness. Kohut uses the examples of the little girl kneading dough in the kitchen next to her mother, and the little boy working with tools in the workroom next to his father, as commonly observed early latency examples of this self-maintaining, self-affirming experience. But, he adds, we need additional data obtained through either observation or introspection, or both, indicating that important alter-ego experiences are self-sustaining events seen not only in childhood but also earlier, in infancy, and later in adulthood and throughout life.

Stern provides observations that support the existence of such a separate category of selfobject experience in infancy. In his developmental progression of the sense of self, Stern identifies the domain of intersubjective relatedness as emerging between the seventh and ninth months of life. At this time the infant reveals a new and powerful motivational force, so strong and vital, says Stern, that it might qualify as a motivational need state. This is the desire to be known by and to know another, to be understood by and to understand another, and to share intimately in intentions and affect states with another. The infant discovers at this time what part of the private world is sharable and what part remains outside of recognized human experience. The difference this sharing makes, Stern asserts, is between the feeling of psychic human membership and the feeling of psychic isolation. While Stern refers to this experience in a general way as "parental mirroring," in relation to affect attunement, it appears more likely to contain the specific and basic roots of the alter-ego selfobject transference of essential human alikeness.

The elaboration in *How Does Analysis Cure?* of the alter-ego transference is a helpful expansion of self-psychological theory, adding significantly to the repertoire of potential selfobject transferences. But just as important, it seems to address and to clarify a concept belonging to classical analysis, the therapeutic working alliance (Zetzel, 1956; Greenson, 1965). The working alliance concept carries with it a basic therapeutic intent on the part of the analyst and a basic wish to get help on the part of the patient; but the force of the alliance is fueled by the selfobject bond, in general, and the alter-ego selfobject bond in particular. The selfobject bond conveys a respectful mirroring of the patient and an idealization of the analyst, but more pervasive, essential human alikeness and relatedness is conveyed in every patient-analyst interchange: the patient reveals his private world; the analyst understands this world as human, believable, and familiar, and conveys this special understanding back to his patient; and in the same instance, the analyst conveys his own identical humanness, as well. This seems to explain better than anything else the power of the alliance and its genetic depths, leading us to contend that the alter-ego selfobject transference, more than the other two, is alive as a background in every successful therapeutic experience, self-psychological, mainstream, or whatever; and, we contend further, its absence puts any therapy in jeopardy.

By creating the basic concepts of the selfobject and the selfobject transference, Kohut merely *added* to the armamentarium of all analysts, classical analysts included. But his ideas about conflict and the Oedipus complex impose more of a challenge, requiring rethinking of classical ideas. One can best understand Kohut's reformulation of the Oedipus complex by looking first at the role he posits for conflict in self psychology. While in the classical model inter- and intrasystemic conflict are taken as primary in the organization of pathology, and the alteration and resolution of that conflict are seen as the key mutative factor in the analytic process, Kohut reduces considerably the influence of this central conceptualization. He asserts that all forms of psychopathology are based on defects in the structure of the self, on distortions of the self, or on weaknesses of the self, and that all these flaws are based on disturbances in the self-selfobject relationships of childhood. Thus, conflicts are viewed not as the primary cause of pathology, but as the result of that pathology. So Kohut believes that while conflicts may be pathogenic and need to be analyzed, their influence is secondary.

The place of conflict as secondary but significant can best be illustrated by his most recent understanding of the Oedipus complex. Kohut distinguishes a normal oedipal *phase* from a pathological *complex*. The phase is both universal and nonpathological, with normal, healthy assertiveness and normal, healthy affection in the child being met by adequate selfobject acceptance and affirmation on the part of the parents. On the other hand, the Oedipus complex is characterized by healthy assertiveness being transformed, or broken down, into destructive hostility, and healthy affection disintegrating into isolated, fragmented sexual impulses. The Oedipus complex is created by parental selfobjects who do not function properly vis à vis the heretofore normally developing child who may enter the phase with a self enthusiastically open to new developmental opportunities, but upon experiencing subtle yet repeated deleterious misattunements, becomes overly anxious.

It is thus in the Oedipus complex, not in the oedipal phase, that Kohut sees intense castration anxiety. In work with such patients, the conflicts around castration anxiety are analyzed in the traditional sense, in terms of drive-wish and defense. But Kohut stresses that the more profound analysis is concerned with the underlying selfobject failures. Following a prolonged working through and filling in of the self defects through transmuting internalization, the patient experiences a normal oedipal phase in the transference, characterized by a gender-differentiated firm self. Thus, in the Oedipus complex, the conflicts around competitive hostile destructiveness and incestuous lustful desires, and the attendant anxiety, guilt, and fear of punishment, are secondary to primary defects in the self originating in the oedipal period as a result of inadequate selfobject responsiveness. In the analysis, too, Kohut says, the resolution of conflict is but an intermediate step toward cure.

In order to test and assess the usefulness, reasonableness, and applicability of this reformulation of the derivation of the Oedipus complex, we can turn to child analysis and to infant and child observation. First, a vignette of a child analytic case.

Jordan, a four-year-old, was brought to an analyst supervised by one of us because of his fears about sitting on the toilet and because in nursery school it was noted that from being an outgoing, confident and friendly child he had become excessively anxious, timid, and prone to daydreaming. Jordan had been upset since the age of three and a half when a four-year-old friend of the family died suddenly of fulminating pneumonia. Because he asked so many questions, he was told about the funeral and about how the child had been put into a hole in the ground. He had wondered how the little boy would eat and whether he would be lonely and afraid of the dark. The parents handled these questions and fears in an exemplary manner, hoping the matter would be laid to rest. But the combination of a lively imagination and age-appropriately immature cognitive capacities, together with an uncharacteristic failure on the part of his parents to meet his needs, prevented this from happening. Instead, Jordan formulated the idea unconsciously that the toilet was like the grave and that he himself could fall through the hole, as his feces did, and be flushed away to his death. He also worried, being curious about little girls his own age, that his penis and testicles might fall off when he sat on the toilet. He was aware of and could talk to his parents about the fear about his penis and testicles, but the ideas about the toilet equalling the grave and the fear that his total self could be buried there, and the whole connection to his dead friend, was unavailable to him and of course to his parents as well. Then, after some months, Jordan began to worry when his parents were absent that they, like someone dead, would never return, though he could not himself make that connection. After all else had failed, including a lot of talk, behavior modification, and the like, Jordan still remained anxious in school and fearful of the toilet, so the parents came in for consultation and subsequently agreed to analysis for Jordan.

Jordan is an only child raised by working parents, both lawyers and both involved in their professions, but who had gone to great lengths to spend adequate and equal time with their son. However, six months earlier, his father, because of an important legal trial taking place out of town, had had to be away from home for a three-month period for a case that was unexpectedly difficult, lengthy, and absorbing of his time and energy. Both Jordan and his mother missed his father during this period. Jordan sought solace in his mother's bed, and his mother, more lax than usual and more needy herself, permitted him to join her. However, she too was busy with her work and not always available. It was during this period that Jordan developed a fear of being on the toilet alone and would ask his mother to be nearby, to leave the door open, and sometimes to sit in the bathroom with him while he had a bowel movement.

When Jordan came to his first analytic hour, he had some difficulty leaving his mother; he had brought a toy bird with him, which, in play, like the bird in *Hansel and Gretel*, led him back safely to his mother's side. His analyst noted that when Jordan was involved with his mother, he seemed inordinately sexual and seductive, touching her breasts and kissing her passionately, an attitude that remained characteristic of him for several months but gradually subsided. In his beginning sessions, Jordan revealed in the transference his preoccupation with the death of his friend. He would throw the analyst away and bury him, doing to the analyst what he was afraid would be done to him—what had been, from his point of view, actually done to him by his father. It was relatively easy to put together his connection of the toilet and the grave, and his fear of the toilet disappeared. Transference issues around separation and death then became prominent, Jordan tying the analyst with Scotch tape to the furniture before the weekends to insure that he would not disappear. As his fears of death subsided, oedipal themes emerged. Jordan expressed a wish to grow extremely tall and strong and, like Superman, possess large muscles, the ability fo fly, and the ability to inspire awe, especially in his mother.

In an hour that most impressively demonstrated the urgency of his wishes and illusted the ingenuity of his creation, Jordan had a puppet eat the analyst's tie, telling him that this would make the puppet strong. Then, slipping out of the play into direct action, he began to eat the tie himself, gleefully, teasingly, but insistently. Analyst and patient talked about the tie's potent powers to make the puppet, and, yes, to make Jordan too, a man of importance, with, as he said, "big muscles and everything." In working through his desire to acquire the strength of a man, they came up against his fear of women. Jordan used a witch puppet to bite off his analyst's nose.

When the analyst wondered nervously if he should be afraid of the witch for any other reason, since he valued not just his nose, but indeed his whole body, Jordan warned that the witch bites off penises too. Patient and analyst were both very relieved to throw the witch far away behind the desk.

As the oedipal themes were worked on repeatedly, Jordan's anxiety lessened, and the analysis proceeded fairly rapidly to a satisfactory conclusion. Oedipal conflicts and struggles within an Oedipus complex can be easily demonstrated, but in this case, the most significant aspect of the pathology was the apparent inability of Jordan's parents to sustain his self-needs through the oedipal phase. While they were more than adequately able to understand and respond to this child during earlier phases, circumstances combined to make them less than optimally available during the oedipal period. As for Jordan's getting better, we see this as attributable to several factors. There was a resolution of Jordan's oedipal difficulty within the transference and within his life. This resolution resulted from Jordan's having been understood and having had explained to him his confusions about death and desertion, his traumatic disillusionment with his heretofore idealized father, and his injured self-esteem at feeling this idealized father had lost interest in him and was unwilling to impart to him his full strength. This was all relived in the transference, including his coming to understand his ambivalent oedipal wishes for his mother and concomitant fears of retaliation from both his father and mother. An important aspect of the transference, as the analysis proceeded, was its idealizing selfobject nature, which aspect helped Jordan to deal with his disappointment with his father. Another significant contribution to the child's resumption of normal development was that the parents themselves, through their work with the analyst, became better able to respond to Jordan, once again achieving the empathic attunement that had characterized their earlier relationship with him.

No case can prove any theoretical proposition but we hope it illustrates the important emphasis Kohut brings to the oedipal phase, that the oedipal self is significantly influenced by selfobject responsiveness, or lack of it, by the oedipal parents; that oedipal pathology carries with it on an oedipal level concomitant selfobject failures that must be attended to in therapy in addition to the oedipal conflicts themselves. Whether selfobject failures are primary and the conflicts secondary, as Kohut asserts, cannot be determined by Jordan's case. Certainly the castration anxiety was more prominent at the onset, and only after it had abated somewhat did the striving for an idealizable oedipal selfobject emerge in the foreground, along with an attendant understanding of how Jordan had experienced his father as letting him down.

Kohut goes on to say that in a child whose self-development is normal, oedipal conflicts would not be pathogenic were there sufficient support from the surround. Given that a multitude of children navigate the oedipal shoals without visible calamity, it seems difficult to fault Kohut's reasoning in this regard. And, as a matter of fact, psychoanalytic research on infants and toddlers into the derivation of castration anxiety and destructive aggressiveness validates this contention inasmuch as the intensity of the anxiety is related to primary difficulties between the child and the surround. We can point to Galenson and Roiphe (1974), who note excessive castration anxieties and concerns in both boys and girls who have difficulties with their mothers; to Parens (1979), who sees assertiveness as normal and destructive aggressiveness as a pathological response to an inadequate relationship between parent and child; and to our own observations over the years in a normal nursery school setting, which indicate that *excessive* expression of either sexuality or hostility is associated with children who are having difficulty negotiating the oedipal phase related to child-parent disharmonies. This is not to say, however, that a normal child in the normal oedipal phase adequately responded to by his parents feels no more than a joyful affection toward them, nor that the child does not experience intense sensual and sexual longings, fantasies, and attendant conflicts toward both parents. Such a contention would fly in the face of our own experience with children. The point is that such conflicts need not be pathogenic.

Another clinical issue that Kohut addressed with considerable emphasis at the first self psychology conference in 1979 was most significant in distinguishing his developmental framework from mainstream analysis in general and from the work of Margaret Mahler in particular: the issue of autonomy from supporting objects, recognized by mainstream analysis as a goal of normal development, versus Kohut's assertion of lifelong dependence on selfobjects. Kohut's position regarding the normality of lifelong selfobject needs would, on the face of it, seem to be confirmed by infant observation. Stern (1985) notes that from the very beginning, the person's life is always social. With the development of the core self taking place when the infant is two to six months old, most of what the infant does, feels, and perceives occurs in the context of human relationships. And with cued memory setting in at that time, henceforth subjective experiences throughout life are largely social, whether we are alone or not: the experience of self with self-regulating other and self-attuning other as a subjective reality is almost pervasive. Hence, the normal person from birth to death seems almost always to be reliant on the presence of others, either external or internal, for self-sustenance. But, on the other hand, Stern writes, in regard to the Mahler-Kohut disagreement concerning autonomy as a goal of development, that a frontiersman would value independence from the presence of the external self-regulating other because that is what is required for survival, whereas in an interdependent culture no such independence is necessary for survival. Thus, autonomy from, or dependence on, others is best understood as a relative issue depending mainly on the values of the subculture. A moralistic stance either way is uncalled for, as Kohut implied.

It is clear that in the "subculture" of American mainstream psychoanalysis, autonomy from the presence of affirming and sustaining selfobjects is held in high regard still as an incontrovertible, valued sign of maturity and thus as an analytic goal. We would like to emphasize that to the extent that such attitudes are held moralistically, either consciously or unconsciously, they will iatrogenically interfere with both smooth and healthy development and with the analytic relationship. Two brief vignettes will illustrate this point.

CASE ILLUSTRATION

In the first, one of us supervised the intensive psychotherapy of a 25-year-old actress, Ms. B, who suffered from inhibitions that interfered with her performance. She also had difficulty relating to her live-in boyfriend. Ms. B was the younger of two children, her older brother strongly favored by both parents and supported by them in his graduate education. She too had initially been supported in her career; but when she persisted in the theatre well into her adult life, her parents withdrew their former encouraging stance, suggesting she choose something more stable and lucrative, though they did not offer financial support for further education. The analysis proceeded well in the exploration of the patient's sense of being unfairly treated by her parents and her strong envy of men, which was reexperienced in the transference with her male therapist. Ms. B looked up to her therapist as a successful professional and as one who she sensed was sympathetic to her own aspirations. In fact, he did appreciate her goals as an expression of her full potential, although he did not tell her so directly, in contrast to her boyfriend's attitude of persistent and direct derogation of her choice of career.

At a particular moment in treatment, the patient's dedication to acting threatened to wane as her lover and her parents joined forces to tell her she was wasting her time, and she toyed with the idea of just chucking it all to do fulltime office work. In this session, her therapist asked why she seemed so unable to persevere on her own. In supervision, he noted that Ms. B had appeared not only low key, but also withdrawn by the end of the session. His supervisor told him that the patient must be discouraged because she perceived herself without backing from anyone. The supervisee agreed, but the two differed theoretically and technically about how the therapist should have handled it. What he had said to her was to the effect that she should not need to have someone else to support her in her career. He explained to the supervisor that he felt she should be able to go it alone, that to rely on others was neurotic and regressive; she should have enough pride in her own ambitions, and enough strength within herself, to remain undaunted by her boyfriend's obvious lack of encouragement. Both supervisor and supervisee understood that he was attempting to remain neutral, that he was quietly on her side, and that, in fact, she had gotten sustenance from him in the past without either of them acknowledging it openly. The supervisor saw his questioning her need for support now as under-mining her view that it was justifiable to want such support and that she probably had experienced him in the session at that moment withdraw his own support. The supervisor suggested that as an alternative the therapist might have said, or might consider saying at some future time, that the patient must find it difficult to pursue her acting goal in the face of such discouragement. The supervisee felt that such a comment would have given Ms. B the feeling that she should expect such encouragement, that she was entitled to it. The supervisor could only agree that this was possible and wondered with the therapist if, indeed, she wasn't entitled to it. Wasn't that a reasonable expectation from her lover, if not from her parents? More to the point, wasn't it reasonable for her to have needed such support, especially given its rarity at crucial times in her life in the past? Isn't it likely, the supervisor asked him, that the remark would lead eventually to crucial memories of disillusionment? The supervi-see, admirably unintimidated, thought that a salient goal in therapy was independence from such regressive wishes. The supervisor was left wondering whether sometime in the future Ms. B might experi-ence with her therapist a traumatic reenactment in the transference.

CASE ILLUSTRATION

The next illustration concerns just such a traumatic reenactment. Laurren, a late adolescent girl, was referred to one of us by her analyst of six years, Dr. G. In describing the case, he said that, inexplicable to him, an unbridgeable stalemate had been reached between him and his patient; Lauren wanted to terminate, and Dr. G felt that more work was needed, although the patient was unwilling to continue with him.

With her new analyst, Lauren seemed open and eager to talk about her inner life and did so avidly, but paradoxically was often late to her sessions. When she was told that her analyst was puzzled by this, Lauren picked up what she felt was a difference from Dr. G in the way such issues were addressed. She expressed gratitude that her analyst was neither judging her as bad, nor suggesting that the lateness was in itself harmful to the analysis. In her next hour, Lauren began by wondering why she had, to some extent, to sabotage the analysis by coming late. She said that she was experiencing with her new analyst what she had already experienced with Dr. G: conflicting needs and fears of getting close. With Dr. G she had had the least painful and disappointing relationship in her life; things had gone very well between them and she could always count on Dr. G's being silently proud of her. Her paretns had not been proud of her when she made good grades, or scored well on the SATs, or won her college scholarship.

But lately she had felt that Dr. G had become subtly disapproving of her. She thought it had to do with her still needing things that had been all right to need when she was younger but were not appropriate now. For instance, Lauren brought her kitten with her to her hours with the new analyst on a few occasions. She felt that this analyst was accepting without the edge of disparagement that she sensed would have been there with Dr. G. The disparagement would have been connected to her still clinging to childish ways. Lauren saw this most clearly in relation to her clinging to her boyfriend, Bob. Dr. G had been quite open in assessing the relationship as no longer appropriate. Lauren felt that Dr. G blamed her and withheld approval from her because she was unable to be emotionally self-sufficient and still seemed to need Bob for more than just "boyfriend" needs. Dr. G had inferred that Lauren used Bob for achieving a sense of security that she should by now have within herself. He saw her persistent need for Bob as a regression to earlier behavior, when she had insisted on looking to her father or mother for approval she feared from experience would not be forthcoming. She knew Dr. G felt she should drop Bob because he was not a good boyfriend for her. She realized that she had to leave Dr. G because it had come down to either giving up Bob or giving up Dr. G. She was faced with a quandary: she still needed both of them. And that she still needed both was seen as a flaw. Lauren concluded that her lateness with her new therapist was an effort to avoid a repetition of the disappointment she had experienced with Dr. G.

It is obviously hard to judge all the factors that had led to the stalemate in the analysis, but one aspect seems clear: Dr. G had a definite idea of what was age- and phase-appropriate for Lauren in terms of neediness toward others. He felt that by this time, and with this much admirable progress in her treatment, Lauren should have achieved more independence. Kohut's suggestion that autonomy is not an invariant goal of analysis might have proven helpful to this analyst and to his patient.

But what about the larger question of whether autonomy is a legitimate goal in analysis, or whether the more appropriate goal is an expanded circle of mature selfobjects? Stern's (1985) notion that the answer is embodied in the standards of the culture or subculture may be correct theoretically, but insofar as the clinical situation goes, the answer must come, as Kohut implied at the first conference on the psychology of the self, from the expressed needs of the patient and from the flexible responsiveness of the analyst.

REFERENCES

Emde, R. N. & Sorye, J. F. (1983), The rewards of infancy: Emotional availability and maternal referencing. In: *Frontiers of Infant Psychiatry*, Vol. 2, ed. J. D. Call, E. Galenson & R. Tyson. New York: Basic Books.

Galenson, E. & Roiphe, H. (1974), The emergence of genital awareness during the second year of life. In: *Sex Differences in Behavior*, ed. R. Friedman, R. Richart & R. Vandervides. New York: Wiley, pp. 223–231.

Greenspan, S. I. (1981), Clinical infant reports: No. 1. *Psychopathology and Adaptation in Infancy and Early Childhood*. New York: International Universities Press.

Greenson, R. R. (1965), The working alliance and the transference neurosis. *Psychoanal. Quart.*, 34:155–181.

Herzog, J. (1980), Sleep disturbances in father hunger in 18-to-20-month-old boys. The Erlkoenig Syndrome. *The Psychoanalytic Study of the Child*, 35:219–236. New Haven, CT: Yale University Press.

Kohut, H. (1959), Introspection, empathy and psychoanalysis. In: *The Search for the Self*, Vol. 1, ed. P. Ornstein. New York: International Universities Press, 1978, pp. 295–232.

——— (1971), *The Analysis of the Self*. New York: International Universities Press.

——— (1977), *The Restoration of the Self*. New York: International Universities Press.

——— (1984), *How Does Analysis Cure?* ed. A. Goldberg & P. E. Stepansky. Chicago: University of Chicago Press.

Lichtenberg, J. D. (1983), *Psychoanalysis and Infant Research*. Hillsdale, NJ: The Analytic Press.

Mahler, M. (1968), *Infantile Psychosis*, Vol. 1. New York: International Universities Press.

——— Pine, F. & Bergman, A. (1975), *The Psychological Birth of the Human Infant*. New York: Basic Books.

Parens, H. (1979), *The Development of Aggression in Early Childhood*. New York: Aronson.

Piaget, J. (1923), *The Language and Thought of the Child*. Cleveland: World.

—— (1973), The affective unconscious and the cognitive unconscious. *J. Amer. Psychoanal.*, 21:249–261.

—— & Inhelder, B. (1966), *The Psychology of the Child*. New York: Basic Books, 1969.

Pine, F. (1981), In the beginning: Contributions to a psychoanalytic developmental psychology. *Internat. Rev. Psycho-Anal.*, 8:15–33.

Shane, M. & Shane, E. (1980), Psychoanalytic developmental theories of the self: An integration. In: *Advances in Self Psychology*, ed. A. Goldberg. New York: International Universities Press.

Stern, D. N. (1985), *The Interpersonal World of the Infant*. New York: Basic Books.

Stoller, R. (1976), Primary femininity. *J. Amer. Psychoanal. Assn.*, 24:59–78.

—— (1979), *Sexual Excitement*. New York: Pantheon.

Zetzel, E. R. (1956), Current concepts of transference. *Internat. J. Psycho-Anal.*, 37:369–376.

Chapter 6

Eating Disorders and Female Development: A Self-Psychological Perspective

Susan H. Sands

Eating disorders are overwhelmingly women's disorders, with females accounting for more than 90% of all bulimics and anorexics. Attempts to explain this quite remarkable gender bias have focused on three areas: first, our culture's slim standard of bodily attractiveness for women (Orbach, 1978; Wooley, Wooley, and Dyrenforth, 1980; Chernin, 1982; Polivy and Herman, 1987)—a standard that became even slimmer between the late 1950s and the late 1970s (Garner et al., 1980); second, the tendency of anorexic and bulimic women to overidentify with the female role, including the slim bodily standard (Bruch, 1973, 1978; Boskind-Lodahl, 1976; Orbach, 1978; Chernin, 1981, 1985; Steiner-Adair, 1986); and, third, the increasing pressures on modern women to juggle competing and often conflicting role demands (Boskind-White and White, 1983; Chernin, 1985; Steiner-Adair, 1986). Yet none of these cultural explanations has thoroughly answered the more fundamental questions of why *women* are so much more influenced by the slim cultural standard than are men, why certain women are so much more influenced than other women, or why the role pressures of modern life contribute to eating disorders in some women and to different disorders in other women. While these questions obviously cannot yet be answered completely, this essay is an attempt to add another piece to the puzzle.

The author wishes to thank Karen Peoples Ph.D., Deborah Weinstein M.F.C.C., Linda Cozzarelli L.C.S.W., and Abby Golomb Ph.D. for their helpful critiques of the manuscript.

We must look to early female self-development in our search for answers. I have chosen to use the perspective of psychoanalytic self psychology for two reasons: first, it is the most highly developed theory of the formation and maintenance of the self; and, second, self psychology views the processes of self-formation as fundamentally the same for girls and for boys, and, thus, by factoring out the biological determinism of classical Freudian thinking, it can more clearly elucidate psychological and cultural influences on gender development. With a few brief exceptions, however (Lachmann, 1982; Lang, 1984; Sands, 1986; Lothstein, 1988), self psychologists have not yet looked closely at gender differences in development and how these may influence the later development of gender-related pathology.

In elucidating the development of the self, self psychology has stressed the crucial importance of empathic responsiveness from the selfobject environment. Kohut (1971, 1977) has focused primarily on the need for mirroring and idealizing responsiveness: mirroring referring to admiration and confirmation of the child's sense of specialness and greatness, and idealizing referring to the child's need to merge with the calmness and power of an admired other. According to a recent reformulation by Stolorow, Brandchaft, and Atwood (1987), the overarching selfobject need is for affect attunement, which leads over time to affect integration and which subsumes mirroring and idealizing needs.

It is the dual hypothesis of this essay that (1) there are special problems for little girls in general along the mirroring and idealizing lines of development and that these gender-based vicissitudes help predispose little girls to the development of eating disorders later on; and (2) in eating-disordered families, these special problems may be seen in exaggerated form. My observations are based on clinical material from 27 eating-disordered patients seen by me over the past seven years—including bulimic, anorexic or anorexic-like (severely restricting food intake) patients.

I will explore three particular problem areas in female development and their contribution to later eating disordered symptomatology and will suggest how eating-disorder symptoms can serve to compensate for deficits resulting from these early female vicissitudes.

MIRRORING DISTORTIONS OF THE BODY SELF

In general, our society fails to adequately confirm and admire little girls' exhibitionism, except within narrowly prescribed, gender-based norms. Laboratory evidence suggests that little girls' exhibitionism is actively interfered with. In the interests of safety and learning to be "ladylike," little girls are discouraged from showing off, being cocky, acting "smart" or aggressive (see, for example, Block, 1973; Mahler, Pine, and Bergman, 1975). In their exhaustive review of the sex-differences literature, Maccoby and Jacklin (1974) conclude that "adults respond as if they find boys more interesting, and more attention-provoking than girls . . . perhaps because boys are valued more" (p. 348). In addition, girls learn early in life, and continue to relearn throughout their lives, that they must subordinate their own exhibitionistic strivings if these strivings are perceived to be in conflict with the needs of others (see, for example, Miller, 1976). The result of such prohibitions is that exhibitionistic experiences (and the affects, like pride, that accompany them) may continue throughout development to evoke conflict and shame (Boden, Hunt, and Kassoff, 1987).

Unfortunately the dampening of the little girl's exhibitionism begins early in life, at the very time when she has a strong developmental need to let her sense of omnipotence ripen and flower. Kaplan (1978) writes:

> Little girls are often deprived of the full grandeur of the love affair [of the "practicing" subphase]. The pride that shines on the jumping and leaping little boy does not shine on the little girl who might want to jump and leap. Most mothers worry more about the physical safety of daughters. The worry and hesitation in the mother's face makes the little girl cautious, thus making it hard for her to let go with daring and abandon during this period. . . . Elation cushions disappointments and disenchantment, and many little girls simply haven't had enough elation [p. 176].

I would add that the little girl is also learning certain excitement boundaries: she is learning that she is only allowed to build up to a certain level of stimulation, then she must hold herself back. Moreover, as Mahler (1976) suggests, girls' lack of a certain aggressiveness and "motor-mindedness" (which seem to help little boys maintain their self-esteem) contributes to the too abrupt deflation of the little girl's omnipotence as she moves from the illusions of grandeur of the "practicing" subphase to the disappointing reality of the rapprochement subphase. Thus it appears that a number of factors conspire to bring about deflation of the little girl's grandiose exhibitionistic self before adequate *inflation* has taken place.

There is, however, one arena in which little girls *are* generally expected to express their exhibitionism, and this is the area of physical appearance. The girl is encouraged to show off her body, her clothes, her hair, her "smile," and in general to think a great deal about how she appears to other people. She learns to offer her body for admiration by others, rather than to use her body to achieve a sense of mastery or prowess. I submit that it is precisely because females have been encouraged to offer this particular fragment of their total experience—their physical appearance—for mirroring that women later on in life tend to reveal their psychopathology through bodily symptoms, such as eating disorders. Women use their bodies to express exhibitionistic concerns because it is one of the few avenues of expression reliably open to them.

However, even this avenue is fraught with conflict, for the mirroring of female bodies, particularly the sexual aspects, continues to be distorted by ambivalence and embarrassment. Little girls are encouraged to be sexually attractive but not sexual—an attitude perhaps epitomized by dressing girls in little dresses with very short skirts and then telling them to keep their skirts down. Parents have for centuries had difficulty naming female genitals, while they have had no trouble concocting amusing and affectionate names for the penis. Normal, universal female events such as menstruation, breast development, and pregnancy continue to be treated with shame and secrecy. These two related problems—the focus on female bodies to the exclusion of other parts of their selves and the fact that the focus is so ambivalent—can lead to difficulties in integrating the body-self into the total self-structure.

Another way that females are allowed and encouraged to express exhibitionistic strivings is through taking care of others. Indeed, in adult narcissistic personalities, female grandiosity may often appear as an exaggerated and lavish serving of others, as opposed to the DSM-III-style male grandiosity, which often manifests as interpersonal exploitativeness and arrogance (Johnson, 1988, personal communication). Girls learn early in life that one of the most rewarded of the "female" ways of taking care of others is to feed them. Moreover, women's bodies come anatomically equipped to feed others. That women are both trained and biologically equipped to become feeders may help explain why "feeding" has such profound meaning for women and why so many adult women in psychological distress, in a misguided attempt to give themselves something, use food to do so.

Adolescence can bring with it further insults to the girl's exhibitionism. Girls at this age suddenly learn that from now on they will be expected to behave according to new rules, rules that may seem foreign and incomprehensible. They are asked to develop new ways of talking and moving their bodies, their hands, their eyes, their mouths in order to make themselves "attractive" to males. They learn that much of the way they may have been—forthright, strong, "natural"—is not attractive to males. They are asked to give up much of what may have provided the basis of their self-esteem and to take on a new way of being for which they feel woefully unequipped. The "tomboy"—who may have received a great deal of admiration from peers for her adventureousness and boldness—may feel suddenly bereft of mirroring responsiveness.

In the early family environment of eating-disordered patients, we often find an exaggerated version of this picture of mirroring distortion. There is often an inordinate preoccupation with bodily appearance, including weight (e.g., Bruch, 1973, 1978; Goodsitt, 1985; Geist, 1985). In these families, how you look seems to determine how you are, who you are, how you feel, and what others will think of you. Other family members often have weight problems and are chronically dieting. Moreover, there is often a pathological focus on body *fragments*. The child looks into the mirror of her parent and sees what Geist (1985) has called "a prismatic image of isolated parts." What the mirror reflects back to the child is too often what is missing or wrong: *protruding* tummy, *fat* thighs, or (in the words of the parent of my patient) *"treetrunk* legs." As Kohut (1977) discovered, the impact is insidious when fragments of our selves, rather than our total selves, are responded to. The focus on fragments results in an immediate loss of the experience of self-cohesion and, over time, can seriously compromise the building of self-structure. Finally, the literature suggests that, in the families of eating-disordered patients, the patient's actual bodily needs and affect states are often not acknowledged nor appropriately differentiated; for example, food is given whether the patient is hungry, depressed, or tired (Bruch, 1973; Goodsitt, 1975).

In our eating-disordered patients, we see numerous and vivid examples of the problems deriving from impaired or distorted mirroring: that is, serious deficits in self-esteem and ambition and an excessive need for mirroring responses from the environment (Kohut, 1977, 1978). Mirroring failures can also push the little girl toward an unhealthy identification with her mother (Geist, 1975), since, without encouragement to develop her own unique capacities, the girl will instead look outside herself and develop attributes *just like* those of her mother. For example, many of my patients have admitted to wearing the same style clothes, sometimes the very same clothes, as their mothers, having never had a chance to develop a sense of their own, unique style of dress. In addition, the failure of the caregiving environment to mirror the *affects* associated with exhibitionism, such as pride, expansiveness, efficacy, and pleasurable excitement leads the child to split off and disavow these affects (Stolorow et al., 1987). Such unintegrated affect states then become the source of enduring inner conflict because, whenever they arise, they are experienced as threats both to the girl's established psychological organization and to the maintenance of her vitally needed selfobject ties.

In eating-disordered patients, the impact of the mirroring failures on the *body*-self is particularly pronounced and will be explored later in the case of Gina. The ambivalent focus on bodily appearance and body fragments, to the exclusion of other parts of the self, leads to both the loss of cohesion of the body-self and its lack of integration into the total self-structure (Goodsitt, 1985; Geist, 1985). Body exhibitionism becomes a continuing source of shame. In adolescence, when bodily concerns take center stage in development, the girl whose body-self-esteem is less intact because of early failures in attunement will have greater difficulty accepting her body's changing and its imperfections. She will experience her limitations as cruel, narcissistic injuries and, in an attempt at restitution, may develop such self-regulatory mechanisms as eating disorders. It is because the body-self has not been integrated into the total self-structure that our patients so often experience their bodies as somehow foreign and almost extraneous to the rest of their self-experience and why they are strangely indifferent to the needs of the body and to the damage inflicted by behaviors like binge eating and purging.

Eating-disordered symptoms themselves often are vehicles for the expression of thwarted exhibitionistic longings. Many writers, particularly Bruch (1973, 1978), have described the inordinate sense of pride with which the anorexic regards her superhuman ability to control her food intake. No investigators to my knowledge have commented on the grandiosity that often accompanies the act of vomiting—an act that some of my bulimic patients regard as a highly developed and refined athletic skill. In the words of one of my patients:

> I was the Miss America of purging. I was the best. Friends of mine got exhausted after two times. I could do it nine or ten. I could *always* make the food come up. If it wouldn't I would reach down in my throat, open the flap and bring it up! It was amazing what I could do. . . . Some girls felt really good about being a cheerleader. I never felt proud of that like I did about purging. And purging was mine. No one knew about it so they couldn't criticize me for it.

Case Illustration: Gina

A good example of how an early ambivalent focus on bodily appearance can interfere with the development of the body self is Gina, a 26-year-old, severely bulimic patient, who at the time she entered treatment had been bingeing and vomiting for nine years and using a dangerous combination of emetics, laxatives, and diuretics for the past three years. She was referred by her physician, who was concerned about her deteriorating physical condition and suicidal ideation. She was living with her parents, after having been recently divorced from a man who battered her. Intelligent, charismatic, and attractive despite being perhaps 35 pounds overweight, she was underemployed as an office worker.

Gina came from an outwardly intact, stable, middle-class home, with two parents and a brother. Throughout three years of treatment, however, the father and brother remained shadowy, and her mother dominated Gina's analytic life. From as early as Gina could remember, her mother had been preoccupied with Gina's weight and her appearance—even though Gina had never been seriously overweight. Her mother focused obsessively on Gina's "hippo hips," telling her she looked "obese and disgusting." She put her daughter on her first Metrical diet when she was in the fifth grade. When Gina became more noticeably overweight around age 14, her mother wrote her a note saying, "You've ruined yourself. You'll never find a man." Over the years Gina felt compelled to weigh herself each morning, and when, a year into treatment, Gina decided to stop weighing herself, her mother literally wept and pleaded with her daughter to get on the scale again.

At the same time, Gina's own attempts as a child to exhibit her body were either discounted or actively rejected. She cannot remember either parent's ever attending one of her school performances. When she would become excited and energetic, she was told that she was "too much" and to "go run around the block." Her sexual exhibitionism seems to have been particularly threatening for both parents. Her mother routinely dressed her in rather old-fashioned, dark-colored, ostensibly "slimming" clothes, and in fact her mother continued to pick out sensible clothing for her until the second year of treatment. Starting around puberty, Gina's father began calling Gina by a supposedly humorous "pet name"—a name that suggested that she was extraordinarily large and awkward.

Something else also happened around puberty. According to Gina, she was suddenly expected to transform herself from a tomboy into something called a "young lady," a status for which she felt unprepared. "Something was stolen from me at puberty," she told me. "I wilted. I became a nonperson." This is when she began to make what she and I came to call "the lists." She literally drew up lists of the attributes of the perfect "social person," the perfect "student," the perfect "daughter," and, later in college, the perfect "career person." Each "person" had different mannerisms, language, even hairstyle. She would consult these lists in order to choose the proper role for the proper situation, having completely lost sight of her own needs and wants. She described having no idea of who she really was—just knowing that she had to do everything perfectly. The lists continued into adulthood. As Gina later came to realize, being overweight was her most obvious imperfection, and it functioned to fend off the dire necessity of absolute perfection. If she lost weight, she would, according to the fantasy manufactured by her and her mother, then have to have the perfect figure, the perfect career, the perfect man, the perfect life. A frightening prospect. Thus in Gina we see clear sequelae of a distorted mirroring process: a self vainly striving for perfection while remaining vertically split-off from her deeper needs and wants.

In the course of treatment, mirroring needs were the first to emerge, and they have predominated throughout. Her profound need to have her specialness acknowledged and confirmed emerged dramatically and unexpectedly during the eighth session after an unfortunate—and serious—mistake on my part. Owing to a series of bureaucratic errors, I had mistakenly told her that she was part of a research protocol and that her first 15 weeks of treatment would be free. When I discovered the error and was forced to tell her that she would be charged for subsequent sessions, she reacted with a surprising (for her) display of outrage. "I felt special being in a research project," she cried. "Because of me science would advance! It elevated my status. . . . For once in my life I thought I got something for nothing, without having to struggle for it. . . . Therapy's not worth the same thing anymore. The value of me is not the same anymore!" This early, major empathic break had brought the grandiose self to its feet, crying out for recognition.

She made dramatic life changes within the first six months of treatment—moving out of her parents' home, meeting and falling in love with an extremely appropriate man, stopping the binge-purge cycle, and normalizing her eating—and she would present her considerable accomplishments to me for mirroring confirmation. Early on she said, "You confirm what I say I want. I'm not used to that." She did not ask for my feedback or opinion—her grandiose sense of self-sufficiency would not allow it—and I offered only those interpretations which she had all but stated herself. She was also pleased that

I could remember what she had told me from week to week, pleased that I could hold all of her in my consciousness. After about a year, a new self-disclosure made it clear that she had also been tremendously afraid that I could not or would not mirror her adequately. She admitted that during the initial phase (when she had seemed to be enthusiastically presenting her ideas and plans to me), she had actually been presenting only *part* of the picture, so that "if you got it wrong, you couldn't mess up the whole thing." We understood together how her current fear stemmed from earlier wounding times, when her developing sense of self had been "messed up" by her parents' distorted responsiveness, particularly her mother's focus on fragments of her total being and projection onto her of her own needs and expectations.

Gina's *body* exhibitionism, perhaps because it was the most abused part of her, did not emerge directly until we were a year and a half into the treatment. She began buying more stylish, feminine, flamboyant clothing—which she announced to me was *her* style, not her mother's—and she began modeling the outfits for me at the beginning of each session, turning around to permit me to admire every inch of her. She told me during one session that she felt like she was "prancing." Her purchase of a T-shirt with a picture of Garfield the Cat on the front seemed particularly apt, for Garfield is perhaps the world's most entitled, exhibitionistic, and nonguilty eater. The focus then shifted to her sexuality. She reported buying sexy lingerie, enjoying glances from men at work, initiating sex with her boyfriend. Most important, she began experiencing sexual feelings for the first time in her life. She also began working out at a health club and reported feeling more physical, as she had as a child. Gina's body self was becoming more integrated into her total self-structure. It was during this period that she told me, "This body has never been O.K. I always felt trapped in my body. I hated this body. When my body wanted things I always told it, 'No. You're just a body!' " I was struck at the time by the distance between her self and her body suggested by her use of the phrase "*this* body." It is also noteworthy that her ex-husband had battered "this body" she hated.

It was only after this important phase of therapy, during which her body self received empathic confirmation and became more integrated into her self-structure, that she was able to exhibit other competencies and potentialities to me. She began talking about her work life for the very first time: "I want to be taken seriously. I want to be more ambitious. I decided last week that I actually may be intelligent." She reported a dream in which she was in a class on eating disorders with a slender, compassionate-type teacher in her early 40s (whom we quickly recognized as me). She wanted to hurry up and finish this course so that she could take other courses with this teacher (a desire we understood as moving beyond her bulimia to explore more deeply other parts of her self). She began showing new signs of being able to mirror herself—her actual, imperfect self—saying, "Nobody has a perfect body. My waist is great. I like the top half. I'll work with what I have." It was also during this time that she decided to lose weight—"for myself and not for anyone else"—and, miraculously to her, her weight began a slow, steady decline.

During the session marking the one-year anniversary of her last purge, Gina came in bursting with excitement and then, with some embarrassment and tears in her eyes, told me: "I wanted to buy you a gift. I looked around and nothing seemed quite right. Then I realized that I could just say 'thank you.' I don't want to say thank you for curing my bulimia but for giving me the belief in myself so I could cure my bulimia. Sometimes I came in here wanting to die and saying 'everything's fine' but *I knew you saw through me,* and you seemed to believe that I could do it." Gina was thanking me for the gift of being *seen.*

Case Illustration: Jerry

Jerry, whose early exhibitionism was severely thwarted, also first used her *body* to express her exhibitionism during the psychoanalytic process. This patient is unique in my experience in that she developed an ingenious, if bizarre, means of literally displaying her grandiose fantasies on her body: she had her body *tatooed.* Although minor tatooing is not particularly deviant within Jerry's New Age women's subculture, her dedication to the project of having her entire body eventually covered with tatoos was unusual. The tatoo imagery, which was beautiful and feminine, often appeared to her first in her dreams. She frequently fantasized about showing her tatoos to her father, who had never been able to provide mirroring of her female self. I came to understand that her emerging needs for her female body-self to be mirrored were so intense and at the same time so forbidden that she had apparently had to invent a compromise solution: she would "concretize" the existence of her inner greatness by literally exhibiting her self on her body and yet she would still keep it hidden from all but her husband.

I first saw the tatoos during the second year of treatment, when on her way out of my office she unexpectedly opened her blouse to reveal her latest tatoos. During the period which followed, in which we were discussing her lifelong needs to be "seen," she began bringing in drawings of her naked body as she visualized it at some future date completely covered by tatoos. Then during the fourth year of treatment, as she more and more actively "put herself out there" in building a career (which we both felt sprang from her nuclear needs), the fantasies of tatooing disappeared. Once she was able to display her talents to the world, to be "seen" and acknowledged for her abilities, she no longer needed to use her body to express her exhibitionistic strivings. To my mind, a two-stage process had taken place. First, Gerry "somaticized" her exhibitionistic needs and through the tatoos was able to proudly display her emerging but still frightened and shy self in beautiful imagery on her body. Then, once she was able to make these needs conscious, she was able to *de*somaticize her exhibitionistic strivings and express them through meaningful work that brought her the acknowledgment she really needed.

LACK OF IDEALIZABLE FIGURES

A second problem for girls growing up in contemporary society is the lack, relative to boys, of figures who can provide idealizing selfobject functions. Let us begin with the mother. Given current childrearing practices and continuing patriarchal trends in our society, almost all mothers are likely to pass through two different stages of deidealization that may be described as "traumatic" for both girls and boys but that are particularly traumatic for the little girl since the mother, being of the same sex, is her primary idealization figure. The first deidealization occurs during a cognitive shift around the age of 15 or 16 months, when the recognition of growing separateness from mother leads not only to the puncturing of the child's grandiosity but, at the same time, to the deflation of the *mother's* omnipotence in the child's mind (Mahler, Pine, and Bergman, 1975). During this period, the toddler may experience intense feelings of helplessness and depression. The second "traumatic disillusionment" with the mother occurs in the ensuing years as the child discovers that the revered mother of the family environment is of decidedly secondary status in society at large (Lang, 1984), and the child has most likely internalized the cultural devaluation. The term traumatic disillusionment is Kohut's (1971) and refers to a degree of disappointment in the idealized parent that is too great to be processed psychologically and that leads to disavowal of the idealizing needs. This kind of massive disillusionment is to be distinguished from that which occurs in the normal course of events, when the inevitable, incremental disappointments in the idealized other allow the child slowly to internalize the parental functions. The extent and severity of the disillusionment, of course, depend on the supportiveness of the selfobject environment, particularly on the extent to which the mother's self-esteem allows her daughter to let herself be idealized as opposed to denigrating herself or retreating in shame in the face of her daughter's efforts to idealize her. Both stages of disillusionment with the mother—but particularly the latter—are bound to be more crushing for the girl than for the boy, since the girl, threatened with the loss of her primary idealization figure, has more to lose.

In families where the female selfobject is herself severely narcissistically vulnerable, as she is in many families of eating disordered patients, the outcome is grimmer. The girl's idealizing needs may be thwarted by a mother who is so seriously self-devaluing that she says in effect, "I am nothing. I am not worthy of your idealization." Or even more often we see in these families a mother who is herself so anxious that she responds with panic to every anxiety signal displayed by the daughter (Geist, 1985) and through her interventions actually makes the daughter's anxiety worse. Such a child will be left with chronic deficits in tension regulation. Moreover, the child whose mother cannot attune to her anxiety states will soon abandon hope of getting the help she needs and will develop a precocious independence characterized by an "I'll do it myself" mentality. In still other cases, the mother's narcissistic equilibrium is so dependent on her being the Good Mother, the model of perfection, that the daughter is prevented from undergoing the gradual, phase-appropriate deidealization process that allows the internalization of the mother's functions.

It is my impression, along with that of Chernin (1985), that this generation of mothers of our patients may have been unidealizable in unique ways, since they were "betwixt and between" the old order and the new and may have felt ambivalent about their traditional roles as wives and mothers or, if they were in the labor force, their untraditional roles as workers. Mothers who are confused about their position as women and the value of their lives and who are envious of their daughters' widening opportunities are not only hard to idealize but can also cause anguish in the daughters, who fear they will damage their mothers by surpassing them.

Now, if the mother is found to be unidealizable, the girl, like the boy, can of course turn to the father in search of an idealizable selfobject. However, while the father can be idealized and his functions internalized, he cannot provide gender-idealizing functions since he is a man. During the oedipal phase in particular, the developmentally crucial selfobject needs are for the *same sex* parent to be idealizable and for this idealized parent to be able to delight in the child's gender-linked values and attributes (Ornstein, 1985). Regardless of the father's idealizability, the little girl has a specific developmental need to idealize her mother in order to consolidate her sense of femininity. This is why the girl usually holds onto the same selfobject, the mother, to meet both her mirroring and idealizing needs (Kohut, 1977). Thus, if the mother is inadequate as a selfobject, the little girl does not have the same second chance to find an idealizable selfobject as does the little boy, who may recover from his disillusionment with his mother by idealizing his father. If the little girl does choose her father as her primary idealization figure, her self-esteem regarding her value as a woman, as well as her valuation of other women and her comfort around other women, may suffer.

For these reasons, the idealization process is a rockier road for the girl than for the boy. In our eating-disordered patients, we see numerous examples of the kinds of enduring problems that signal early derailments along the idealizing line: problems with tension regulation, inability to find inspiration and meaning in life's activities, and an excessive need to attach themselves to admired others. Having been chronically and traumatically disappointed in the ability of the selfobject environment to provide soothing and comfort, these patients have learned to look outside the realm of selfobject relatedness for attempted solutions (Gehrie, 1987; Zadylak and St. Pierre, 1987). Compulsive eating, according to Kohut (1984), is "an attempt to replace the selfobject (and the transmuting internalization it provides) with food (and the activity of eating)" (p. 20).

I would add that disordered-eating patterns are often an attempt specifically to replace the *idealized* selfobject. The food is often characterized in terms similar to those used to describe an idealized person—soothing, perfect, omnipotent (that is, capable of solving all problems). Patients often describe what sounds like a passionate love affair with their favorite foods. On one occasion, when I naively asked an anorexic-like patient if she could let herself eat a *little* of her favorite binge food, she looked worried, hesitated for some seconds, and then said, "But if I could just eat it like that, any time I wanted to, it wouldn't be so wonderful. I have to have *something* to love." The person who has an eating disorder has "given up" on receiving empathic attunement from the caregiving surround and has turned instead to a nonhuman (and thus more reliable) substitute to find the comfort and inspiration she seeks. As one of my patients put it, "There was no one who I could trust to share the deep pain. Food was more trustworthy, because food was always there." Food, of course, is a particularly compelling substitute since it is the first bridge between self and selfobject—the first medium for the transmission of soothing and comfort.

Because the food rituals are seen as the only truly reliable selfobjects, they are defended with as much ardor as a selfobject connection to a human being. The rituals take on a sacrosanct quality. "My purging is the one thing I won't let *anyone* mess with," one of my patients explained. This patient, when faced with the prospect of her mother's new husband's moving into the house with them, explained that by far her greatest fear was that his presence would somehow limit her freedom to purge. At a later date, this same patient reported an incident in which she was at a party vomiting in a bathroom when a male friend accidentally walked in on her. Without thinking, she wheeled around and punched him in the face. The purging ritual is defended so desperately because the patient unconsciously knows that if she is deprived of the ritual before genuine selfobject responsiveness can be substituted, she is seriously endangering her self-cohesion. Thus the ritual is defended as fiercely as one would defend a part of the self.

Case Illustration: Dorothy

Some eating-disordered patients whose idealizing needs were thwarted early in life develop the rudiments of an idealizing transference almost immediately upon entering treatment. Dorothy, on the other hand, was so frightened by the intensity of her needs and her fear of being injured again by further rejection that she could not begin to admit my importance until well into the third year of treatment. Indeed, it was her resistance to idealizing that most eloquently told the story of her early traumatization.

Dorothy, who was 48 years old when she entered treatment, wept throughout the first hour, explaining that she had not been able to stop crying since her husband's death two years earlier. She was highly articulate, conservative in dress and manner, a manager in a small business. This was her first time in psychiatric treatment. While she had been obsessed with her weight since early adolescence and had been through many periods of weight loss and regain, she had begun vomiting only a year earlier. Following her husband's prolonged and painful death, she had gone into an agitated depression, spending every evening in front of the television set, eating and vomiting sometimes three times a night to slow down racing thoughts and relieve feelings of loneliness and emptiness. She was also having trouble sleeping and had frequent thoughts of suicide. Her husband, she explained, although he had not been affectionate or sexual, had been "the only one who had ever cared," the only one who had ever tried to "make it better." His loss was devastating for her. She also complained of having no direction in life and of never knowing what she wanted to do, in life in general or on the everyday level.

Her mother was, as Dorothy put it, "incapable of mothering" and "incapable of love." She could not express affection, give advice, soothe Dorothy, or even *talk* to her daughter about anything of emotional significance. According to Dorothy, the "path was too wide"—that is, her parents offered no guidance or help in finding a direction. Dorothy still carried a mental picture of her mother with a serious, frightened expression and furrowed brow. Her mother spent all her time doing household chores, and she seemed incapable of having fun under any circumstances. Later, as an adult, Dorothy was told by an aunt that her mother had not wanted to have children. The mother had no apparent skills or talents or hobbies and often expressed the opinion that she was "not good at anything." According to Dorothy, her mother's anger was violent, uncontrollable, unpredictable, "on-and-off."

Her mother was also unable to talk about anything having to do with sex or reproduction. Her mother's silence, plus a failure to get information from peers, left Dorothy woefully unprepared for the onset of menses, which frightened her our of her wits, and, at age 20, for the birth of her first child. One memory in particular stands out. When Dorothy found a beautiful dress in her mother's closet and asked about it, her mother turned her back and walked out of the room, refusing to even acknowledge the question. The reason, she found out much later, was that the dress was a maternity dress. Dorothy herself remains, to this day, disgusted by and cut off from her body and her sexuality. She feels her breasts are too large and will not undress in front of anyone.

Her father seldom appeared in her childhood memories, and after three years of treatment, I still knew very little about him. She said that he was not capable of showing or verbalizing any feelings of affection for her but that she still knew that he loved her. She could still evoke the cozy pleasure of those rare moments when she and her father shared an evening snack together. In general, however, her father appears to have been more absent than present within the family system, and, most important, he seems not to have been able to comfort Dorothy or help her with her struggles—with her mother, her sister, or her feelings.

Dorothy was the middle of three daughters, the oldest of whom was always in trouble as a child and always screaming at her mother.

(As an adult this sister has been diagnosed schizophrenic.) As a result, Dorothy fashioned her own role in the family as the one who did not make trouble. She felt she had to hold her breath and tiptoe around so she would not get noticed and yelled at too. She did not get yelled at, but she also did not receive any attention. When she herself was angry or scared, she showed these feelings to no one. Dorothy was also the one in charge of taking care of her younger sister every day after school, so that she was never able to develop activities with friends. The result was that Dorothy felt she was "grown up by age five."

Clearly, Dorothy's mother had been pitifully hard to idealize because of her inability to provide mothering functions, her self-devaluation, her fear of her own sexuality, and her unpredictable moods. Dorothy's somewhat idealizable father had not been very available. Another possible candidate for idealization, her older sister, was mentally disturbed. And owing to the family's social isolation, it was unlikely that Dorothy had been exposed to many other idealizable figures. Having had no one to idealize wholeheartedly as a child— no one to soothe her and help her integrate painful affects—she was left with severe deficits in her ability to regulate internal tension states and to find direction and meaning in life's activities. Then, two years ago, another cruel blow of fate was dealt Dorothy—she lost her husband, the only person in her life whom she had come close to idealizing.

Food had always functioned as a selfobject in her life. According to Dorothy, the only way family members were able to show love for each other was through food. The single memory Dorothy retains of her mother's being "caring" was when Dorothy was sick, at which time her mother would bring her hot lemonade with honey in a green mug—a ritual she maintains to this day. Her most treasured memories with her father were of eating "potato bug sandwiches" together. Food was further overvalued in her family by being treated as in short supply except during holidays, when Dorothy was encouraged to eat to the point of doubling over with intestinal pain. "Food," she told me, "was really the only mother I ever had."

Precisely because Dorothy unconsciously yearned for an idealizing transference so much, she fiercely defended herself against it for almost three years. She maintained that her relationship with me meant nothing to her and that because I was so "professional" she could not know me at all, much less care about me. "I can't rely on getting help from anyone," she told me during the first year of treatment, tears streaming down her face. "I have to do it alone." Her dreams, which were only vaguely remembered, were often of moving about a world filled with faceless people or of riding endlessly on buses, unable to find her destination, with no one to guide her. Her waking experience was also one of almost unbearable loneliness, particularly during the evenings alone in her big house. However, some seven months into treatment, she brought in a poem she had written entitled "The Wall" in which she described the wall she chronically felt surrounding her and cutting her off from other people. The last line of the poem, significantly, was "I cannot scale it alone." At that time, when I commented that she would not be alone *here*, she again pooh-poohed my suggestion that my presence could be of consequence to her at all.

More than a year and a half into treatment, her conflict between seeking help or "doing it alone" intensified within the transference over a four-month period. The majority of the time she steadfastly maintained that I meant nothing to her and that she meant nothing to me, but every now and then a tear would appear in the fabric of her defenses. Following my month-long winter vacation, for example, she admitted for the first time that "it wasn't fair for you not to be here during the holidays when they were so hard." In the next session, the question of whether there was any "caring" between us emerged again. "You couldn't care or you couldn't do your job," she said. I then asked her if it *felt* to her as if I didn't care. "It doesn't matter if you do or you don't," she answered in a bored fashion. I replied, "It does matter to you." She hesitated, then said, "I don't think there can be caring in a professional relationship . . . do you?" I hesitated, then replied, "Yes." She flushed deeply, then covered her reaction with a quick smile and said, "I don't know if I'm glad to hear that or not. It makes it more complex."

A month later, after she told me about an emotional crisis that had occurred over the weekend, I asked her if she had thought of calling me. She answered coldly, "No reason to call. What can you do? Besides, I couldn't reach you anyway." I asked her whether she meant that I might be in session and would have to call her back. "Yes," she replied in an angry staccato voice, "people can *die* in an hour. . . . I learned a long time ago that there was no one. . . . Other people can feel support. I can't." When I commented that she seemed to feel that she could not learn to let that support in, she replied without hesitation, "No. It has to be *given* to you. . . . I'm not sure how long I can keep on—a child without love or nurturance eventually dies. I think it can happen to adults too." That session ended with my talking with her about how frightening it was to dare hope that she could be helped, because she might be let down again.

The next session she told me that she had cried in the parking lot outside my office for ten minutes before she could drive home. "I was trying to think about what I wanted. I wanted someone to give me a hug, to say it's going to be all right." I asked her if she had wanted that from me, and she said, "No, not especially. I wanted it from someone who would be there. You talked about hope. Well I have to say honestly that I don't really have any hope because I have never experienced it, but what I've decided to do is to *pretend* that I believe things can change and go on making an effort."

This, then, was the ingenious means by which this extremely frightened patient worked her way out of her dilemma: by pretending that she could change, she could hold on to some hope and perhaps begin to take some risks; at the same time she could still protect herself against the possibility of being disappointed or rejected again as she had been throughout her life. In the sessions that followed, she began to wonder if support had perhaps already been offered to her at different times but that, because of her fear, she was not able to "see" it when it came her way. Then during one session she came in with agonizing lower-back pain and asked me for an aspirin. The next session she admitted that asking for the aspirin was "a big deal, because I never ask for anything." Several months later, she called me for the very first time to ask for an appointment that evening (an appointment she had previously canceled). When she came in, she said for the first time, "I knew I needed to ask for help." She had begun vomiting again following a period of four months of abstinence, and she had called me immediately after she vomited. We acknowledged together what a big step she had taken in asking for my help. The session ended with her talking about the need to replace "the wall" with a more flexible shield, "so I can let people in to comfort me and still be protected.

A few months later, Dorothy had a dream about "a baby, then a child who everyone thought was dead." The child was "sewn together" with thread (arms to body, finger to finger), put in a white cardboard box and placed on a shelf in a closed room. But then someone decided the baby was not dead, and the box was opened. The child's skin had patrified and turned brown. Dorothy, in the dream, is trying laboriously to clip the threads that bind the child's fingers together. She feels the presence of someone else with her as she works. She is very frustrated because her scissors are not small enough to get at all the stitches, but somehow, despite her inability, the child is "being released" and "coming alive." The last dream image is of the child, alive but still awkward, tottering down a hallway.

DAUGHTER AS NARCISSISTIC EXTENSION
OF MOTHER

A third developmental problem for girls stems from the simple fact that they are the same sex as the most usual primary caretaker. Unlike boys, girls do not have to go through a process of disidentification from their mothers in order to establish their gender identity. As a consequence, they remain throughout life more psychologically connected to their mothers than boys do (Stoller, 1968; Chodorow, 1978). According to Chodorow (1978), "primary identification and symbiosis with daughters tend to be stronger and cathexis of daughters is more likely to retain and emphasize narcissistic elements, that is, to be based on experiencing a daughter as an extension or double of the mother herself" (p. 109). If the mother is herself narcissistically disturbed and requires a narcissistic extension, she is more likely to use her daughter than to use her son to provide this function. The daughter's greater psychological closeness to her mother and hence greater sensitivity to relational nuance (Surrey, 1985) also makes her less likely to be able to refuse the narcissistic demands of her mother.

In families of eating-disordered patients, the narcissistic use of the daughter by the mother is often striking. Practically every writer on eating disorders has remarked on the striking degree of "symbiotic attachment," "merger," or "enmeshment" in families of eating-disordered patients, particularly between mother and daughter. The daughter (who later develops an eating disorder) is often seen as the "special child," mother's special confidante. She is asked to give up her own needs in order to meet those of her mother—in short, to become her mother's self*object* rather than a self.

If the girl does not adapt to the needs of her mother and pursues her own developmental goals, she not only fears hurting the mother but dreads rupturing the selfobject bond upon which her own psychological integrity depends. I agree with Friedman (1985) that with eating-disordered patients, we more often hear a fear of harming the parent than of being harmed, but I think these fears are largely indistinguishable, since damaging the mother damages the selfobject bond, which in turn endangers the integrity of the self.

The daughter, then, is torn between the urgings of her own developmental strivings and her equally strong need to meet the narcissistic needs of the mother. In this context, the function of eating-disorder symptoms is to give her the sensation of differentiation without having to separate psychologically from the mother. Many writers, like Bruch (1973), Minuchin, Rosman, and Baker (1978), and Masterson (1977) have viewed the restricted eating of the anorexic as an attempt to define her self by taking rigid control of what comes into her; others (Palazzoli, 1978; Sugarman and Kurash, 1982; Brenner, 1983) have conceptualized the purging of the bulimic as an attempt to *de*merge from mother, following a merger through bingeing. I would add that the attempted merger-through-bingeing is with the fantasied *adequate* mother; the demerger-through-purging, with the unempathic mother. Through the distorted eating patterns, the patient creates the temporary illusion of differentiation while at the same time maintaining the archaic selfobject bond.

To illustrate the striking degree to which many eating-disordered patients become narcissistic extensions of their mothers, I would like to return to the case of Gina, discussed earlier in the section on mirroring failure.

Case Illustration: Gina, Continued

Throughout her treatment, Gina's father and brother remained shadowy, and her mother—a remarkably controlling and opinionated woman—dominated Gina's intrapsychic life as well as her everyday life. Not only did Gina's mother expect her daughter to provide selfobject functions, she made it clear that her daughter was to be her *primary* selfobject. Gina's primary role in maintaining her mother's psychological equilibrium became apparent early on in treatment when Gina was planning to go on a weekend trip with her boyfriend. Her mother became extremely agitated, saying, "How can you go off and leave me all alone?" ignoring the fact that her husband and son would be in the home with her.

Her mother expected her daughter's needs to mirror her own. In the arena of eating, if Gina did not eat the same thing in the same amount and at the same time, her mother would consider her "disloyal" and would give her "the evil eye." When her mother announced at the breakfast table, "Well now I'm finished and I'm not going to eat until dinner time," this was meant as a prescription for Gina's behavior. (Father and brother were given more leeway.) Perhaps the most striking example of the mother's merging of her own needs with Gina's was her telling her daughter each year, "For my birthday all I want is for *you* to lose weight." Similarly, Gina's mother could not tolerate Gina's affects when they conflicted with her own. When Gina became depressed as a child, for example, her mother would tell her to "snap out of it; be strong," and, as a consequence, Gina's depressive affect was split off, and she developed a falsely cheerful face to present to the outside world.

When Gina first came in for treatment at age 26, she was living in her parents' house, following her marital separation, and she was also expected to spend every weekend helping her mother around the house. Every decision in Gina's life—including what clothes to buy—was made jointly by her and her mother. After just three sessions, however, Gina was considering moving out of her parents' house, presenting idea after idea for my confirmation. Her bulimic symptoms began to decrease. When her mother learned of Gina's decision to move out, she became cold and attacking, questioning every facet of Gina's ability to survive on her own and telling her that if she wanted to leave she must really hate her parents. Gina's guilt did increase, but she still managed to move out and into an apartment with a friend. Following the move, there was a dramatic decrease in her bingeing and vomiting.

Gina continued nevertheless to see her mother often, but after each visit she felt a desperate need to binge and vomit. The connection between the visits and the purging became too obvious to ignore, and for the first time she was able to acknowledge how the feelings she experienced of being suffocated and controlled when she was around her mother led to attempts to rid herself of these feelings through purging. During the course of therapy, every time Gina contemplated a move toward separation she would experience an upsurge of bingeing and vomiting. Together we came to understand how these symptoms represented her response to the impossible conflict she felt between the needs of her self to move on toward differentiation and mature functioning and the equally imperative need to maintain the selfobject connection.

Soon after moving out, she met and fell in love with a man who proved to be an excellent mirroring selfobject, nicely attuned to her feelings and accepting of her bulimia. Gina was shy in telling me about Randy and realized over time that she feared I might be like her mother and not be able to share her with him. At one point she asked if she could bring him in to meet me, and I sensed that she wanted concrete proof that I could tolerate her having another important connection. I said yes, and apparently I passed the test, for she never did need to bring him in. Her mother began a crusade against Randy, criticizing everything about him, telling Gina she could "do much better" and confessing that she "had a bad feeling around him," as she had had around Gina's first husband (who had ended up battering her). Gina's anguish became unbearable at this point. She decided that she had to make a decision to give up either Randy or her mother; but every time she considered giving up Randy, she was filled with uncontrollable rage, and every time she considered giving up her mother, she had terrifying fantasies that her mother would "freak out" or kill herself or that, without the selfobject connection, she herself would disintegrate. Despite the fact that her moods and her bulimia were veering out of control, she and Randy decided to become engaged and live together. One evening, with barely controlled rage, she told her mother off, and to her surprise her mother not only did not fall apart, she "flipped her off," Italian-style. Shortly after this incident, Gina came into our session and handed me a bag of chocolates, saying "a strange phenomenon has occurred: I ate just one chocolate." One week later, she stopped vomiting. Soon after, she came in and announced that she had figured out that she felt best when she ate at 8 AM, 11 AM, and 4 PM, whether anyone else ate at those times or not. She was becoming empathic to her own food needs.

The first major setback occurred when Gina and Randy, because of a logistical problem with their housing, moved in with Gina's parents for two weeks. During this time, Gina again fell under her mother's sway, felt less connected to Randy and began bingeing and vomiting daily. She also canceled two sessions with me. She later told me how close she had been at that point to stopping treatment because she had not wanted me to get in the way of her bulimia. She had scared herself badly, and there followed a period of her describing in excruciating detail the binge/purge ritual, trying to make painfully conscious its horror as well as its seductiveness to prevent herself from relapsing again.

Several months of anger followed—first at Sam's family, then at me, finally at her mother. During this period, Gina called one evening and left a message asking me to call her, but I failed to pick up the message. The next morning she left a message at the clinic saying, "Cancel all future appointments." After I called and persuaded her to come in, she told me that she had urgently needed my help when she called me and when I did not call her back that evening, she had actually heard herself make a decision mentally, saying "All right. I'll do it *myself*," after which she proceeded to binge and vomit for the first time in six months. This incident led to many weeks of discussion of how her Mother had not been able to accept her anger—in fact, to accept anything separate about her—and how she had had to rid herself of this offending affect to maintain the connection with her mother. She also understood how it was that she had given up on getting help with her feelings and had developed a defensive precocity, saying in effect, "I'm on my own." She tearfully told me then and many times afterwards how my calling and asking her to come in showed I "cared" and, more than anything else I did, helped her trust me.

Shortly after this incident she had a dream that revealed her continuing struggle with her mother's intrusions into her growth process. In the dream, she could feel a "catastrophic" binge coming on and knew that if she could just make it to my office everything would be all right. But her legs were like spaghetti; she could barely walk. Her parents appeared outside my office and asked her what she was doing there. She made up an excuse, refusing to tell them about her treatment (as she has in reality), and continued into my office. In this dream she affirmed once again her right to a private life.

There followed the period of exhibiting and confirming her body self and then her professional self, described earlier. A later dream revealed an even more profound sense of autonomy. In the dream, which followed a difficult evening during which she had desperately wanted to vomit, she found herself on a ward filled with anorexics and bulimics. "You were there wearing some kind of white coat. I was glad you were there because you know I don't belong there. I kept looking for the guy with the keys so I could get out, then I realized I could just walk out."

TREATMENT CONSIDERATIONS

In eating disorders, food or eating rituals, rather than people, are turned to for meeting selfobject needs, because previous attempts with caregivers have brought disappointment and frustration. By turning to food, the eating-disordered person negates the need for selfobjects and circumvents further hurt. The problem is that the new restitutive system organized around food does not "work" because it cannot provide the selfobject responsiveness and thus the structure-building that the patient really needs. Kohut (1978) writes:

> It is the tragedy of all these attempts at self-cure that the solutions they provide are impermanent, that in essence they cannot succeed. . . . They are repeated again and again without producing the cure of the basic psychological malady . . . no psychic structure is built; the defect in the self remains. It is as if a person with a wide-open gastric fistula were trying to still his hunger through eating. He may obtain pleasurable taste sensations by his frantic ingestion of food, but, since the food does not enter the part of the digestive system that absorbs it into the organism, he continues to starve [p. 846–847].

In his last book, Kohut (1984) tells the story of how the unorthodox physician Schwenniger cured Otto von Bismark's insomnia by sitting by his bedside from the time he went to sleep to the time he woke up. Schweninger subsequently became a part of Bismarck's entourage and Bismarck, who had been obese, remarkably began to lose weight steadily—demonstrating, according to Kohut, that in the presence of a sustaining selfobject, the food could be abandoned as replacement.

The first goal of treatment, therefore, must be to "convince" the patient through our understanding of her hopes and fears that she should give human beings another chance—to rekindle the hope that at least one human being, the therapist, can provide the attuned responsiveness that will allow her development to begin again where it was derailed early in life. This can be accomplished only through empathy—through the therapist's seeking to understand the patient's utterances from within the patient's own frame of reference. The therapist's empathic-introspective stance allows the remobilization of the early selfobject needs that have long been unconscious and that can now within the transference begin to peek through the repression barrier.

I will now address clinical issues within the context of the special considerations regarding women discussed earlier. First, it is particularly important for the therapist to be aware of the thwarted exhibitionistic needs of many female patients and the shame attendant upon expressing their exhibitionism through other than culturally proscribed channels, like bodily appearance or serving others. Our patients' body self-esteem may be particularly fragile given the culture's distorted, ambivalent, and fragmented mirroring of women's bodies. We should, therefore, encourage the total body-mind self to present itself for mirroring confirmation and not get in the way of this process. We have to be particularly careful not to respond to fragments of the body self, by, for example, joining with the patient in her concern about her wide hips or large thighs or by focusing on her "temper," as others have done. Rather, we need to empathize with her concerns within the context of the total self, saying for example, "It is hard for you to feel good about yourself when you feel that your hips are too large" or "When someone treats you like that, it makes you feel angry." We should try to avoid interpretations at the level of physical appearance and instead address our comments to the subjective, affective experience of our patients to let them know that we can see their total selves and to help them recognize, label, and differentiate affect states and bodily needs. For example, if a patient gets a new job the therapist might focus not on the fact of the patient's having landed the job but on the patient's inner, affective experience of the process she went through to get the job—for example, how proud the patient may feel to have been able to assert herself in this new way. As Stern (1985) has shown us, the process of affect attunement involves the crossmodal sharing of inner affective experience. Thus, it is the therapist's attunement to the patient's *affect* states surrounding grandiose-exhibitionistic experiences that will allow the patient to integrate these experiences into her self structure.

We must be careful not to view the patient's emerging grandiosity as a defense against dependency or low self-esteem (as a traditional analyst might), but as the expression of a valid developmental need that did not receive adequate responsiveness at the appropriate age and that now needs to be acknowledged so that it can be transformed from its archaic form to more mature forms of healthy assertiveness and self-esteem.

The question that arises at this point is *how* to let oneself be used as a mirroring selfobject for our patients. Does one preserve the nongratifying analytic stance, as Kohut counseled, and only interpret the patient's need to be mirrored? Or does one actively mirror—that is affirm and admire—the patient? It is important to remember that a therapist should not be trying to *do* anything to the patient but, rather, should be making every effort to respond to the needs of the patient. One immerses oneself in the subjective world of the patient and lets oneself be used as the specific kind of transference figure she needs. Thus, to let oneself respond to the patient's needs to be mirrored does not necessarily imply actively delighting in or admiring the patient. On the other hand, not to respond with a gleam in one's eye when the patient reports a major developmental achievement is not an example of maintaining neutrality; it is wounding. Hence, my answer to the question of how much to mirror is necessarily inexact and situational; it is closest to Bacal's (1985) idea of "optimal responsiveness," which he defines as the "responsivity of the analyst that is therapeutically most relevant at any particular moment in the context of a particular patient and his illness" (p. 202). However, I have come to believe that we must respond with enough of a gleam to let the patient know that we share in her inner experience of accomplishment yet not respond with so much pleasure at the accomplishment itself that the patient believes that we are personally receiving narcissistic gratification from her action. If the patient senses that the therapist wants or needs something from her, the patient will be forced into a mode of either compliance or defiance and in either case will give up her own nuclear needs. Johnson (1988) gives a poignant example of the uncanny ability of eating-disordered patients to sense the needs of their therapists: he discovered after many months of treatment that an anorexic patient had been routinely coming 10 minutes late to her sessions in order to give *him* time to go to the bathroom. It is also true that our responses to mirroring needs may be different in the earlier "understanding" phases than in the later "explaining" phases of treatment (Ornstein and Ornstein, 1985). During the understanding phase, one more often simply responds with a gleam, that is, minimally provides the needed selfobject function. Once this bond of responsiveness has counteracted the patient's fearful expectation of disappointment and failure, one can move on to the explaining phase of treatment, in which one actively collaborates with the patient in explaining the meaning of the patient's selfobject needs in terms of their genetic origins.

As therapists, we need also to be aware that many women have not had adequately idealizable female selfobjects because of society's devaluation of women and that they remain chronically in need of such soothing and inspiring connections. Particularly if we are women, we must be able to let our female patients idealize us as models of calmness, strength, and perfection when and how they need to. We must use our empathy to "hold" the patient's distress, vulnerability, and anxiety so that these affects can be integrated into their self-structure. We need also to recognize that our patients' devaluations of us often mask idealizing needs—idealizing needs which the patient is afraid to express for fear that the longed-for idealized other will disappoint her now as in the past. We must also be aware of how our patients' thwarted need for a soothing, idealized merger may have led to its apparent opposite—a false and brittle "independence." With these precociously independent patients, we need to encourage attachment and dependency through interpretation of our patients' fears of what will happen to them should they allow the therapist to become important to them.

It is crucial to allow full expression of the idealizing needs and to be careful not to thwart this idealization process by either deflecting the idealization due to our own discomfort with adulation and the grandiosity it arouses in us, or by interpreting the patient's idealization as a defense against hostility. In general, we should confirm, when appropriate, our patients' perceptions about society's devaluation of women and convey through our empathic attunement our wholehearted acceptance of female experience.

SUMMARY

I have tried to suggest how an understanding of three problem areas specific to female development can help explain women's greater susceptibility to pathological eating behavior. The distorted mirroring of little girls' exhibitionism, particularly the selective and ambivalent focus on physical appearance, creates a body pathway for expressing exhibitionistic concerns later on. Interferences in female idealization processes result in functional deficits in tension regulation which may necessitate self-soothing mechanisms like eating disorders. The fact that little girls are usually the same sex as their primary caretakers can lead to their misuse as narcissistic extensions and, consequently, to the need to create self-definition through disordered eating patterns. These gender-based vicissitudes, very often in combination, can help predispose girls to the development of eating disorders later in life.

REFERENCES

Bacal, H. (1985), Optimal responsiveness and the therapeutic process. In: *Progress in Self Psychology: Vol. 1*, ed. A. Goldberg. New York: Guilford Press, pp. 202–227.

Block, J. H. & Van der Lippe, A. (1973), Sex role and socialization patterns. *J. Consult. Clin. Psychol.*, 41:321–341.

Boden, R., Hunt, P. & Kassoff, B. (1987), The centrality of shame in the psychology of women. Presented at meeting of the Association of Women in Psychology Conference, Denver, CO, March 6–8.

Boskind-Lodahl, M. (1976), Cinderella's stepsisters: A feminist perspective on anorexia nervosa and bulimia. *Signs*, 2:342–356.

Boskind-White, M. & White, W. (1983), *Bulimarexia*. New York: Norton.

Brenner, D. (1983), Self-regulatory functions in bulimia. *Contemp. Psychother. Rev.*, 1:79–96.

Bruch, H. (1973), *Eating Disorders: Obesity, Anorexia Nervosa, and the Person Within*. New York: Basic Books.

——— (1978), *The Golden Cage: The Enigma of Anorexia Nervosa*. Cambridge, MA: Harvard University Press.

Chernin, K. (1982), *The Obsession: Reflections of the Tyranny of Slenderness*. New York: Harper & Row.

——— (1985), *The Hungry Self*. New York: Harper & Row.

Chodorow, N. (1976), *The Reproduction of Mothering*. Berkeley: University of California Press.

Friedman, M. (1985), Survivor guilt in the pathogenesis of anorexia nervosa. *Psychiat.*, 48:25–39.

Garner, D., Garfinkel, P., Schwartz, D. & Thompson, M. (1980), Cultural expectations of thinness in women. *Psychol. Rep.*, 47:483–491.

Gehrie, M. (1987), Eating disorders and early pathology: An hypothesis. Presented at the 10th Annual Conference on the Psychology of the Self. Chicago, October 23–25.

Geist, R. (1985), Therapeutic dilemmas in the treatment of anorexia nervosa: A self-psychological perspective. *Contemp. Psychother. Rev.*, 2:115–142.

Goodsitt, A. (1985), Self psychology and the treatment of anorexia nervosa. In:

Handbook of Psychotherapy for Anorexia Nervosa and Bulimia, ed. D. Garner & P. Garfinkel. New York: Guilford Press, pp. 55–82.

Johnson, C. (1988), The treatment of character disorders among eating disordered patients: transference and countertransference issues. Presented at Eating Disorders Conference, Berkeley, January 22–23.

Kaplan, L. (1978), *Oneness and Separateness.* New York: Simon & Schuster.

Kohut, H. (1971), *The Analysis of the Self.* New York: International Universities Press.

———— (1977), *The Restoration of the Self.* New York: International Universities Press.

———— (1978), Preface to *Der falshe weg sum Selbst. Studien zur Drogenkarriere* by Jurgen vom Scheidt. In: *The Search for the Self, Vol. 2,* ed. P. H. Ornstein. New York: International Universities Press, pp. 845–850.

———— (1984), *How Does Analysis Cure?* Chicago: University of Chicago Press.

Lachmann, F. (1982), Narcissism and female gender identity: A reformulation. *Psychoanal. Rev.,* 69:43–60.

Lang, J. (1984), Notes toward a psychology of the feminine self. In: *Kohut's Legacy,* ed. P. E. Stepansky & A. Goldberg. Hillsdale, NJ: The Analytic Press, pp. 51–69.

Lothstein, L. (1988), Selfobject failure and gender identity. In: *Frontiers in Self Psychology,* ed. A. Goldberg. Hillsdale, NJ: The Analytic Press, pp. 213–235.

Maccoby, E. & Jacklin, C. (1974), *The Psychology of Sex Differences.* Stanford, CA: Stanford University Press.

Mahler, M., Pine, F. & Bergman, A. (1975), *The Psychological Birth of the Human Infant.* New York: Basic Books.

Miller, J. (1976), *Toward a New Psychology of Women.* Boston: Beacon Press.

Minuchin, S., Rosman, B. & Baker, L. (1978), *Psychosomatic Families.* Cambridge, MA: Harvard University Press.

Masterson, J. (1977), Primary anorexia in the borderline adolescent: An object relations view. In: *Borderline Personality Disorders,* ed. P. Hartocolis. New York: International Universities Press.

Orbach, S. (1978), *Fat Is a Feminist Issue.* London: Paddington.

Ornstein, A. (1985), Mother and daughters: A psychoanalytic perspective on a relationship. Presented at the Northern California Society for Psychological Studies, Burlingame, March 10.

Ornstein, P. & Ornstein, A. (1985), Clinical understanding and explaining: The empathic vantage point. In: *Progress in Self Psychology, Vol. 1,* ed. A. Goldberg. New York: Guilford Press, pp. 43–61.

Palazzoli, M. S. (1978), *Self-Starvation.* New York: Aronson.

Polivy, J. & Herman, P. (1987), Diagnosis and treatment of normal eating. *J. Consult. Clin. Psychol.,* 55:635–644.

Sands, S. (1986), Penis envy revisited: A self-psychological perspective on female development. Presented at meeting of Association for Women in Psychology, Oakland, CA, March 6–9.

Steiner-Adair, C. (1986), The body politic: Normal female adolescent development and the development of eating disorders. *J. Amer. Acad. Psychoanal.,* 14:95–114.

Stern, D. (1985), *The Interpersonal World of the Infant.* New York: Basic Books.

Stolorow, R., Brandchaft, B. & Atwood, G. (1987), *Psychoanalytic Treatment.* Hillsdale, NJ: The Analytic Press.

Stoller, R. (1968), *Sex and Gender.* New York: Science House.

Sugarman, A. & Kurash, C. (1982), The body as a transitional object in bulimia. *Internat. J. Eating Dis.,* 1:57–67.

Surrey, J. (1985), The "self-in-relation": A theory of women's development. *Work in Progress,* 84:02. Wellesley, MA: Stone Center Working Paper Series.

Wooley, S., Wooley, O. & Dyrenforth, S. (1980), The case against radical intervention. *Amer. J. Clin. Nutrition*, 33:465–471.

Zadylak, R. & St. Pierre, A. (1987), A self-psychological approach to the treatment of eating disorders. Presented at 10th Annual Conference on the Psychology of the Self, Oct. 23–25.

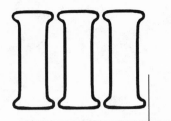

Clinical

Chapter 7

Therapeutic Experiences

Ernest S. Wolf

Almost since its emergence out of the murky past of hypnotism and exhortative psychotherapy, psychoanalytic science, while trying to maintain its dedication to a primacy of values of objective truth-seeking, has struggled against the regressive pull of the human concerns of psychoanalytic practice. Freud himself managed to maintain an uneasy but productive balance between the cool detachment of the laboratory scientist and the compassionate healer of the medical tradition. He knew that his patients came for amelioration of their misery and not because they wanted to advance the cause of psychological science. But he also knew that all the compassion in the world could not cure psychoneurotic suffering. His hope was that a fuller understanding of the mental processes would make treatment more effective. He took the revolutionary step of expanding the concept of the mind to include, in addition to conscious thoughts and feelings, a vast realm of unconscious mental activity. Inevitably, his interest had to shift away from observation of his patient's *behavior* to attempting to feel himself into their subjective experiences.

To examine with objective, scientific detachment the subjective experience of oneself and of others had never before been done consistently and systematically. Thus was born the psychoanalytic method as the scientific study of a person's inner life. Objective data had to be obtained about subjective experiences in order to stay within the canons of those sciences that were regarded as the only legitimate ones. Vicarious introspection into the inner life of others—

105

that is, the process we know as empathy—became the essential method for data collection in psychoanalysis. Empathy is a problematic process because it is experientially private and subjective rather than public and directly verifiable. It is not surprising, therefore, that close to half a century passed before leading psychoanalysts began to acknowledge the central role of empathy in psychoanalytic practice and theory formation (Kohut, 1959). The pursuit of uncontaminated, objective, scientific data saw a tendency to make the clinical analytic situation resemble the natural science experiment by eliminating the emotional subjectivity of the observing scientist—the analyst. Similarly, psychoanalytic theories have tended to ignore the subjective nature of much of psychoanalytic data and to stress the hard facts of verifiable truths over the soft impressions gained experientially. Psychoanalytic theories of cure, especially, have stressed the importance of cognitive insights, the hard truths that can be stated in the objectively defined terms of an appropriate technical language.[1]

In reevaluating psychoanalytic theories of treatment, Friedman (1988) credited Freud with considering understanding, attachment, and integration to be important factors in achieving treatment benefits. Reviewing post-Freudian contributions, Friedman noted a continuing controversy between those analysts who stressed intellectual understanding, including nonverbal emotional understanding, and those analysts who favored emotional attachment to the analyst as the critical factor in cure. Stolorow, Brandchaft, and Atwood (1987) believe that the debate over insight versus attachment represents a false dichotomy that has pervaded Western psychology in general and from which self psychology also has not been free. Instead they suggest that insight through interpretation, affective bonding through empathic attunement, and the facilitation of psychological integration are indissoluble facets of a unitary developmental process.

This essay discusses the disruptions and restorations of the therapeutic process in psychoanalysis and psychoanalytic therapy. Even in a smoothly proceeding psychoanalytic treatment one can observe often, perhaps always, sudden disruptions that transform the relatively harmonious working relationship between analyst and analysand—sometimes referred to as the therapeutic alliance—into an

[1]Psychoanalytic theoreticians usually have not been at ease with the verities embedded in subjective experiences. Indeed, language itself cannot easily be made to express the nuances of the inner life, and we admire the special talents of those who can bend the flow of words to evoke our inner life. We call them poets. Freud himself was richly endowed with this same talent, though he used it to write case histories rather than novellas. Not surprisingly, he received the Goethe prize for literature. No psychoanalyst has ever been honored with a Nobel prize for achievement in science.

adversative ambience. It appears that these disruptions occur during all psychoanalytic treatments regardless of the theoretical convictions of the therapist, that is, regardless of whether the analyst thinks of himself as classically or object-relations or self-psychologically oriented. However, different theoretical frameworks lead to different conceptualizations of the observed phenomena, indeed, sometimes to entirely different observations altogether. I will attempt to conceptualize within the theoretical framework of psychoanalytic self psychology, but I am aware that the described phenomena could be formulated differently. In a properly conducted psychoanalysis, the disruption is followed by a restoration of the collaborative ambience between analysand and analyst. Failing that restoration, the joint psychoanalytic enterprise is likely to founder in a premature termination or in an interminable stalemate.

My examination of the disruption-restoration cycles will attempt to avoid premature theorizing by using an initial focus on the subjective world of analysand and analyst as they are experienced by each. Toward this end, I will address the following questions: 1) What are the effects of the disruption-restoration episodes on the analytic experience? 2) What makes the disruption-restoration episodes healing experiences? 3) What is the experiential difference between the self of the analysand before and after a series of disruptions-restorations? 4) How can one best conceptualize the changes in the self before and after a series of disruption-restoration experiences?

EXPERIENCING THE THERAPEUTIC SITUATION[2]

The Initial Experience.

Prospective analysands come into psychoanalytic treatment because, generally speaking, they feel bad about themselves. Whatever their symptoms—most do have symptoms that often are labeled as neurotic—these patients usually are aware of being more fearful and more distrustfully guarded than they wish to be. They seem to precipitate unsatisfactory relations with others, whether they blame themselves for this or not. They know that they often feel and act blusteringly arrogant on the surface but are full of shame and self-blame inside. Experiencing oneself as so emotionally labile, awkward in action and ineffective in achieving satisfying goals, lowers respect for and pleasure in their own self-image. So does the thought of

[2]See Wolf, 1984, 1986.

having to undergo psychological treatment. The anticipated encounter with the analyst evokes anxiety.

The psychoanalyst at first experiences meeting the new patient with very similar emotions, although probably at a milder level of intensity. Usually there is some awareness of heightened tension or anxiety even before meeting the prospective analysand. Will I be able to respond correctly? Will this unknown person be able to do the work of treatment? Initially many therapist feel themselves becoming defensively in greater need to be in control. They may feel the need to be right rather than to be open to learning something about this new person. Tension, sometimes even anxiety, pervades the beginning therapeutic relationship for both.

This almost palpable tension characterizes the opening phase of psychoanalytic therapy. After some time in treatment it gradually abates. Such amelioration may come about quickly, but more often relaxation does not occur for weeks or months. Very seldom does the tension persist after years of therapist and patient working together. Usually, the analyst empathically recognizes the analysand's specific and nonspecific fears and, by bringing them into the open and explaining them, expects to achieve a gradual amelioration. As the tension slowly ebbs, both participants experience themselves and each other less fearfully, more trustingly, and with diminishing needs to be guarded in their own affects and spontaneity. In short, analysand and analyst experience an enhanced sense of well-being. The tense opening phase of the analysis merges into a phase of cyclically alternating tension followed by relaxation marking disruptions and restorations of the therapeutic relationship.

The Disruption Experience.

This second phase is ushered in when the analysand suddenly experiences the analyst as not being attuned or attentive. The patient feels misunderstood and unable to get through to the therapist. Perhaps the therapist seems more interested in himself and in his theories than in the patient's concerns. Or the therapist may seem to be more involved with the patient's family or other adversaries than being allied to the patient. Sometimes the patient has the impression that the analyst is more interested in the patient's behavior than in how he feels inside or that the analyst cares more about what the analysand does than who he is. For the patient it is an experience of ineffectiveness, perhaps even of total powerlessness.

In the past I have talked about "empathic failure of the therapist" (Wolf, 1984) as the cause for the disruption. Let me now correct the erroneous impression that I was blaming the therapist for the disruption. The disruption is not due to a failure of either but rather to a discrepancy between the analysand's and the analyst's experiences of reality. Here is a condensed clinical example:

> A young lawyer, in his third year of analysis, reported that his cat had died. The cat had never been mentioned before, and rather perfunctorily, without any real feeling, I acknowledged the loss. A period of silence ensued, and I said something like "let's go on." More silence, and I commented that the cat must have been quite important and the loss very painful to the patient. Yes, the cat—he used the cat's name—meant very much to him, but he did not think I could understand that. He sounded upset. During the next session he still was upset, as I could tell by his coldly angry voice. I interpreted that he was angry with me for not having been more sympathetic. Yes, he agreed, he did not think I really cared, but just like his mother I acted as if I did. Mother would put on a great show of concern, especially when other people were watching, but she didn't really care. I confirmed that I did not feel about pets the same way that he and many other people do but that he must have experienced my comments as pretending concern similar to his mother.

In this example of a disruption, one can discern elements of both here-and-now experience and of transference. Both aspects are always present. First, the analysand experiences the analyst as not empathic, as not understanding how the patient feels, and then the patient is reminded of similar painful and traumatic malattunements in childhood. The transference of the expectation of not being understood makes the analyst's lack of attunement a repetition of a childhood trauma: not only is the analyst suddenly not available as a confirming selfobject experience in the present, but instead he seems to endorse and sanction the validity of the mother's lack of empathy as well as her need to pretend. The analyst, for his part, had thought himself well attuned to the patient. He knew about mother's pretending to feelings she did not have, and he had never before been aware that the analysand had any particular interest in pets. His perfunctory response seemed an appropriate acknowledgment. In fact, it was an appropriate acknowledgment, from the analyst's point-of-view, but not from the patient's point-of-view. The analysand unquestionably experienced a lack of empathy and understanding. The analyst must recognize and acknowledge that, because, by so doing, 1) he restores the patient's experience of a bond with the analyst and 2) he provides the patient with an experience of having effectively communicated to the analyst.

Generally speaking, it is a consequence of such malattunement that patients feel alone and overwhelmed by affects of anxiety, frustration, anger, helplessness, and rage, or hopelessness and depression. The disruption of the therapeutic relationship is associated with crushed self-esteem, that is, a devastating sense of badness characterizes the disrupted state of the analysand.[3] Why is this so?

Within the frame of a self-psychologically oriented treatment ambience, the loss of attunement and the disjointed communication are experienced as a loss of intimacy, that is, as a threat to the attachment of analysand to analyst. The experience of a selfobject bond is lost and with it the experience of a cohesive self. Indeed, numerous observations over many years allow us to assert with a high degree of reliability that a selfobject bond—whether of a mirroring, or idealizing, or alter-ego variety—is a necessary condition for a self-state that is experienced as being whole, cohesive, balanced, and energetic.

The Instinct of Mastery in Psychoanalysis.

Freud (1905) mentioned an apparatus for obtaining mastery and an instinct of mastery. Elaborating in 1913 he wrote, "Activity is supplied by the common instinct of mastery, which we call sadism when we find it in the service of the sexual function" (p. 322)) and, "Indeed it is at bottom a sublimated off-shoot of the instinct of mastery exalted into something intellectual, and its repudiation in the form of doubt plays a large part in the picture of obsessive neurosis" (p. 324). And again, in 1920, in the discussion of the *fort-da* game, he speculated, "These efforts might be put down to an instinct for mastery that was acting independently of whether the memory was in itself pleasurable or not" (p. 16). However, he did not pursue this line of investigation. Angyal (1941) in a similar vein discussed a "trend to autonomy," which was mentioned by Hendrick (1943) when he elaborated on what he chose to call an instinct to master. Hendrick characterized it as a fundamental drive of human beings to control the environment and associated with a specific pleasure experience that he termed work pleasure. Hendrick (1942) referred here to "an inborn drive to do and to learn how to do. This instinct appears to determine more of the behavior of the child during the first two years than even the

---

[3]The self-experience of the analyst will qualitatively include some similar feelings, if he allows himself to become aware of them, although one may reasonably hope he will be able to resist the regressive and fragmenting pull of the disruption more successfully than the patient can.

need for sensual pleasure" (p. 40). However, Hendrick's view received little acceptance. Recent data reported from researches on infants strongly suggest a reexamination of the relevance for psychoanalytic theories of structure formation of the mutual interaction between infants and mothers.

Infant Observations

White (1959) studied what he called the "concept of competence" based on infant observations. He concluded that activities in the ultimate service of competence must therefore be conceived to be motivated in their own right, proposed this motivation be designated "effectance," and characterized the experience produced as a feeling of efficacy.

Furthermore, research in infant development suggests the consideration of other needs in addition to the array of needed selfobject experiences. Lichtenberg (1985, 1989) has shown that more recent studies in infant development are suggestive of the role of efficacy pleasure in the consolidation of self experience.[4] Citing the work of the Papouseks, Lichtenberg reports a classic example demonstrating infants' pleasure in their own efficacy. Four-month-old infants were exposed to five seconds of multicolored bursts of light. They oriented themselves toward the stimulation with interest, and then, typical of responses to unvaried stimuli, their orientation diminished after repetition. One might say they got bored with just being passively entertained. But then the experiment was arranged so that when the infants in the course of their movements rotated their head 30 degrees to a predetermined side three times successively within a time interval, the light display was switched on. The infants' apparent awareness of their having an effect on the bursts of light changed the boredom to excited interest: as soon as the infants turned on the light presentation by their own head movements, their behavior changed dramatically. Their orientation reactions increased in intensity, and they continuously made all kinds of movement to try to switch on the visual stimulation again. The infants, after a few successes, might leave their heads turned 90 degrees even though the lights were to be seen in the midline. Furthermore, the infants did not seem to be watching. Nonetheless, they continued to turn on the display and

[4]Various infant researchers have used different terms in reporting on the phenomena here discussed. Efficiency, competence pleasure, efficacy pleasure, effectance pleasure are among these (White, 1959, 1960; Papousek, 1975, Broucek, 1979, Sander, 1983).

responded to their success with smiles and happy bubbling. The pleasure appeared to originate more from the effectiveness of their light-swtiching actions than from the visual stimulation itself.

Other infant researchers also observed that when infants have contingent control over events in the external world, they begin to smile. Broucek (1979) believes that the source of pleasure does not lie in problem solving alone but in those experiences when the infant's activity is the cause of the result. He concludes that awareness of being the cause and the sense of efficacy and pleasure associated with it are the foundation of self-feeling. Lichtenberg (1989) has identified the sense of achieving physiological regulation due to a satisfactory match between caregiver ministrations and the infant's awareness of need as a foundation of self-feeling. He indicates that achieving intimacy in attachment and affiliation is another foundation of self feeling. The characteristic patterns of mutual influence of mother and infant come to be recognized and expected by the infant (Stern, 1985; Beebe and Lachmann, 1987) Thus there exists now a body of data that illuminates structure formation in infancy and, by extension, may also illuminate the restoration of structure in psychoanalytic treatment.

The Experience of Efficacy in Psychoanalytic Treatment

From the awareness of having an initiating and causal role in bringing about states of attachment and intimacy, the infant acquires an *experience of efficacy* that, in addition to the responsive selfobject experiences, becomes an essential aspect of the cohesive self-experience. It is as if the infant were able to say to himself (with apologies to Descartes), I can elicit a response, therefore I am somebody. The regression facilitated during the analysis of adults opens the way to reexperiencing on an archaic level the pleasurable experience of efficacy and the painful self-destroying experience of the loss of efficacy.

The Restoration Experience

The therapists's responses to the patient's and his own affects determine the future course of the analytic enterprise that has become disrupted. One can expect the analyst to have undergone a psychoanalytic experience himself and to have absorbed the attitudes and principles that guide a proper analytic ambience. He will thus become aware of the disruption and its effects on his and his patient's experience. Introspectively in contact with his own inner psychic reality and empathically attuned to his patient's different reality and suffering, the analyst is in a good position to discern what actions committed or omitted may have precipitated the present impasse. Perhaps he will come to realize that the disruption is due to a break in correctly sensing each other's inner experiences: not only an erroneous attunement of the analyst to the patient's needs, but the patient's equally erroneous reading of the analyst's intentions, often as a result of transference of archaic fears and expectations. The therapist therefore will explore and feel out for clues to explain the disruption and will grope for ways of communicating his understanding, that is, conveying his insight to the patient via interpretation. This exploratory and explaining effort of the analyst is experienced by the patient as evidence that his concerns are being taken seriously. For both, but especially for the analysand, this is an experience of his own efficacy in eliciting an attuned response, of having made a dent, of being somebody, a confirmed self. Healing experiences in psychoanalytic treatment require 1) a sense of being understood by the other and 2) a sense of one's own efficacy regarding the other. We cannot, with our present state of knowledge in psychoanalytic psychology, say much about the relative contribution of the various types of mirroring, idealizing, or alter-ego selfobject experiences nor of the experience of efficacy to the cohesion of the self. But it seems clear that all of them are essential for the emergence of a strong self. One could conceptualize the need for efficacy pleasure as a variety of a needed mirroring experience. However, in view of its extraanalytic validation by mother-infant observations involving responses from a nonliving object, the need for efficacy experiences is best considered a separate kind of need.

Interpretation as a Total Experience

An effective analyst provides for his patients a healing experience by using his insights into himself as well as into his patient. Expressing these insights to the patient verbally, that is, through verbal interpretations, can enhance the healing experience and facilitate its absorption and fixation into the patient's memory. Making such interpretations also enhances the therapist's self-esteem, because he feels he is doing something actively in harmony with his value system of being truthful as well as helpful. Moreover, interpretations carry the stamp of science and philosophy, under whose aegis the whole enterprise is lifted out of the tawdry underside of human interactions.

Thus, cure in psychoanalytic treatment is for the analysand effective evocation from the analyst of a suitable selfobject experience of interested and benevolent concern as well as an experience of his own efficacy in evoking it. Many analysts are able to fashion such a needed response by making a verbal interpretation. The effect of these interpretations rests more on the meaning of the interpretive experience for the analysand rather than simply on its cognitive-verbal content. However, since the meaning of experiences can be conveyed only by using metaphors, the verbal interpretation becomes a useful tool for evoking and communicating mutative experiences. To the analysand, the meaning of the analyst's interpretation and its expression of concern may be an acknowledgment of the analysand's importance, that is, a mirroring selfobject experience; or it may mean being accepted by an admired other, that is, an idealizing selfobject experience; or it may be an experience of essential likeness with the analyst, that is, an alter-ego selfobject experience; or it may be an experience of his own efficacy. All of these entail a firming or restoration of a needed bond to the selfobject together with an confirmed experience of being somebody. An enhanced feeling of well-being is the almost universal accompaniment.

CONCEPTUALIZING THE THERAPEUTIC PROCESS

The Necessity of Metaphoric Descriptions

Having described the events during psychoanalytic treatment as they are experienced by both analysand and analyst, I shall now discuss the result of these therapeutic events from an objective-descriptive point of view. In other words, I shall try to come to some conclusions about how the state of the patient's self is different—has changed—by virtue of the therapeutic experience. How can we think about a self that is not a thing but an organization of experiences?

We can know about the self only through the phenomena of direct self-experience or by inferences derived from these as we attempt to think about these self-experiences and form theories about them. In other words, to objectify, manipulate, and communicate about these subjective experiences, we use metaphorical constructions. Freud wrote in 1926, "In psychology we can only describe things by the help of analogies. There is nothing peculiar in this; it is the case elsewhere as well. But we have constantly to keep changing these analogies, for none of them lasts us long enough" (p. 195). Just as Freud asked us to picture the ego as a kind of façade, as a frontage, as a cortical layer, so in psychoanalytic self psychology we have to picture the self as a *structure*, specifically as a structure with two poles connected by an arch (Kohut, 1977; Kohut and Wolf, 1978). Unless we conceptualize in such metaphorical images, we will find it very difficult to talk about the self. Even Atwood and Stolorow (1984) cannot wholly free themselves of this need to use metaphorical language, as evidenced by the use of such words as structure and pattern when they speak of the organization of subjective experience. Substituting the term structuralization for structure does not make the sentence and the implied thinking process any less metaphorical.

The analysand comes into treatment because the functioning of his self is impaired. This impairment may be chronic or acute. It may signify 1) a developmentally incomplete self-structure, 2) a mostly developed but fragmented self-structure, or 3) deficient functioning of a developed self because of imbalances among the self's components. The impairment may be due to faulty development, developmental arrest or injury to the developed self. Trauma during early development or later may have occurred in acutely intense and even overwhelming dosage or, more likely, chronically over longer periods of time in small but cumulative doses. In clinical self psychology, perhaps too simplistically, we have lumped all these impairments together under the term "fragmentation."

The therapeutic experience results in the self's becoming less fragmented. Within the terms of our inquiry that is a clear statement about the self's structure: it has become more continuous, its parts more smoothly coordinated with each other, its boundaries more clearly delineated, its various constituents more evenly balanced. Its functioning has become more efficiently integrated.

Transmuting Internalization?

But how did this increased cohesion come about? Kohut (1971) related these changes to the formation and accretion of structure; he termed the process *transmuting internalization*. In the therapeutic situation, optimal frustration facilitates a transference to the selfobject analyst, whose imago is cathected with the patient's interest. Due to the frustrating aspects of the intraanalytic transference relationship, the imago is broken up, decathected in fractions, and internalized by a process of identification, the internalized structures now performing the functions the transferential object had previously performed. Kohut (1977) elaborated this view by adding that the patient uses the analyst as a selfobject, that is, as a precursory substitute for the not-yet-existing psychological structures, until new structure are formed in the ego under the impact of archaic strivings. In a further elaboration of the optimal frustration-internalization sequence, Kohut (1984) pointed to the optimally frustrating loss of the selfobject/analyst's omniscience when the analysand discovers that his own understanding of his mental states and attitudes is at times better than that of the analyst. The analyst's occasional failures, then, constituting optimal frustrations, lead to the building up of self-structure. Kohut never wavered from the conceptualization that cure in psychoanalysis entailed the accretion of structure by a never clearly defined process of internalization. He also never doubted the importance of optimal frustration as a spur to this internalization, although in his last book (Kohut, 1984), he left as a question to be resolved by future research whether abiding psychic functions can also be acquired by the self without preceding frustration. Indeed, the work by Bacal (1985) and Terman (1987) point to the mainly gratifying nature of the optimally effective therapeutic relationship, and they are proposing the term *optimal gratification.*

Kohut (1984) gave an example of an optimal frustration the analysand's discovering

> that his own understanding of his mental states and attitudes is at times better than that of the analyst, that the analyst is not omniscient, that his empathy is fallible, and that the patient's empathy with himself, including, par excellence, his empathy with his childhood experiences, is often superior [p. 72].

This example is paradigmatic for transference disruption-restorations generally as they occur in psychoanalytic treatment. There always is the analysand's disappointment in the analyst, which is then accepted by both analysand and analyst during the subsequent restoration phase.

What is being internalized by the patient during such a disruption-restoration? In Kohut's (1984) description, it is the information that the analyst is not as ideal as the patient had thought that becomes new self-structure. I think we can expand that description. To be sure, the patient discovers that the analyst is not omniscient, that he falls short of the idealized grandiose imago the patient has of him. The patient's image of the analyst shrinks and seems more like the disappointing selfobjects of childhood. But the patient obtains additional information about the analyst—that the analyst, probably unlike the archaic selfobjects of childhood, does not reject or deny the patient's perception of him as less than ideal. Thus, the patient gains two pieces of information that are at variance with his earlier expectations about the selfobject analyst. Moreover, the patient also learns that he can communicate his unflattering knowledge about the analyst to him and still have the analyst accept it. The internalization of the new knowledge about himself and about the idealized selfobject takes place under conditions of a therapeutically facilitated regression. It is accompanied by intense affects and therefore penetrates to the deepest layers of the patient's psyche, resulting in a modification of the patient's image of himself and of his selfobjects. Consequently, a change occurs in the patient's expectations from the relationship between self and selfobjects.

Accretion versus Rearrangement.

Does the internalization of this information about self and selfobjects result in an accretion of self-structure, or is the result a rearrangement of the existing structures? I am not sure that this is a meaningful question, since we are dealing with a metaphorical picture of the self and the selfobjects. Clearly, the self, as an organization of experiences, will now function somewhat differently than before the disruption-restoration. What has changed to account for this improved functioning?

Perhaps we can come to some conclusions by looking at people who have had a good analysis or other good psychotherapeutic experience. Such people appear to feel and function better, but their basic personality patterns seem unchanged. They are still the same persons, and one would not mistake any of them for someone else. Often they are less labile and less easily upset. They are less anxious, but the old fears are still detectable in an ameliorated state. They are less defensive, yet the old defenses can be brought into play whenever old dangers threaten or seem to threaten. Probably defenses are not triggered as easily or as strongly. These people are no longer driven by affective storms. The highs of elation and the lows of depression are neither as intense nor as long lasting as before treatment, but they have not disappeared completely. In short, they are the same people, not different but perhaps more expressively themselves than before.

These observations lead me to conceptualize the change as a strengthening of the self by way of rearrangement rather than as an accretion of self-structure. Our observations do not support a need to postulate an accretion of structure. It is sufficient to think of the self's increased strength through reorganization. Perhaps that means a rearrangement of the constituents and an integration of split-off parts. Perhaps a better fit of the various parts of the self makes for tighter cohesion, and better coordination results in greater balance.

All these rearrangements by integrating diverse aspects of the self reduce internal tension. Most likely, a shift away from "accretion" to "rearrangement" is the kind of change in metaphoric image that Freud had in mind when he told us we need to change the analogies often because they do not last us long enough.

REFERENCES

Angyal, A. (1941), *Foundations for a Science of Personality*, New York: Commonwealth Fund.

Atwood, G. & Stolorow, R. (1984), *Structures of Subjectivity*. Hillsdale, NJ: The Analytic Press.

Bacal, H. (1985), Optimal responsiveness and the therapeutic process. In: *Progress in Self Psychology*, Vol. 1, ed. A. Goldberg. New York: Guilford Press, pp. 202–226.

Beebe, B. & Lachmann, F. (1988), Mother-infant mutual influence and precursors of psychic structure. In: *Frontiers in Self Psychology: Progress in Self Psychology, Vol. 3*, ed. A. Goldberg. Hillsdale, NJ: The Analytic Press, pp. 3–25.

Broucek, F. (1979), Efficacy in infancy: A review of some experimental studies and their possible implications for clinical theory. *Internat. J. Psycho-Anal.*, 60:311–316.

Freud, S. (1905), Three essays on the theory of sexuality. *Standard Edition*, 7:130–243. London: Hogarth Press, 1953.

—— (1913), The disposition to obsessional neurosis. *Standard Edition*, 12:317–326. London: Hogarth Press, 1958.

—— (1920), Beyond the pleasure principle. *Standard Edition*, 18:7–64. London: Hogarth Press, 1955.

—— (1926), The question of lay analysis: Conversations with an impartial person. *Standard Edition*, 20:183–250. London: Hogarth Press, 1961.

Friedman, L. (1988), *The Anatomy of Psychotherapy*. Hillsdale, NJ: The Analytic Press.

Hendrick, I. (1942), Instinct and the ego during infancy. *Psychoanal. Quart.*, 11:33–58.

Kohut, H. (1959), Introspection, empathy, and psychoanalysis. In: *The Search For the Self*, Vol. 1, ed. P. Ordstein. New York: International Universities Press, 1978, pp. 205–232.

—— (1971), *The Analysis of the Self*. New York: International Universities Press.

—— (1977), *The Restoration of the Self*. New York: International Universities Press.

—— (1984), *How Does Analysis Cure?* ed. A. Goldberg & P. E. Stepansky. Chicago: University of Chicago Press.

—— & Wolf, E. (1978), The disorders of the self and their treatment: An outline. *Internat. J. Psycho-Anal.*, 59:413–425.

Lichtenberg, J. D. (1983), *Psychoanalysis and Infant Research*. Hillsdale, NJ: The Analytic Press.

—— (1989), *Psychoanalysis and Motivation*. Hillsdale, NJ: The Analytic Press.

Sander, L. (1983), To begin with: Reflections on ontogeny. In: *Reflections on Self Psychology*, ed. J. Lichtenberg & S. Kaplan. Hillsdale, NJ: The Analytic Press.

Stern, D. (1985), *The Interpersonal World of the Infant*. New York: Basic Books.

Stolorow, R., Brandchaft, B. & Atwood, G. (1987), *Psychoanalytic Treatment*. Hillsdale, NJ: The Analytic Press.

Terman, D. (1987), Optimum frustration: Structuralization and the therapeutic process.

In: *Learning from Kohut, Progress in Self Psychology, Vol. 4*, ed. A. Goldberg. Hillsdale, NJ: The Analytic Press, pp. 113–125.

White, R. W. (1959), Motivation reconsidered: The concept of competence. *Psychol. Rev.*, 66:292–333.

—— (1960), Competence and the psychosexual stages of development. *Nebraska Symposium on Motivation*, 8:97–141.

Wolf, E. S. (1984), Disruptions in the psychoanalytic treatment of disorders of the self. In: *Kohut's Legacy*, ed. P. E. Stepansky & A. Goldberg. Hillsdale, NJ: The Analytic Press, pp. 143–156.

—— (1986), Discrepancies between analysand and analyst in experiencing the analysis. In: *Progress in Self Psychology*, Vol. 1, ed. A. Goldberg. New York: Guilford Press.

Chapter 8

A Self-Psychological Theory and Approach to Treating Substance Abuse Disorders: The "Intersubjective Absorption" Hypothesis

Richard B. Ulman
Harry Paul

Although short on clearly defined and specifically devised treatment plans, psychoanalysis is long on theories claiming to explain the etiology and psychodynamics of substance abuse. Psychoanalytic theories and approaches to the treatment of substance abuse have gone through three different major cycles, corresponding to the theoretical dominance of id psychology, ego psychology and object relations theory, as well as theories of narcissism and the self. We believe that, together, self psychology and the work of Stolorow and collaborators (see, for example, Atwood and Stolorow, 1984; Ulman and Stolorow, 1985; Stolorow, Brandchaft, and Atwood, 1987) on psychoanalytic phenomenology and intersubjectivity offer possibilities for advancing the psychoanalytic understanding and treatment of substance abuse disorders.

Kohut (1977a) contended that the potential "explanatory power of the new psychology of the self" (p. vii) was especially great in the area of "the addictions". He (Kohut and Wolf, 1978) subsequently mentioned "addictive behavior" (p. 416) as a major symptom of narcissistic behavior disorders. Unfortunately, however, with a few noteworthy exceptions in the application of self psychology to the eating disorders (see, for example, Geist, 1984; Goodsitt, 1984; Brenner, 1986), self psychologists have failed to follow Kohut's lead by

The authors wish to express their thanks to Arthur Malin, M.D., who offered a number of helpful suggestions that were incorporated into the original paper.

121

applying a self-psychological conceptualization of narcissism to understanding and treating the addictions. Our work is an attempt to use the explanatory power of self psychology to understand and treat a wide variety of substance abuse disorders.

We define a substance abuse disorder as the compulsive and habitual use (or, in the case of anorexia, the disuse) of a substance (or substances) for the purpose of altering, either psychopharmacologically or biochemically and physiologically, the sense of subjective self (Stern, 1985). Such abuse is characterized by dependence, addiction, tolerance, and withdrawal.

Our approach to understanding and treating the "addictive personality" (Kohut, 1987) is based on three propositions: (1) all substance abuse disorders (including all forms of drug or chemical dependence and addiction as well as the various food and eating disorders) are manifestations of a subjective disturbance in the unconscious organization of experiences of self in relation to selfobject; (2) the addictive person fantasizes a particular substance as imbued with unconscious meaning whereby it is subjectively experienced as providing selfobject functions; and, (3) self-psychological treatment is effective because the selfobject functions of substances become "intersubjectively absorbed" within the context of the therapeutic relationship in the form of "selfobject transference fantasies" (see Ulman and Brothers, 1987, 1988).

We divide our work into three sections. The first section outlines our new theoretical perspective. Section two describes our treatment approach, and section three contains a discussion of two treatment cases. The cases are designed to illuminate critical clinical processes determining the relative success or failure of the therapy of the always difficult to treat addictive personality.

THEORETICAL OVERVIEW

A careful reading of Kohut's (1959, 1972, 1977a,b, 1987) brief yet insightful comments on addiction or substance abuse reveals several important lines of thought. He (1971) argued that the addict has failed to develop (internalize and transmute, that is "transmuting internalization") the psychological structures required for experiencing the mirroring selfobject functions of self-confirmation and self-validation, nor those required for experiencing the idealizing selfobject functions of self-soothing and self-calming. For example, Kohut (1987) stated that the object of an addiction is needed to perform an important psychological function ordinarily performed by oneself . . . a self-soothing, self-esteem maintaining function that ordinarily in the course of development is internalized as part of one's own psychic structure [p. 131].

As a result of failing to adequately internalize and build up necessary psychological structures, the addict is compelled to depend on an inanimate substance (e.g. drugs, alcohol, food) as a "substitute for a selfobject" (Kohut, 1977a, p. vii). As a substitute selfobject, a substance functions as a "remedial stimulant" (Kohut, 1972, p. 626; see also Geist, 1984) defending against the fragmentation or depletion of the self.

According to Kohut (1977a), the addict, by

ingesting the drug . . . symbolically compels the mirroring self-object to soothe him, to accept him. Or he symbolically compels the idealized selfobject to submit to his merging into it and thus to his partaking in its magical power [p. vii].

[By incorporating the drug, the addict] supplies for himself the feeling of being accepted and thus of being self-confident; or he creates the experience of being merged with a source of power that gives him the feeling of being strong and worthwhile. And all these effects of the drug tend to increase his feeling of being alive, tend to increase his certainty that he exists in this world [p. viii].

In line with Kohut's (1959, 1977a, 1987) thoughts on the addictive personality, we view all substance abuse disorders (including all forms of chemical dependence, as well as the various food and eating disorders) as subjective disturbances in the unconscious organization of experiences of self in relation to selfobject. These disturbances appear in at least two typical forms of self-disorder: the empty, depleted, depressive self; and the fragmenting, disintegrating, manic self. Each of these basic self-disorders arises because of a specific developmental arrest in the structuralization of subjective worlds of experience (see Stolorow and Lachmann, 1980). Such an arrest entails the developmental failure to transform archaic forms of narcissism with resulting "vertical splits" (Kohut, 1971) and tendencies toward painful states of empty and depleted depression or fragmenting and disintegrating mania. Archaic narcissism remains dissociatively split off and "disavowed" (Basch, 1981, 1983) in the form of unconscious fantasies of grandiose exhibitionism, idealized merger, or alter ego twinship.

Thus far we have presented a general theory of self-disorder that is applicable to a number of subjective disturbances in experiences of self in relation to selfobject. A critical question remains, however: What is the specific nature of the subjective disturbance in experiences of self in relation to selfobject of the addictive personality?

We believe that the addictive person fantasizes a particular substance as imbued with unconscious meaning whereby it is experienced as providing selfobject functions of mirroring, idealization, or twinship. According to Kohut (1987), addiction may be "to a drug, to people, to food, to alcohol, to masturbation, or to perverse pursuits" (p. 118). Kohut went on to point out that the addiction, whether to a particular substance, activity, or person, "is not determined by the elaboration of the object, but *by the needs of the self*" (p. 119).

Behaviors and activities may all become compulsive and habitual and take on selfobject functions related to the activation of archaic narcissistic fantasies. The addictive person is unable to perform these necessary selfobject functions because of parental failures in empathic attunement that have disrupted the normal transmuting internalization of these functions. Instead, these selfobject functions either are only partially internalized in the form of fragile and vulnerable psychic structures or are not internalized at all and are therefore entirely missing.

We are proposing that on an unconscious fantasy level the addictive person establishes early in life a primary selfobject relationship with an inanimate object, substance, or activity rather than with another person. In Winnicottian (1951) terms, the addictive person becomes fixated on the use of a "transitional object" from childhood. The exact etiology of such an enduring but archaic selfobject relationship is still unclear. However, the selfobject relationship with inanimate objects or activities usually assumes the form of a fullblown substance abuse disorder during the adolescence or early adulthood of the addictive person. As a result of early narcissistic traumata, the addictive person depends on and trusts only inanimate objects, substances, or activities to provide needed selfobject functions.

Moreover, in line with the "drug of choice hypothesis" (Milkman and Frosch, 1977), we contend that certain persons develop archaic selfobject relationships with a particular substance or substances depending upon their specific psychoactive effects. Expanding upon Kohut's (1972) idea of remedial stimulants, we view the abuse of a substance as a means of psychopharmacologically, biochemically, or physiologically achieving a desperately needed relief from depressive emptiness and depletion or manic fragmentation and disintegration. In other words, we are giving new self-psychological meaning to the idea that substance abuse is a form of self-medication gone awry.

Certain psychoactive substances, acting either as central nervous system depressants or as stimulants, engender a mood of elation, euphoria, and fullness or a mood of calmness, soothing, and wholeness. The mood results from the psychopharmacological, biochemical, or physiological activation of split-off and disavowed archaic narcissistic fantasies. Our conception of archaic narcissistic fantasy is based on Kohut's (see, for example 1966, 1968, 1971) early work on the self. (See also Ulman and Brothers, 1987, 1988 for a more detailed examination of Kohut's early thoughts on archaic narcissistic fantasy.) Following Ulman and Brothers (1987; see also Ulman and Brothers, 1988) we define such "central organizing fantasies of self in relation to selfobject" as entailing "illusions of personally unique attributes and special endowments, superhuman invulnerability and invincibility, magical and uncanny powers (for example, clairvoyance, psychokinesis, and telepathy), as well as union or 'oneness' with supreme and all-mighty beings" (p. 176).

TREATMENT

Our approach to treatment is based on the work of Kohut as well as Atwood and Stolorow. According to Kohut (1987), the addictive person going "into psychotherapy becomes addicted to the psychotherapist or to the psychotherapeutic procedure" (p. 126). Kohut insisted that "there is nothing wrong with it. This is the way it should be, because they lack the necessary structure at this point" (p. 126).

In an early attempt to distinguish the selfobject from the object-directed transference, Kohut (1959) suggested that in the treatment of the addict "the therapist is not a screen for the projection of existing structure; he is a substitute for it. . . . Inasmuch as psychological structure is necessary, the patient now really needed the support, the soothing of the therapist. . . . His dependence cannot be analyzed or reduced by insight; it must be recognized and acknowledged" (p. 225).

In line with this observation, Kohut (1987) warned therapists attempting to treat addictive persons that

> You can say you cannot give them what they need from you. You can give drugs instead of yourself, but then you will not set up the type of situation that in a way repeats the childhood situation by fulfilling for them the functions that they cannot fulfill for themselves [pp. 126–127].

Kohut urged that instead the therapist facilitate a selfobject transference (fantasy) in which the addictive person experiences (fantasizes) the desperately needed selfobject function as being provided. Such a sustaining therapeutic relationship gradually allows the addictive person to experience these selfobject functions as being provided by himself or herself. Kohut concluded that in this way the therapist helps the addictive person to "build up structure" (p. 127).

Atwood and Stolorow (1984) have made the point that after the selfobject bond has been established, it "absorbs" the functions previously provided by the symptom in maintaining the cohesiveness of the self. We have expanded on this idea and developed a self-psychological treatment approach based on the clinical phenomenon of the absorption of selfobject functions in the intersubjective context of the therapeutic relationship.

Our intersubjective absorption hypothesis is consistent with Kohut's description of transmuting internalization as being analogous to the metabolic process of building up protein in the body (see Strozier, 1983). In connection with this biochemical analogy, Kohut claimed that the unconscious process of psychic structure building is analogous to the process whereby foreign protein is ingested, broken down, and molecularly reassembled. Kohut stated, "This is a good analogy for transmuting internalization" (quoted in Strozier, 1983, p. 483).

Finally, in a statement that anticipated our idea about archaic narcissistic fantasies as manifested in selfobject transferences, Kohut (1959) noted:

> In fact, it is a clinical experience that the major psychoanalytic task in such instances is the analysis of the denial of the real need; *the patient must first learn to replace a set of unconscious grandiose fantasies* that are kept up with the aid of social isolation by the, for him, painful acceptance of the reality of being dependent [p. 225, italics added]

At another early place in his writings, Kohut (1968) said, "The central activity in the clinical process during the mirror transference concerns the raising to consciousness of the patient's *infantile fantasies of exhibitionistic grandeur*" (p. 490, italics added). Commenting on a specific case, Kohut described the patient's early childhood fantasy of operating "streetcars via a 'thought control' which emanated from his head above the clouds" (p. 491). Kohut pointed out that this patient's childhood "grandiose fantasy" emerged and underwent transformation in the context of a mirror transference.

In keeping with Kohut's, as well as Atwood and Stolorow's thinking, our treatment approach rests on the proposition that within the intersubjective context of the therapeutic relationship, the selfobject functions of substances become absorbed in the form of selfobject transference fantasies. Such archaic transference fantasies enable the patient to experience the therapist as providing selfobject functions previously performed by a substance. In this way, on the level of the patient's unconscious fantasy life, the therapist replaces and takes over the substance's unconscious meaning.

The analysis of a transference fantasy, as well as the working through and resolution of a selfobject transference neurosis, leads to the therapeutic transformation of archaic narcissistic fantasies and the transmuting internalization of their selfobject functions. A close reading of Kohut (see, for example, 1971; see also Ulman and Brothers, 1987, 1988) reveals that he originally conceptualized transmuting internalization as involving the transformation of archaic narcissistic fantasies ("prestructural objects") into healthy and mature psychic structures.

The fantasmagorical nature of the analytic relationship creates a therapeutic context in which it is possible for the selfobject functions of a substance to be intersubjectively absorbed as part of a transference fantasy. Our treatment approach consists of the therapeutic activation of split-off and poorly integrated archaic narcissistic fantasies in the form of selfobject transference fantasies. The analysis and therapeutic transformation of these transference fantasies entails the transmuting internalization of the selfobject functions of substances. This is critical to preventing future substance abuse relapses. Previous attempts by the substance abuser at achieving integration of split-off and disavowed archaic narcissistic fantasies were unsuccessful because these efforts depended on the use of substances.

The recent work of Ulman (1988) and Ulman and Brothers (1987, 1988) supports our use of the intersubjective field, codetermined by patient and therapist, as the therapeutic medium within which to facilitate and empathically observe the restoration and transformation of central organizing fantasies of self in relation to selfobject. The transmuting internalization of selfobject functions often leads to dramatic improvements in the substance abuser's life outside of the treatment relationship. We present an example of such improvement in one of our treatment case discussions.

Our self-psychological treatment approach centers on three paradigmatic intersubjective configurations. The first has to do with the empty, depleted, depressed substance abuser's selfobject transference fantasy of mirroring. Such an addictive person compulsively and habitually uses central nervous system stimulants (for example, amphetamines or cocaine) to psychopharmacologically activate and intensify grandiose fantasies (see Tolpin, 1974) as well as the accompanying moods of euphoria, elation, and fullness (that is, "being full of oneself").

The second paradigmatic intersubjective configuration focuses on the fragmenting, disintegrating, manic substance abuser's selfobject transference fantasy of idealized merger with an omnipotent figure. Such an addictive person compulsively and habitually uses central nervous system depressants (for example, alcohol and heroin) to psychopharmacologically activate and intensify unconscious fantasies of idealized merger with the omnipotent figure and the accompanying mood of calmness, soothing, and wholeness. Paradoxically, in the case of alcohol and heroin, a subjective sense of wholeness may be psychopharmacologically achieved as a result of an experience of oblivion and loss of self as part of a fantasized union with the cosmos.

A third paradigmatic intersubjective configuration, one with which we have had less clinical experience, involves the selfobject transference fantasy of twinship with an alter ego. At present, we are unclear about the specific selfobject functioning of this transference fantasy as regards its specific psychopharmacological action.

Certain substances, such as alcohol, heroin, amphetamines, and cocaine, because of their inherent psychoactive effect on the central nervous system, are usually subjectively sensed as heightening specific archaic narcissistic fantasies and as providing corresponding selfobject functions. Other substances, such as food, may be subjectively sensed as heightening archaic narcissistic fantasies and as providing selfobject functions based more on personality factors than on their inherent psychoactive effects.

This is also true to a lesser degree of such substances as alcohol. However, in some addictive persons, alcohol intensifies a grandiose fantasy because of the stimulating effect of the substance rather than because of its usual depressing or sedating effect. We have found this phenomenon in a subgroup of our alcohol abusing patients.

It is important to point out that the simultaneous abuse of different substances (that is, what is now referred to as multiple, mixed, poly or crossover substance abuse) is an increasingly common pattern among addiction-prone persons. Multiple substance abuse may be in the service of psychopharmacologically activating the same or different archaic narcissistic fantasies. For example, a common form of multiple substance abuse combines cocaine and alcohol. Cocaine, a central nervous system stimulant, usually activates grandiose fantasies; whereas alcohol, a central nervous system depressant, usually activates fantasies of idealized merger with an omnipotent figure.

The simultaneous and combined abuse of such substances is typically an attempt to modulate fantasy and mood. For example, as a grandiose fantasy is overstimulated and a corresponding mood of euphoria reaches the heights of ecstasy, the abuser attempts to modulate both fantasy and mood with substances that produce a central nervous system depressing effect. There are as many different forms of multiple substance abuse as there are individual substance abusers. Each of these different forms must be understood on the basis of the number and type of substance or substances being abused and the individual personality makeup of the substance abuser.

We also need to comment on anorexia nervosa. The anorexic's selfobject relationship to a substance (that is, food) is based on a compulsive refusal to use rather than on habitual use. Although, we have had limited clinical experience with anorexics, it is our impression that the refusal to eat may be a substance abuse disorder insofar as a clear and distinct selfobject relationship with food can be established.

Paradoxically, the absence rather than the presence of a substance may both biochemically and physiologically activate grandiose fantasies and accompanying moods of euphoria, elation, and fullness. The act of refusing to use a substance may temporarily lead to a subjective sense that poorly internalized or missing selfobject functions are provided. It may be that the anorexic is a captive of a grandiose fantasy that provides her with a subjective sense of fullness, thus psychologically offsetting the absence of a physiological experience of satiation.

The therapist's own subjectivity is particularly important in working with the substance abusing patient who presents special countertransference problems. Understandably, most therapists subjectively experience themselves as separate, autonomous, and independent agents. As a result, it is often difficult to facilitate and tolerate the substance abuser's necessary transference fantasy of the therapist as an inanimate object and substance replacement with which to form a relationship that will provide desperately needed selfobject functions. Recognizing this difficulty, Kohut (1987) stated, "It is very difficult to be the object of an addiction because in order to be such an object one is depersonalized. One is not oneself. All that counts is what one is used for" (p. 127).

Problems arising in the countertransference dimension of the intersubjective context of the therapeutic relationship sometimes lead to reactions on the part of the therapist that may interfere with the emergence and development of the patient's necessary transference fantasy. For example, Kohut (1968) emphasized that

An analytically unwarranted rejection of a patient's idealizing attitudes is usually motivated by a defensive fending off of narcissistic tensions, experienced as embarassment and even leading to hypochondriacal preoccupations, *which are generated in the analyst when repressed fantasies of his grandiose self become stimulated by the patient's idealization* [p. 500, italics added].

Kohut continued:

If the analyst has not come to terms with his own grandiose self, he may respond to the idealization with an intense stimulation of *his unconscious grandiose fantasies* and an intensification of defenses, which may bring about his rejection of the patient's idealizing transference [p. 501, italics added].

We view such reactions on the part of the therapist as a selfobject countertransference fantasy. Kohut warned that if the "analyst's defensive attitude" arising from the selfobject countertransference fantasy "becomes chronic . . . establishment of a workable . . . [selfobject] transference is interfered with and the analytic process is blocked" (p. 501).

The interaction of transference and countertransference produce what Ulman and Stolorow (1985; see also Ulman, 1988) call the "transference-countertransference neurosis." Later in this chapter we provide two examples of such an intersubjective configuration.

The analysis of "specific narcissistic resistances" (Kohut, 1970) to selfobject transference fantasies, as well as the use of selfobject countertransference fantasies, is especially important in treating the substance-abusing patient. The analysis of resistance is crucial to the emergence and development of a selfobject transference fantasy as part of the intersubjective context within which to facilitate the absorption of the selfobject functions of substances. Kohut (1968) stressed the importance of resistance analysis to the emergence of archaic narcissistic fantasies within the transference. He warned:

In view of the strong resistances that oppose this process [that is, the emergence of archaic narcissistic fantasies as part of the transference] and the intensive efforts required in overcoming them, it may at times be disappointing for the analyst to behold the apparently trivial fantasy that the patient has ultimately brought into the light of day [p. 490].

Our treatment case examples will illustrate how we work with the resistance to the formation of a selfobject transference fantasy. Without such a transference fantasy, the substance abuser will be unable to give up emotional dependence on the psychoactive functioning of a substance as a fantasized selfobject substitute. This makes achieving abstinence and sobriety difficult, if not impossible, thus seriously jeopardizing treatment.

In view of the importance of abstinence during the initial phase of treatment, we make the cessation of all substance abuse an immediate topic of discussion. We do not subscribe to what we call the "you can have your substance and abuse it too" philosophy so common among some therapists. At the same time, we do not naively believe that simply addressing the topics of abstinence and sobriety automatically guarantees quick and permanent cessation of substance abuse. On the contrary, the type of substance (or substances) being abused, the intensity and chronicity of the abuse, and the degree of resistance to the transference are all critical in determining the ease and speed with which abstinence and sobriety are achieved.

During the initial phase of treatment, the therapist helps the patient to achieve abstinence and sobriety by encouraging them to take advantage of self-help and peer support groups such as AA, OA, CA, DA, NA, and GA. We view these groups as providing for the substance abuser secondary selfobject functions that in no way interfere with the primary selfobject functioning of an archaic transference fantasy. On the contrary, we find that achieving abstinence and sobriety with the aid of self-help and peer support groups often intensifies archaic transference fantasies and their selfobject functioning.

We do not think that engaging the substance-abusing patient therapeutically in issues of abstinence and sobriety is in any way inconsistent with a self-psychological approach. Indeed, Kohut (1987) maintained, "in the true addictions, one must go about an attempt to cure with the muscular approach of removing the addictive agent and providing a variety of incarcerative procedures that build up some kind of a force to do away with the poison" (p. 127).

In fact, we see initiating a therapeutic dialogue concerning abstinence and sobriety as demonstrative of empathic attunement with the substance abuser's subjective sense of being at the mercy of forces over which he or she has little understanding or control. We also construe such a therapeutic dialogue as communicating to the patient our empathic attunement with painful affective states of depressive emptiness and depletion or manic fragmentation and disintegration.

Failure to make abstinence and sobriety basic treatment issues in the initial phase of therapy is, we believe, grossly unempathic and reflective of a profound lack of attunement to the substance abuser's personal state of mind and subjective frame of reference. We are all too familiar with the unsuccessful treatment of substance-abusing patients caused by the therapist's failure to discuss at the beginning of therapy abstinence and sobriety as basic treatment issues. Actively pursuing these topics in the initial phase of treatment helps to establish a therapeutic context in which central organizing fantasies of self in relation to selfobject may emerge and develop, thereby creating an intersubjective context within which to facilitate the absorption of the selfobject functions of substances. The gradual transmuting internalization of the selfobject functions of substances creates the sturdy and enduring psychological structures necessary for long-term abstinence and sobriety.

TREATMENT CASES

We present two representative treatment cases to illustrate the critical issues in the therapy of the substance abusing patient. Each of the cases explicates one or more of the important theoretical or treatment issues thus far discussed. We have selected an alcoholic and a bulimic patient because they are clearly representative of a larger group of substance-abusing patients.

Case #1: Teddy

This case illustrates two important points: 1) the entrenched resistance to establishing a selfobject transference fantasy as a means of achieving abstinence and sobriety; 2) a discussion of the psychoanalytic treatment of the substance-abusing patient using the intersubjective field as codetermined by respective selfobject transference and countertransference fantasies of patient and therapist.

When Teddy began therapy for the treatment of chronic alcoholism, he was a young man in his early 30s. He reported that he had been an alcoholic for the past 12 years and that his drinking problem included blackouts, tolerance, and withdrawal. He also described a pattern of marked and progressive deterioration in his psychosocial functioning.

Teddy said he had worked for 10 years as a salesman for his father's successful real estate business. He had begun working for his father after dropping out of college. He noted that he was uninterested and unmotivated in his work, was unsuccessful, and, as a result, felt that he was a source of great embarrassment and humiliation for his father.

Teddy had been married for five years but described his marriage as rocky and about to break up. He admitted to alcohol-induced verbal and physical abuse of his wife.

Teddy said he had been close to his mother, who died of brain cancer when he was 19. Teddy dated his alcoholic drinking to his mother's death, which he never fully mourned. Early in treatment, Teddy reported a dream in which he was sucking pleasurably at his mother's breast. He associated this dream fantasy to the soothing, calming effect of alcohol. It may be inferred that he had made a powerful unconscious and symbolic connection between sucking at his mother's breast and the selfobject functioning of alcohol. The presence of this dream fantasy so early in treatment reflected the emergence of an archaic transference fantasy that Teddy would vigorously resist.

Teddy noted that he had a very poor and distant relationship with his father. He felt that his father looked down on him, constantly belittling him before family and friends. He spoke sadly of feeling like an incompetent idiot as a result of his father's abuse. Lacking self-confidence in his own mental and verbal capacities, he had been a poor student, who had had to repeat a grade in elementary school.

Throughout the first year of treatment, Teddy steadfastly resisted what appeared, on the basis the powerful dream image of sucking pleasurably at his mother's breast, to be a selfobject transference fantasy of idealized merger with an omnipotent, maternal figure. He was deprived therefore of the potential of the transference fantasy to help create an intersubjective context in which the selfobject functions of alcohol could be absorbed, thereby providing him with a desperately needed sense of calming, soothing, and wholeness. He also resisted all efforts to achieve abstinence and sobriety. For example, in a flagrant display of his resistance, he often came to sessions intoxicated.

Teddy continued his alcoholic drinking and downward psychosocial plunge. After becoming intoxicated at a bar, getting into a fight with the bartender over his bar tab, being arrested and spending the night in jail, Teddy finally agreed to be hospitalized for detoxification and rehabilitation therapy. He spent approximately two months in two inpatient treatment centers. Upon discharge from the second program, Teddy returned home and resumed working for his father. He also became active in AA but did not return to treatment for over a year.

After Teddy returned to treatment, he and the therapist together analyzed his prior resistance to forming a sustaining therapeutic bond. They used his dream as a critical intersubjective frame of reference (see Ulman, 1988, on the intersubjective context of dream formation.) It emerged that Teddy resisted looking to the therapist to provide missing soothing and calming selfobject functions because he unconsciously dreaded that he would be forced to repeat the experience of being traumatically abandoned by a maternal figure (the male therapist) as he had been by his mother when she died. (See Ornstein, 1974, on the dread to repeat and the hope for a new beginning.)

As the dread behind Teddy's resistance to the selfobject transference fantasy was analyzed, he reported that he felt more relaxed. He spoke of trusting and feeling comforted by his relationship with the therapist. The therapist read Teddy's remarks as evidence of the emergence of the selfobject transference fantasy of idealized merger with an omnipotent maternal figure. Teddy's selfobject experience of enhanced calmness and wholeness was in marked contrast to a prior subjective state of painful disorganization in which he experienced himself as fragmenting and disintegrating.

As the therapy proceeded into the second and third years, another dimension of the selfobject transference fantasy emerged. This was the paternal dimension of the idealized merger. As previously noted, Teddy reported that his father had been hypercritical of him, making him feel that he could never please him and thus win his approval. The therapist helped Teddy explore his dread that the therapist would be as hypercritical and judgmental as his father, unmercifully belittling him for even the slightest error.

As the dread behind the resistance to the paternal dimension of the selfobject transference fantasy was analyzed, Teddy referred to his relationship with the therapist as a "mentorship." Apparently, on an unconscious fantasy level, Teddy experienced himself as an admiring and worshipful apprentice to the all-powerful and all-knowing mentor/therapist. During sessions, he constantly asked the therapist for the proper pronunciation and meaning of words that he either mispronounced or misused. Together, they often looked up in the dictionary the correct spelling and definition of words.

Teddy also became very interested in self psychology, a theoretical perspective of which his therapist was an active proponent. He attended various self psychology lectures, seminars, and conferences. In addition, he increasingly spoke of his interest in becoming either an alcohol counselor or a therapist like his analyst.

There was abundant evidence of the emergence and unfolding of an archaic transference fantasy in which Teddy unconsciously fantasized an idealized merger with the therapist as an omnipotent and omniscient selfobject extension of himself. However, Teddy maintained a certain subjective distance from the idealized therapist; it was idealization from afar with only a partial merger.

Teddy and the therapist spent most of the third and the beginning of the fourth year of the therapy focusing on his dread of a more complete merger. This was critical to facilitating the therapeutic process of intersubjectively absorbing the selfobject function of alcohol. Teddy feared complete merger with the idealized therapist because of a dread of traumatic abandonment by a maternal figure or humiliating derision by a paternal figure. He experienced himself as whole only by maintaining a safe subjective distance from the idealized therapist.

In looking back at the case, the therapist recognized that he had countertransferentially contributed to the difficulty in creating an intersubjective context in which Teddy could unconsciously fantasize himself as completely merged with the idealized paternal imago. On an unconscious countertransference level, the therapist was more subjectively comfortable in allowing Teddy to idealize him from afar, thus avoiding the intimate experience of a complete merger. He therefore countertransferentially resisted the further and necessary development of Teddy's selfobject fantasy of completed merger. (See Racker, 1968, on "counterresistance.")

With the successful analysis of the resistance to further merger, Teddy and the therapist formed a closer and more intimate relationship. For the first time, they talked about personal matters such as Teddy's sexual relationship with the woman with whom he had been living. They also spoke about his sadomasochistic masturbatory fantasies and his viewing of sexually violent pornography. In addition, Teddy wanted to know more about the details of his therapist's personal life, which the therapist provided whenever possible and appropriate.

During the fourth year of treatment, Teddy and the therapist analyzed the archaic transference fantasy through which the selfobject functions of alcohol had become intersubjectively absorbed. This took place in the context of Teddy's taking over, via transmuting internalization, many of the selfobject functions he had previously experienced as being provided by the therapist, who on an unconscious fantasy level functioned for Teddy as a selfobject replacement for alcohol. With new self-assurance, Teddy spoke of being able to calm and sooth himself. Likewise, he talked with new self-confidence about his intellectual abilities, verbal skills, and capacity for meaningful emotional relationships. Reporting significant success at work and in his personal relationships, he characterized his life as dramatically improved.

Teddy's selfobject transference with the analyst had evolved as a part of the transformation of his unconscious fantasy of the therapist as an omnipotent and omniscient parental figure. Teddy increasingly spoke about his desire to have a more "equal" relationship with the therapist. He said he wanted them to experience each other as peers and friends. The transformation of Teddy's archaic transference fantasy occurred through the processes of intersubjective absorption and transmuting internalization of selfobject functions. Both of these processes led to psychic structure building.

After five years in a still ongoing therapy, it seems clear that Teddy progressed from one type of transference fantasy to another. As part of his original transference fantasy, he had experienced the therapist as providing needed selfobject functions in his role as a replacement for alcohol. Now, Teddy transferentially experiences the therapist as a more separate object with whom he wants to have an "equal" relationship.

Case #2: Mary

The case of Mary, a 38-year-old bulimic patient, is illustrative of the resistance to and emergence of a fantasy of grandiose exhibitionism in the form of a transference fantasy of mirroring. It is also another example of how a therapist's countertransference fantasy can seriously interfere with the unconscious organizing activity of a transference fantasy, leading to an interruption in the therapy. (See Ulman and Brothers, 1987, 1988 for a discussion of transference and countertransference as determined by the unconscious organizing activity of archaic narcissistic fantasies.)

Early in treatment, the therapist sensed that Mary was intensely resistant to the unfolding of a transference fantasy of mirrored grandiosity. The therapist subsequently realized that throughout the early phase of treatment, Mary had dreaded risking that the therapist would not mirror her grandiosity. According to Mary, she had learned from early interactions with her mother that only good or positive affects could be tolerated. Apparently, any display on Mary's part of negative feelings was experienced by her mother as a threat to her mother's sense of self. Her mother had labeled such feelings as bad and unacceptable. Her mother could not tolerate affect states if the feelings involved conflicted with her need for Mary to serve as her selfobject.

On those rare occasions when Mary did express negative feelings towards her mother, she recalled feeling overwhelmed by a sense of emptiness and self-hatred. Mary said that she assumed that the therapist, like her mother, needed her to be well-behaved and to express only positive feelings. Negative feelings that Mary had toward the therapist or those that she felt toward herself made her feel like a bad and worthless person. Within the context of an archaic maternal transference fantasy, Mary imagined that exhibiting her grandiosity and expecting mirroring risked the painful experience of herself as once again unmirrorable.

The early phase of this 15-month, twice-weekly treatment was dominated by the self-hate and self-denigration Mary had for her bad, imperfect, and flawed self. Mary's experience of herself as unmirrorable prevented the emergence of a grandiose fantasy in the form of a mirroring selfobject transference. Mary's negative feelings toward herself made it very difficult for her to feel special or desirable. She was absolutely convinced, she said, that her therapist looked at her with the same disgust with which she viewed herself.

In this context, her bulimic symptoms were not a problem to be understood, but rather another reason to hate herself. She was adamant in her belief that the therapist also found her bulimic bingeing and purging disgusting. How could someone who stuffed herself with food and then forced herself to vomit expect to be seen as grand and wonderful?

For the first four months of treatment, Mary continued to binge and purge almost daily. Regardless of the manifest content of her sessions, the main latent issue was the terrifying vulnerability Mary experienced in any human contact. She was exquisitely sensitive to what others felt and thought about her. Both her powerful need to be seen as good and acceptable and her equally strong belief that she was viewed as disgusting, repulsive, and unacceptable filled her with self-hatred. Mary's self-loathing left her feeling empty, depleted, and depressed.

By bingeing, Mary attempted to use food and satiation as a means of filling the inner emptiness she experienced. Bingeing was always followed by a sense of disgust with herself for overeating. She immediately felt compelled to purge herself of the contents of her stomach in an attempt to magically undo her overindulgence. Having purged, however, she was consumed with self-loathing.

The binge/purge cycle kept Mary locked in an empty depression and consumed by narcissistic rage. It also prevented her from obtaining psychologically nourishing narcissistic supplies in the form of a pleasant feeling of being full of herself, that is, achieving healthy self-worth as a means of normal self-esteem regulation. If Mary could fill up psychologically on a sense of herself as acceptable (that is, become inflated by the selfobject fantasy of mirrored grandiosity) as part of her transference experience, then she would be less dependent on bingeing in a futile attempt to raise her spirits and uplift herself.

Yet time after time in the early phase of the treatment Mary was consumed by self-loathing. During this period, she often spoke midway through a session of wanting to end it abruptly. In response, the therapist asked her, "Why, when you feel in the most pain, must you leave my sight?" The choice of the word "sight" was intentional. According to Mary, she did not want to be seen by the therapist as such a disgusting creature. Mary dreaded that if the therapist saw her as she saw herself, he could not possibly be available to her in the transference fantasy as a mirroring selfobject.

Mary gradually realized that the therapist understood the subjective danger she experienced in being with him. More specifically, she realized that he understood her need to make sure that he could accept and tolerate her dysphoric affect states, and that negative feelings would not drive him awy in disgust and revulsion.

The therapist's empathic understanding of Mary's concerns helped to create an intersubjective context in which it was possible for Mary to lower her resistance to the emergence of a transference fantasy of the therapist as a mirroring selfobject. As Mary increasingly exhibited her grandiosity in the intersubjective context of this transference fantasy, the experience of being mirrored filled her with elation. As she filled up psychologically on a subjective experience of her own grandiosity, she reported a gradual decrease and eventual cessation of all bingeing and purging. She stopped using laxatives and made significant changes in her life. Mary made excellent progress. The selfobject functions of food had begun to be absorbed within the intersubjective context of a mirroring selfobject transference fantasy.

Mary was making significant therapeutic progress as a result of experiencing herself as mirrored in the context of the selfobject transference fantasy. However, she continued to express fear that the therapist would demand even more progress as the price for the continued experience of herself as mirrored. In other words, Mary dreaded becoming enslaved as the therapist's selfobject much as she had experienced herself in her relationship with her mother. For Mary, such enslavement meant that unless she made progress deemed adequate by the therapist, she risked losing him as a mirroring selfobject.

Another factor further complicated the therapeutic situation. Mary became involved for the first time in many years in a relationship with a man whom she experienced as providing many of the selfobject functions previously provided by her transference fantasy of the therapist.

Another issue important at this point in the therapy was related to a three-week vacation the therapist was planning. Discussion centered on Mary's feeling that in taking the vacation the therapist was satisfying his own needs and making himself completely unavailable to her. Mary also worried that in even broaching this subject she was expressing negative feelings toward the therapist and thus was rendering herself unmirrorable and seriously disturbing the transference fantasy.

As the other subjective presence in the intersubjective field created by patient and analyst, the therapist was aware of a particular strain he was under at this time. His principal mirroring selfobject, his wife, had been sick and bedridden for a number of months. As a result, he felt unmirrored in his personal life, leaving him at times feeling empty, depleted, and depressed. The impact on his work was particularly noticeable when he was expected by a patient to function within a transference fantasy as a mirroring selfobject. Initially, he was aware of this problem as having only subtle effects. However, there were dramatic effects for patients, like Mary, who were especially sensitive to any hint of reproduction of a situation in the therapy in which they experienced themselves as required to provide selfobject functions for parental figures.

In a session just prior to the interruption in treatment, Mary came in quite upset, crying, and once again attacking herself. Although her narcissistic rage at herself was less intense than before, it reappeared whenever Mary experienced herself as vulnerable to the criticism of others. (See Ulman and Brothers, 1988, for a discussion of self-directed narcissistic rage.)

In this particular session, the therapist did not understand some of the issues being discussed. With Mary's permission, he had periodically tape recorded. He had not taped in approximately two months. In the next session he decided to tape. Immediately upon seeing the tape recorder, Mary became upset and worried about why he had decided to record.

With the tape recorder on, the therapist interpreted Mary's concern as reflecting her fear that he felt threatened by the discussion of her negative feelings about vacation and her narcissistic rage in the previous session. Mary, however, was convinced that the therapist's failure to immediately turn off the tape recorder reflected his greater concern with his own needs than with her needs. The iatrogenic recreation of Mary's disturbed relationship with her mother seriously interfered with the mirroring transference fantasy. The therapist's countertransference need to experience himself as mirrored by Mary as his fantasized selfobject seriously interfered with the unconscious organizing activity of the transference fantasy.

During the remainder of this particular session and in the next session, Mary remained firmly convinced that the therapist was concerned only with satisfying his own needs and at her expense. She spoke of fearing that continuing the therapy under these conditions would jeopardize her recently won abstinence and sobriety. She also stated that her new boyfriend had taken over the therapist's earlier role of helping her to feel acceptable. In spite of the therapist's recommendation that Mary remain in treatment, she insisted on "taking a break."

With hindsight, it seems that the therapist's need to experience himself on a countertransference level as mirrored by Mary as a fantasized selfobject created an "intersubjective disjunction" (Atwood and Stolorow, 1984) that triggered a negative therapeutic reaction (see Brandchaft, 1983). Mary's transference fantasy of being mirrored for the strength of her own feelings, regardless of how negative, had not been in operation long enough within the intersubjective field to completely absorb the selfobject functions of bingeing and purging on food. The process of the transmuting internalization of these selfobject functions via the analysis and transformation of this transference fantasy of mirrored grandiosity was not complete. The tenuous and fragile nature of the archaic transference fantasy left it extremely vulnerable to interference from countertransference. The result was the dissolution of a previously sustaining selfobject transference fantasy and a disruption of the therapeutic relationship.

REFERENCES

Atwood, G. E. & Stolorow, R. D. (1984), *Structures of Subjectivity*. Hillsdale, NJ: The Analytic Press.

Basch, M. F. (1981), Psychoanalytic interpretation and cognitive transformation, *Internat. J. Psycho-Anal.*, 62:151–175.

——— (1983), The perception of reality and the disavowal of meaning. *The Annual of Psychoanalysis*, 11:125–153. New York: International Universities Press.

Brandchaft, B. (1983), The negativism of the negative therapeutic reaction and the psychology of the self, In: *The Future of Psychoanalysis*, ed. A. Goldberg. New York: International Universities Press, pp. 327–359.

Brenner, D. (1986), A self-psychological approach to understanding and treating the eating disorders. Presented at meeting of The Society for the Advancement of Self Psychology, New York.

Geist, R. A. (1984), Therapeutic dilemmas in the treatment of anorexia nervosa: A self-psychological perspective. *Contemp. Psychother. Rev.*, 2:85–110.

Goodsitt, A. (1984), Self psychology and the treatment of anorexia nervosa, In: *Handbook of Psychotherapy for Anorexia and Bulimia*, ed. D. Garner & M. Garfinkel. New York: Guilford Press, pp. 55–82.

Kohut, H. (1959), Introspection, empathy and psychoanalysis, In: *The Search for the Self*, Vol. 2, ed. P. Ornstein, New York: International Universities Press, 1978, pp. 205–232.

———— (1966), Forms and transformations of narcissism, In: *The Search for the Self*, Vol. 1, ed. P. Ornstein. New York: International Universities Press, 1978, pp. 427–460.

———— (1968), The psychoanalytic treatment of narcissistic personality disorders: Outline of a systematic approach, In: *The Search for the Self*, Vol. 1, ed. P. Ornstein. New York: International Universities Press, pp. 477–509.

———— (1970), Narcissism as a resistance and as a driving Force in psychoanalysis, In: *The Search for the Self*, Vol. 2, ed. P. Ornstein. New York: International Universities Press, 1978, pp. 577–588.

———— (1971), *The Analysis of the Self*, New York: International Universities Press.

———— (1972), Thoughts on narcissism and narcissistic rage, In: *The Search for the Self*, Vol. 2, ed. P. Ornstein. New York: International Universities Press, 1978, pp. 615–658.

———— (1977a), Preface to *Psychodynamics of Drug Dependence*, ed. J. D. Blaine & D. A. Julius. National Institute on Drug Abuse Research, Monogr. Series #12, Washington, DC: Govt. Printing Office.

———— (1977b), *The Restoration of the Self*, New York: International Universities Press.

———— (1987), The addictive need for an admiring other in regulation of self-esteem, In: *The Kohut Seminars on Self Psychology and Psychotherapy with Adolescents and Young Adults*, ed. M. Elson. New York: Norton, pp. 113–132.

———— & Wolf E. (1978), The disorders of the self and their treatment: An outline. *Internat. J. Psycho-Anal.*, 59: 413–425.

Milkman, H. & Frosch W. (1977), The drug of choice, *J. Psychedel. Drugs*, 9:13–14.

Ornstein, A. (1974), The dread to repeat and the new beginning: A contribution to the psychoanalysis of the narcissistic personality disorders. *The Annual of Psychoanalysis*, 2:231–248, New York: International Universities Press.

Racker, H. (1968), *Transference and Counter-transference*, New York: International Universities Press.

Stern, D. (1985), *The Interpersonal World of the Infant*. New York: Basic Books.

Stolorow, R. D., Brandchaft B. & Atwood G. (1987), *Psychoanalytic Treatment*. Hillsdale, NJ: The Analytic Press.

———— & Lachmann F. M. (1980), *Psychoanalysis of Developmental Arrest*. New York: International Universities Press.

Strozier, C. B. (1983), Fantasy, self psychology, and the inner logic of cults, In: *The Future of Psychoanalysis*, ed. A. Goldberg. New York: International Universities Press.

Tolpin, M. (1974), The Daedalus experience: A developmental vicissitude of the grandiose fantasy, *The Annual of Psychoanalysis*, 2: 213–228. New York: International Universities Press.

Ulman, R. B. (1988), The transference-countertransference neurosis in psychoanalysis: The intersubjective context of dream formation. In: *The Borderline and Narcissistic Patient in Therapy*, ed. N. Slavinska-Holy, New York: International Universities Press, pp. 203–219.

———— & Brothers, D. (1987), A self-psychological re-evaluation of posttraumatic stress disorder (PTSD) and its treatment: Shattered Fantasies, *J. Amer. Acad. Psychoanal.*, 15:175–204.

———— ———— (1988), *The Shattered Self*. Hillsdale, NJ: The Analytic Press.

———— & Stolorow. R. D. (1985), The "transference-countertransference neurosis" in psychoanalysis: An intersubjective viewpoint, *Bull. Menn. Clin.* 49:37–51.

Winnicott, D. W. (1951), Transitional objects and transitional phenomena, In: *Through Paediatrics to Psycho-Analysis*. New York: Basic Books, 1975, pp. 229–242.

Chapter 9

Analysis Terminable and Interminable Revisited: On Self/Selfobject Fixations

Hyman L. Muslin

Our interest in self/selfobject fixations stems from an abiding concern with the difficulties we experience with patients who suffer throughout their life within the prison of their fixated selves. They petition for help, they wish to be free from the strictures of their self-distortions and they struggle mightily in their analyses to obtain relief; but the limited capacities of some of these patients to enter into a potentially curative bond—a self/selfobject merger—will not permit this bonding. In others, the resistance to development may become manifest only in the working-through phase of analysis, and in still others the difficulties may be seen in the termination phase of their analysis, when they demonstrate difficulty in removing themselves from their selfobject transferences (Muslin, 1986, 1987).

Self/selfobject fixations involve the self's development in relation to its selfobjects and therefore to the successes or failures of those dyads. Whenever there has been failure in either the establishment of the self/selfobject bond or the interiorization of specific selfobject functions, the self will be devoid of those internalized selfobject functions; the self will not have gained structure and therefore continues to need and to search for the missing functions to maintain optimal self-life.

Our basic research query centers on the attraction that compels people who have been deprived of selfobject support repeatedly to seek out or unconsciously manufacture (resurrect) the dyad of deprivation in which, as in the early days, the self will posture itself in an

143

attitude designed to evoke selfobject relief of its specific tension of self-need. These incessant repetitions, setting up dayds in an attempt to establish a hoped-for self/selfobject bonding and internalization of the selfobject functions, represent the central ingredient in self/selfobject fixation. Deprivation without the accompaniment of the self's repetitious reenactment with a hoped-for gratifying selfobject does not stand for the fixation process; deprivation by itself does not necessarily usher in the self/selfobject repetition compulsion.

FROM DEPRIVATION TO FIXATION

We now turn our attention to the forces that transform deprivation into the compulsive seeking process that we call self/selfobject fixation. We are, of course, speaking of those persons so attracted to the reestablishment of these malignant dyads of infancy and childhood that they remove themselves from mature selfobject gratifications that are available to them in adult life. Several queries present themselves: 1) Is the movement of deprivation to fixation determined by the intensity of the deprivation? 2) What is the role of surrogate figures in fixation? 3) What occurs in those instances of deprivation in which a compensatory selfobject is present or not present? 4) Are there constitutional factors that influence the reaction to a deprivation, such as an adhesiveness factor, the plasticity factor, or psychic inertia? 5) What is the impact on the analysis of empathic failures on the analyst's part leading to faulty understanding or misattuned interpretations? While this chapter is an attempt to delineate those factors which influence the fixation process from the side of the patient, we are of course mindful of the role that the analyst's understanding and its vicissitudes play in removing a patient from his fixations. However, as important as the analyst's activity may be to the success or failure of the analysis, we will consider here only the patient's contributions to the fixation.

The Intensity of the Selfobject Deprivation as a Factor in Fixation

Selfobject deprivations range from minor selfobject failures to massive rejections. In those instances of so-called optimal (nontraumatic) frustrations that initiate the process of accretion of the self-structures through interiorization, a positive mutative effect is achieved through deprivation. In those instances in which deprivation is followed by fixation, the deprivation is, of course, of intense proportions. It is prolonged; it is unremitting as the selfobject shows massive and constant failures in its functioning as a mirroring presence or in other selfobject functions. Perhaps in some instances of massive selfobject deprivation, this variable alone constitutes the necessary and sufficient factor to cause a fixation. In addition to the quantitative aspect of the deprivation, other variables are ordinarily essential for the development of the fixation syndrome (Kohut, 1971; Tolpin, 1971; Wolf, 1980).

The physiology of deprivation important in self/selfobject fixations centers on the inability of the self to accrete selfobject functions. A selfobject that is not in harmony with its charges exhibits behaviors inimical to the internalization process, including behaviors that do allow the self/selfobject bond to take place. The self, attempting to bond and begin the internalizing process reflective of a well-working self/selfobject dyad, will instead be constantly and severely rebuffed and will, at least temporarily, withdraw. In subsequent interactions, the self will begin to exhibit those specific behaviors and attitudes in an attempt to evoke the selfobject infusions necessary for a cohesive self—the process of fixation.

The Impact of Surrogate Figures in Deprivation

Surrogate figure here refers to selfobject surrogate. Thus, in an instance of a mirroring selfobject loss such as in death or a prolonged absence (illness), a surrogate selfobject would refer to a person who performs those exact selfobject functions—mirroring, for example— that previously were performed by the now missing selfobject. In any selfobject loss, temporary or permanent, the presence of a selfobject surrogate in the environment may interfere with the deprivation– fixation process. The variables to be considered are the vulnerabilities and ability of the self to form these substitute archaic selfobject bonds. Has the developing self become bound to the original archaic selfobject, that it will not permit or eaily permit transfer to a surrogate selfobject to furnish the necessary archaic needs? At what stage in an infant's self-development does the self achieve selfobject constancy that does not permit any substitute selfobjects to perform the archaic functions of mirroring or calming? In these developmental scenes in which a self/selfobject bond has been established, a self/selfobject rupture would usher in an episode of either fragmentation or fear of punishment. A timetable for these experiences cannot be established since the depth of archaic self/selfobject attachment is a reflection of each unique archaic dyad, a combination of the capacities for affinity in a relatively unformed self and a particular selfobject's capacity for fusion with the self of the infant.

A surrogate selfobject may be crucial in the maintenance of the cohesive self if the suddenly deprived self is still capable of forming a merger with the surrogate. In those situations in which a self/selfobject bond has formed—a selfobject constancy in the view of the self—the surmise we are advancing is that the infant, if massively deprived of its selfobject, will not be able to form a relief-giving bond with a surrogate selfobject but instead will experience the ruptured bond only as a fragmenting experience.

The Role of a Compensatory Selfobject in Fixation

In Kohut's (1977) view, a self/selfobject rupture or failure in the primary self/selfobject bond would not result in the empty self of a infant vulnerable to a narcissistic personality disorder if a compensatory selfobject were present and could abort the pathologic process of an uncohesive self. Kohut was alluding to the failure of a primary, mirroring bond that could be attenuated by an idealizing selfobject bond. The compensatory selfobject is an important entity in the sustenance of a self suddenly bereft of its source of worth or calming. With the advent of this selfobject, a potential self-catastrophe can be averted. However, in each instance of deprivation ensuing from the lost or defective primary selfobject, the compensatory selfobject's contributions must be separately evaluated. In some situations of this sort, the compensatory selfobject's mission is successful; in others, it is not. At times, success or failure depends on the timing of the loss (selfobject constancy); at other times, the result relates to the quality of the compensatory selfobject's functioning.

The Influence of Constitutional Factors on Fixation

When Freud (1937) wrote of factors influencing untreatability in psychoanalytic treatment, a prominent factor in his view was the presence of a constitutionally acquired libido that he described as adhesive. In these patients there was little capacity to detach libidinal cathexes from one object to another. He described other processes in the ego determined by heredity (mobile libido) as well as processes in the id determined by heredity (resistance from id) that influenced treatability.

In this view of self psychology theory, the interminable attachment of the self to an archaic selfobject is best interpreted as a sequel to a rupture or failure of the self/selfobject bond where the impact of a surrogate or compensatory selfobject is minimal or absent, initiating a lifetime of re-creating the archaic bonds in the hope of finally getting the required selfobject supplies to interiorize. However easily one can reconstruct the scenarios of deprivation ostensibly leading to deprivation, the onus is on us to understand and explain those instances in which the deprivation is not, at least not on the surface, massive or protracted; and we are at a loss to understand the self-object loyalty of a deprivation and fixation process that has been instituted in an unremitting search for a specific selfobject with whom to bond. When one adds up the various environmental and learned factors in the initiation of a deprivation–fixation process, there still remains an area in which constitutional abilities or inabilities may influence the process of fixation.

LITERATURE REVIEW: FIXATIONS

The subject of fixations linked with interminability of analyses was a preoccupation of Freud's (1937) in one of his last papers, "Analysis Terminable and Interminable". There Freud outlined four areas of resistances to change, which he said depended on "fundamental conditions in the mental apparatus" (p. 241). The four areas of resistances are: 1) the adhesiveness factor of the libido, defined as the capacity to detach libido from one object and displace it onto another; 2) a mobile libido, characterized by lack of sufficient adhesiveness so that cathexes onto an object are soon withdrawn; 3) a depleted capacity for change and further development, psychic inertia (psychical entropy); 4) the death instinct (pp. 241–242).

Freud was alluding to the limitations imposed on the mental apparatus by heredity rather than to those resistances to change reflecting the "defensive struggle of the early years" (p. 240). Freud further noted that, in general, "the stronger the constitutional factor, the more readily will a trauma lead to a fixation and leave behind a developmental disturbance" (p. 220). Concerned with the variable results of analytic therapy, Freud concluded that if the quantitative factor of instinctual strength—the intensity of the instincts—is excessive, then the analytic cure, ensuring of control over instinct by "replacing repression with ego-syntonic control" will fail. He wrote:

> . . . the answer to the question of how to explain the variable results of our analytic therapy might well be that we, too, in endeavouring to replace repressions that are insecure by reliable ego-syntonic controls, do not always achieve our aim to its full extent—that is, do not achieve

it thoroughly enough. The transformation is achieved, but often only partially: portions of the old mechanisms remain untouched by the work of analysis. . . . But we must not take the clarity of our own insight as a measure of the conviction which we produce in the patient. His conviction may lack "depth," as one might say; it is always a question of the quantitative factor, which is so easily overlooked. If this is the correct answer to our question, we may say that analysis, in claiming to cure neuroses by ensuring control over instinct, is always right in theory but not always right in practice [p. 229].

Thus, Freud's final commentaries about the results of analytic therapy were that there are major limitations, from constitutional endowment as well as from ontogenetic variables, on the capacity for termination or cure in analysis. As many observers have pointed out, Freud's views were sober (Blum, 1987), pessimistic (Strachey, 1955), somber (Jones, 1957) and perhaps related both to the year that preceded the Nazi Putsch and to his 81st year, which was filled with the suffering of a major illness. Although these allusions to pessimism are important, the major contributions of this paper, in my view, was to call attention to the "variable results of analysis" (p. 229), an attempt to delineate which variables were crucial in rendering a patient amenable to eventual cure and termination of the analysis.

Freud's comments on the limits of analysis and the focus on fixation clearly ushered in the subsequent movement toward lengthening analysis and deepening the therapeutic ambitions from symptom removal to character change. Certainly, since 1937 many aspects of the analytic process of cure and knowledge of the resistance to change have been illuminated or at least addressed. As Blum (1987) pointed out in his half-century retrospective, "Since 1937, many dimensions of psychoanalysis have changed, and the whole body of psychoanalytic knowledge has been greatly enriched by subsequent psychoanalytic experience, and the proliferation of psychoanalytic research and education following World War II" (p. 38).

Freud's attempts to understand the phenomenon of fixation and its effect on development, as well as its part in resistance to cure in analysis, were certainly unfinished work, for they lacked the direct development observation that took place in later years by Spitz (1959), Winnicott (1965), Mahler (1971), Stern (1985), and others (Sander, 1964; Greenspan, 1981). The 1937 essay was of course also without the more sophisticated ideas of Hartmann (1939), Winnicott (1965), Anna Freud (1936), Blum (1987), Greenacre (1967), Furst (1967), and Kohut (1971, 1977).

And, finally, although Freud did allude in the 1937 work to the libidinal attachment to an object, the areas of attachment between the self and its selfobject were not known in Freud's world; the need to receive an infusion of selfobject supplies to develop as a cohesive entity was not yet recognized in psychoanalysis (Kohut 1971, 1977).

In the years since 1937, significant changes in psychoanalysis—theory, practice, and research—have mightily altered the concept of fixation in development and interminability in psychoanalytic therapy. The views of the ego psychologists (Hartmann, 1939; A. Freud, 1936), the object relation theorists (Winnicott, 1965), and now the self psychologists (Kohut, 1971, 1977, 1984) have modified Freud's views how the mental apparatus functions and develops. In a sense, now that we "know" a great deal more of the complex steps of development—or at least attempt to isolate the variables integral to development—can highlight more facets of the fixation process. We now know more of what is fixed, or is still being worked on, or is still being clamored for. A self psychology theorist working on his patient's deficient archaic self/selfobject mirroring bond will center his understanding of his patient's repeated search for (and defense against) "the perfect union" on the patient's experienced missing sources of self-input and his Sisyphus-like behavior in his current surround while still attempting to derive archaic inputs to add to the self. An object relations theorist will be drawn to understand the problems of his patients vis-à-vis fixation in a manner that would be quite different from Freud's global view of libidinal adhesiveness onto an object. Thus, Balint (1937) would understand a common fixation to be expressive of the infant's frustration in relation to an object; the infant is from the beginning in a state of primitive relatedness to another object (primary love, primary object-love). Winnicott (1965) relates the cohesion of the infant self to a surround that is empathic and responsive to it—the "holding" environment, the good-enough mother, the ego-supportive environment. The ego psychologist would stress the influence of deprivation on the development of various ego functions, such as secondary autonomy, ego governance, and the capacity for adaptation (Hartmann, 1939).

A notable advance in the psychoanalytic understanding of man since 1937 has been in the area of child development. The findings of the developmentalists have made analysts aware that the phases of child development can be viewed not as libidinal phases, but in terms of the maturation of the infant's physical and mental capacities. From the viewpoint of Sander (1964), Greenspan (1981) and Stern (1985), the developmental phases parallel the unfolding of the parent-child dyad through the development of the social adaptations that occur as

a result of the maturation of observable capacities. Developmentalists, on the whole, have discarded the phases of orality, anality, and
so on, along with the concept that insults and traumas at a certain
libidinal stage result in specific types of problems at a later date,
because no evidence seems to exist for those notions (Stern, 1985).
Although these researchers do not speak specifically about fixations,
their observations include self/selfobject dyads that are tailored to a
maternal selfobject's capacity to perform selfobject functions (Stern,
1985).

Over time, disagreement with one or other of the positions taken
by Freud in 1937 emerged (Gutman, 1963; Kanzer, 1975; Blum, 1987).
However, the essential position advanced by Freud—that in some
patients the attraction to the past is so compelling that living in the
present is never a sufficiently complete or gratifying experience—has
never been discarded. Granted that a great deal has now been
observed, described, and formulated that helps to define the intrica-
cies of phases and subphases of development, there remains Freud's
central finding that there are those who cannot be extricated from
their past, even with longer and "deeper" analyses.

CLINICAL MATERIAL

In the view of psychoanalytic self psychology advanced in this
chapter, each analysis measures its success by the patient's ultimate
freedom from self/selfobject fixations. What the therapist struggles
with in an analysis in which he becomes aware that a particular
patient's self/selfobject bonds are not amenable to ordinary ministrations is the lack of self-change over a long period of therapeutic time.
In such analyses, many attempts to illuminate the archaic bonds in
its many forms, including the repeated presentation of the archaic
bonds in the transference, have been unproductive. These cases
represent instances of the self/selfobject fixations we need to study.
The research query is framed in this manner in our minds as well as
articulated in some form to our patients: What is the attraction to
structuring current human encounters in a manner that resurrects
the old disappointments, fears of abandonment, and emptiness?
Further, after many attempts on our part to highlight the reentry into
the past, the retreats continue. These illuminations are combined
with the focus on the here-and-now, which situations may have
triggered the reentry into the past. At times only after the working-
through process becomes joined can the analyst become aware that
the patient's self is entrenched in a seemingly interminable struggle

(against the goals of analysis) to maintain the past, the self/selfobject loyalty. No one is unmindful of the, one might say, ordinary difficulties of self-retreat into the past throughout patient's experience. Patients who present with interminable selfobject addictions challenge our empathic capacities to appreciate the self-workings of these people, who reflexively and repeatedly turn from the present to the past in their attempt to resurrect their archaic struggles.

Thus, presented with each of our patients, but especially with those with archaic selfobject addiction, we are challenged to understand their attraction to the past in the hope that our understanding will enable them to live with safety in their current circumstances without retreating. In the cases of interminability, the analyst can often not ascertain what ushers in the retreat to the past, and the analyst ordinarily pursues one or many of the usual surmises relating to retreats. At times movement begins or resumes; at times not, there is no movement at all; at still other times therapeutic movement resumes at a later point and therefore makes it difficult to assess what the liberating forces were. Often in these clinical situations it is a case of "non liquet" (Freud, 1926, p. 11).

We are therefore obliged to examine our case material in greater depth to enlighten us. To that end, we will now explore a few typical clinical situations that, it is hoped, will aid us to understanding 1) the nature of fixations as we see them in analysis, and 2) the nature of the "cure" of fixation—essentially the study of the multidetermined nature of the resistance to movement away from the points of fixation.

Case I: An Interminable Case

Ms. M was a patient whose episodic anxieties and overeating were traceable early in her analysis to the deprivations she had suffered as a result of her mother's inattention to her infantile and childhood needs. Fear had dominated each of her interactions with her mother since her early days. They always centered on whether her mother would once again be in a rejecting mood and dismiss her. Ms. M always described her mother as an "Ice Queen," imperious, never showing affect and always quick to dismiss her, especially her wishes for affection, which she became afraid to show. Ms. M's older and younger brothers both apparently adapted early in their lives to their mother's limitations by joining with their father, a sports-minded stock broker, in many athletic activities. The patient quickly identified herself as her mother's lady-in-waiting and went underground with her wants; she had early learned to be silent about her longings lest her mother once again dismiss her. Her interactions with her mother were frightening, always accompanied by the concern that she might explode with her appetites for an embrace or a kiss. She does not remember when she made the connection between the contents of the refrigerator and emotional relief from tension, but it was early in her life. Even in eating she feared exposure, since it involved receiving direct gratification for her appetites, which she now experienced as aspects of herself that must be hidden lest mother find out and again threaten her with abandonment. Soon she learned the prophylactic use of food, of becoming "filled up" to restrain herself from petitioning her mother with any request. Once she felt her insides were loaded up with food, her other appetites—and therefore her emotional tensions—were quiescent. When her mother's denial finally broke down—the patient was now 10 and obese—and she became aware of her daughter's use of food, she began frantically taking her from one physician to another, of course to no avail. Throughout adolescence Ms. M continued to become larger in spite of all her mother's and father's rages at her public embarrassment of them and the value they placed on attractiveness. Although she was frightened by their near-violent rages at her obesity, Ms. M continued to do what kept her in equilibrium, going on surreptitious late night and early morning binges, sometimes followed by induced vomiting. And, playing the role of the devoted and mute lady-in-waiting, she continued to follow her program-of-action designed to keep her mother in equilibrium.

At the end of adolescence Ms. M met a sympathetic young man bound for a career in business; they were married when she was 19. She worked in several different settings as typist and file clerk and finally became a real estate broker five years prior to starting her therapy. The diagnostic data revealed a highly intelligent woman who suffered with episodes of total self-bankruptcy, during which times she could not get out of bed. Her relationship with her husband was cordial but unfulfilling. A man driven to achieve monetary success, he spent each working hour on money-making activities. The compulsive eating, especially at night, had waned for a few years directly after the marriage but was again dominating her life. The eating now throughout the day began with provocation. However, she continued to be plagued by violent reactions to her mother's daily phone calls. These reactions consisted of severe anxiety during her mother's call, followed almost immediately by a rush to the refrigerator for anything to "fill me up." She still had a recurring dream from childhood, a nightmare in which she found herself inside a huge refrigerator attempting unsuccessfully to grab frantically at all of the food within it.

The first phase of her analysis found her able to report her inner life without tension and to join in an exploration of deeper mental contents. However, shortly after this interlude, she began centering her comments on her mother and her husband; they were, of course, interchangeable. These comments were filled with her list of disappointments in her mother's and her husband's inability to attend to her. They were, in her view, too busy, so that their attention was never able to satisfy her. Before long, the analyst was added to the list, and now she complained that the analyst was too busy or too distracted or too involved with others to attend to her. These complaints were never accompanied by requests for direct gratification; they were always "empty" complaints, simply statements of what she was not deriving from any of her relationships.

The analyst's initial interpretations of her urges to structure her significant relationships to fit her ancient self/selfobject patterns were somewhat successful in that she saw her strivings for the past and could pull herself away sufficiently to begin to study her archaic strivings. She began pursuing old and near-forgotten ambitions to pursue a degree in economics. There were other signs of entering into a calming and uplifting selfobject bond: her mood became elevated, she started going to cultural and artistic activities she had never attended, and she began taking more self-fulfilling vacations. Side-by-side with this movement, the patient continued to report that she communicated with her mother each day with a little less trepidation and a little less rushing to the refrigerator. Nonetheless, the obesity continued without change. It seemed as if she was going to continue to her mother's death her reminders to her mother that she was going to be her unattractive lady-in-waiting and then enter a convent.

And so the cycle began: the patient had begun to move into a therapeutic bond, an idealized self/selfobject transference. But then the snag developed; the patient resumed the archaic bond. Cycle after cycle of the ancient bond was repeated: the patient would be in good harmony with the analyst for considerable periods, only once again to reenter the self of the shabby, lonely, and unattractive girl in a relationship with the "Ice Queen" analyst. And each time she entered into the archaic bond, she reexperienced the painful, tense self of the youngster who was always concerned lest she lose her grip and reveal her inner appetites for being cherished or guided or calmed. The question then became, is this self capable of removing itself from the fear of the selfobject mother's destructiveness and live in the present? To begin with, of what does the fear consist? Once illuminated, the fear must be experienced in this fashion: "If I grow away from her (= you) and no longer am subservient to her and take support from other peopel, my mother (= you) will desert me; and since she is the only important source of my worth, I must stay with her." Straying away from mother's purview amounts to being abandoned, and so one does not stray far.

The aim of an analysis is that increased awareness of the emergence of the strivings for these types of bonds will ultimately render the reappearance of those strivings ineffectual. That is, once one becomes aware of the reentry of the archaic, the "imperative" experience recedes as the self-of-the-present assumes control. These latter remarks are, however, schematic; in practice, prior to the establishment of the therapeutic bond, the analyst works with the self of a patient that has "become" the self of the child attempting to merge with her targeted selfobject. Therefore, for long periods—sometimes interminable periods—there is no self-observing, since sophisticated self-functions are not operational in an archaic self. Feeling safe and involved in the ambience of the self/selfobject bond with the analyst is the result of the working-through phase of an analysis (Muslin, 1986); after a selfobject bond is achieved (or in situations where there is no massive emergence of the archaic self) and the self of the patient becomes more cohesive, the self-observing functions are effective and patient and doctor can become aware of the intrusions of the archaic self. Kohut (1984) described the process by which a patient develops vital and missing self-structures through internalization of the analyst's selfobject functions:

> In response to the analyst's errors in understanding or in response to the analyst's erroneous or inaccurate or otherwise improper interpretations, the analysand turns back temporarily from his reliance on empathy to the archaic selfobject relationships (e.g., to remobilization of the need for merger with archaic idealized omnipotent selfobject or remobilization of the need for immediate and perfect mirroring) that he had already tentatively abandoned in the primary selfobject transference of the analysis. In a properly conducted analysis, the analyst takes note of the analysand's retreat, searches for any mistakes he might have made, nondefensively acknowledges them after he has recognized them (often with the help of the analysand), and then gives the analysand a noncensorious interpretation of the dynamics of his retreat. In this way the flow of empathy between analyst and analysand that had been opened through the originally established selfobject transference is remobilized. The patient's self is then sustained once more by a selfobject matrix that is empathically in tune with him.
>
> In describing these undulations, the researcher must show how each small-scale, temporary empathic failure leads to the acquisition of

self-esteem-regulating psychological structure in the analysand—assuming, once more, that the analyst's failures have been nontraumatic ones. Having noticed the patient's retreat, the analyst must watch the analysand's behavior and listen open-mindedly to his associations. By listening open-mindedly, I mean that he must resist the temptation to squeeze his understanding of the patient into the rigid mold of whatever theoretical preconceptions he may hold, be they Kleinian, Rankian, Jungian, Alderian, classical-analytic, or, yes, self psychological, until he has more accurately grasped the essence of the patient's need and can convey his understanding to the patient via a more correct interpretation [p. 66–67].

However, to arrive at this point in the therapeutic bond, the patient's archaic self-interests directed toward the archaic selfobject analyst have to come to an end. No small passage! Once the archaic self emerges to seek its selfobject in a defense transference posture— whether, as Kohut said, in response to an unavoidable empathic failure or as an unfolding and modal process in analysis—the patient's self is joined with its selfobject—at times in cement, understandably, it demands what was held back from it in its development, its quota of "immediate and perfect" mirroring, or merger with the archaic idealized selfobject. These considerations are well known to analysts who understand and observe patients from the view of their self-deficits and weaknesses. So often in patients who demonstrate the proneness to interminability the mystery is what will terminate their struggle for selfobject supplies once they have joined the transference selfobject in the repetition compulsion to achieve past needs? Especially, as we have reminded, the patient's self that is caught up in these struggles is an archaic self unable to self-observe, not joined in the rapport needed for mutual investigation.

Ms. M demonstrated this interminability in her analysis. In her case it was the process of struggling for her life against the hostile Ice Queen/selfobject analyst. And so, as soon as an initial rapport was established, the analysis became filled with repeated reenactments of her painful times with the unempathic and demeaning mother/ analyst. And what of her ability to use interpretations of the transference reenactments? There was sufficient self-capacity at times to effect a therapeutic split and derive some benefit from the analytic interventions. However, the long-term benefits expected of the analytic process were missing; the defense transference was not altered by repeated interpretations. Rather, in this case and others exhibiting the proneness to interminability, the patients continue to relive and reenact the thrust to the past, the structuring of the malignant self/ selfobject dyad of the past.

Case II: A Terminable Case

The patient, Ms. H came to analysis after experiencing what she called a depression that had persisted for over six months. She was at that time in mourning for her father, then dead for a year. At the time of her first visit with me, she was 32 years old, a slightly built, fragile appearing woman. She related that she had been in both analysis and psychotherapy since she was 20; her mother, who died of a breast cancer when Ms. H was a senior in college, had been ill with a depression since her daughter's high school days and had become more depressed when she entered college.

The major information that she revealed was that she had had a depressing life from the earliest of her remembrances, a life without the uplifting of any adequate mirroring presence throughout her development. Her mother, she recalled, was unable to calm her at any time. She became in fact so distressed over her mother's inconsistent and rejecting ministrations that she cried and became agitated when her mother did attempt to hold her. The patient was told innumerable times that her first years had been marked by her being a colicky infant and that she had been considered as a candidate for surgery in her first year of life (probably due to a diagnosis of pyloric stenosis) for this condition. Her only memories alluding to their early experiences were that she was afraid of being picked up and held by her mother. She recalled vividly a scene at her third birthday party when her mother picked her up and she panicked and could not be calmed. She recounted often in her analysis that her mother had picked her up only when she was in dire distress and then immediately put her down when the distress was ended.

From the beginning of the analysis the childhood pattern unfolded—that she continued to be distressed over the possibility of anyone's spontaneously reaching out to touch or embrace her. It was only through the reconstruction in the third year of her analysis that the pattern became clear: she associated her mother's presence and touch with the psychic pain of forced isolation—when her mother picked her up, she always carried the threat of ultimately rejecting her either by placing her in the crib or by putting her down without further contact. Undoubtedly, her mother's intimate presence was further associated with the physiologic distress, a pain that could not be eased. How much of an impact on her mother's functioning this infant who could not be soothed made we do not know, but clearly neither the patient nor her mother had a gratifying relationship. Ms. H never experienced her mother as a source of warmth or nurturance. She was always vigilant and fearful around her mother lest her mother find something amiss in her behavior and become critical and eventually put her in the crib of isolation, where she would cry without the prospect of someone giving her succor.

Thus, the major instigator of her lifelong psychic distress was revealed to be her experience of her mother as an imprisoner. While the patient could and did clamor for interest throughout her life, including in her analysis, the capacity to receive, and therefore accrete self-structure, was always interfered with by the prospect of feared dismissal. She complained only that she was not being given the proper attention, but actually she was confined to the outside in all her relationships, a victim of the unconscious equation of close-ness with imprisonment. It is, of course, no surprise that she never came to her mother for aid for fear of either coldness or criticism, and so she became an isolate in her own home, always lonely, always feeling cold. She was also usually agitated in school and at home, could not sit for any length of time, and therefore could not comfort-ably sink into books, movies or conversations. On the other hand, she was not totally without stimulation. It was just that she was unable to unfold herself and be lifted up, physically or emotionally. It was always too frightening for her to be receptive to her mother. The stimulation that she did get was that her mother, a former piano teacher, ran the house, until she became ill when the patient was 12, like a military installation with rules and fines. Ms. H's sibs, she reported, somewhat less awed or frightened by her mother, were less nervous than, she but the emotional atmosphere was always a cold one. No one touched, hugged, or kissed—or, even more significantly, smiled—at one another when mother was around.

Her father, whom she felt more positively toward, was a warmer person. He showed good humor and tried to engage her later, in her early teens in his sports, fishing and boating, to which she re-sponded. However, in the first several years of her life, he was not home a great deal, being away on business and coming home mainly on weekends. In later years, he took the entire family on trips, when she participated with pleasure in fishing and boating and hiking; but naturally, as one of the family, she did not have an exclusive relation-ship with him. More simply and to the point, her father did not function as a mirroring presence.

He remained in her self-experience as a person idealized from afar. He did not use his talents to teach, guide, or even influence her destiny in any of her activities from early learning experiences to choice of friends or college or marriage. We are, of course, reporting what he was for her; that he might have been more of a leader or calmer we can only speculate, since with him also she was vigilant and therefore never able to engage in a merging relationship.

Her experiences in school paralleled those at home. She became superficially attached to a group of young women and practiced what she had perfected at home—being the accommodating friend, never displaying self-needs. Unfortunately for her learning, her capacity to "take in" from her instructors and the books continued to be impeded. She did not enter into a dialogue with either teachers or authors. In high school, she did not date, nor did she enter into any social activities. One reason was that since Ms. H's early high school days her mother had become more and more isolated and was diagnosed as suffering with a depression. The patient and her siblings had for several years only minimal supervision since the mother was chronically depressed and received regular psychotherapy from the time the patient was 15. Her home situation was so depressing that neither she nor her siblings ever brought friends home. When she was 18 and started college in her home town, her mother's condition worsened, necessitating hospitalization. It was at this time that Ms. H started psychotherapy. In her senior year at college, it was discovered that her mother had a cancer of the breast, which had already widely metastisized. The patient reacted to her mother's death a year after the discovery of cancer with a mixture of sadness and relief at the end of suffering. Her mother had not been able to receive any relief from her psychic and physical distresses for many years.

The patient's first analysis was, as had been noted, helpful to her in many ways. She became able to relate to men at her workplace— she had become a elementary school teacher—albeit with anxiety; and she began going to group parties and dances. Her first analyst, she informed me, concentrated on her special feeling of competitiveness with her mother for her father's interest and did not focus on her isolated childhood.

In a nutshell, as Kohut often said, the entire analysis concerned itself with the vicissitudes of her fixation on restraint and vigilance against potential invaders of her life space. Her previous work in analysis had not given her the knowledge or the experiences necessary for her to extricate her from her self of isolation, a self filled with fears of being touched and therefore surrounded by barricades to intimacy in many forms—toward mirroring, toward calming, toward being led. Her fixations onto this self had led to her experience of life as being empty, but she was unaware that she was functionally unable to partake of the supports that were offered from her milieu. She was filled with "empty complaints," complaints she could not pursue to gratification. Many other methods of maintaining this self of isolation became evident through the analysis—dueling with me, withholding information, curtailing the length of her sessions by coming late and leaving early—as well as when panic emerged and her walls became permeable.

The analysis began with the patient expressing fear of allowing me to enter into her psychic life. From my side, I witnessed a person who was remarkably responsive to any physical movement on my part, to which she would react with intense anxiety. I vividly recall the first years of analysis, when her voice would approach the intensity of shrieking. Her anxiety, centered on her responses to me, dictated that the analysis concern itself with her immediate entry into the defense transference, in which I was experienced as the agent of punishment. I quickly learned that my task was to provide a milieu without overt interventions so that over a long period of time she could begin to experience a safe environment free of any unprecipitated "controlling" on my part. Little by little, the manner in which she structured her life was revealed; that is, she managed to keep everyone, emotionally speaking, at bay. While seeming to have many complaints about her longings, the complaints, as mentioned earlier, could not proceed to fulfillment since the necessary posture of receptivity could not be experienced without panic. She attended to all of her "duties" pro forma, without joy, since the pathway to discharge of her strivings was foreshortened. In this way she maintained herself—empty, lonely, but safe. She of course began now to repeat this defensive pattern with complaints of loneliness and defenses against gratification, sometimes nonverbally—coming late, leaving early; other times rejecting all comments of mine. I was able at times—very tentatively and only infrequently—to explain the repetitiousness in her experience of me as another potential imprisoner.

At the end of the second year, she responded to these interventions and the milieu by recounting her remembered early days with her mother—the fear of her embraces—and we reconstructed those early fears of being cast away. Over the next long period of time, this archaic pattern of protection waned, and she began to experience not just complaints of my indifference, but wishes for more and more comforts. Finally the actual experiences of being calmed emerged in the analysis. She could now enter into the analytic work with enthusiasm, since, as she said, she was no longer involved in my "put-downs," which had blocked her in the past. Now the work centered on the emergence of her assertive strivings, quickly followed by the psychological "looking backward" to see if I was still there and approving, followed usually by a dip into the old experience of empty complaining and back again in the here-and-now benevolent milieu of analysis. A typical pattern was her telling me of a weekend with her husband in which she had a love experience with him that was "good." This recounting was followed by associations to worries about an impending separation from me and then to an experience of a sad memory of bringing her mother a homework assignment only to have it taken over by her mother. Finally, she would "wake up" and remind herself of the distance between then and now. When she announced that she now wished to terminate, it seemed to be a reasonable decision. The termination phase ended satisfactorily.

DISCUSSION: SELF/SELFOBJECT FIXATIONS

The emphasis in this essay has been on the fixations of the self to its original selfobject, the original deprivor, rather than the so-called libidinal fixation notion of classical psychoanalysis. Although Freud (1937a) spoke of "libidinal cathexes from one object" and "cathectic loyalty" when he described fixations (p. 241), he was referring to the constitutional differences in libido supply and distribution, the "lines of development . . . already laid down for it" (p. 240). The thesis advanced here is that in those instances where there have been significant selfobject deprivations, the process of fixation will ensue if certain other conditions are met. It is postulated that there are at least four major variables operating from the psychological side alone in any fixation: 1) a massive deprivation at the hands of an archaic selfobject over a considerable length of time, 2) the absence of surrogate selfobjects to substitute for the deficient selfobject, 3) the absence of a compensatory selfobject, such as an idealized parent imago, that can alleviate the distress of a defective mirroring selfobject, 4) the critical time span of the ongoing deprivation—the surmise is that, beyond a critical period, no selfobject can diminish the fixation-effect of the deprivation, 5) the impact on the analysis of the analyst's successes or failures in empathic recognition of the material and the therapeutic activities extending from his empathic cognition.

The uniqueness of the self/selfobject fixation lies in the archaic self's unleashing of its demand for the missing selfobject functions. It is a self driven by urges appropriate to its infantile state to achieve its end. As every analytic observer ascertains, once the archaic self is in control, only the monolithic concerns of this self are present, searching for supplies of worth or soothing. This archaic self now exerting its control cannot be reasoned with, since reality considerations and considerations of causality do not fuel its preoccupations, only the needs for the missing functions of the archaic selfobject. Thus, each analysis becomes a research project on fixations—cause and cure—since each analysis involves fixations of different magnitudes and characteristics and varying degrees of resistance to the formation of a therapeutic bond leading to self-development.

Comparisons and Contrasts

As we begin a psychoanalysis, we cannot determine from our initial assessments which of our patients will be able to undergo the analytic treatment successfully to the point of termination and which will not. From the diagnostic data and data in the beginning of an analysis, we cannot determine such factors as the intensity of the adhesiveness of the pathologic self/selfobject dyad nor any of the other factors necessary in the formation of an intractable fixation. The processes involved in fixation are intrapsychic and proceed without manifestations that can be observed, even through the direct observations employed in research on the development of children (Stern, 1985).

Comparison and contrast between the foregoing cases of a terminated analysis and an interminable analysis reveal that in the analysis of Ms. M the transference to the analyst was never able to be studied through self-observation by the patient, which in itself revealed the frozen nature of the self when she entered into her selfobject transference. In the analysis with Ms. H, although it offered severe difficulties, the selfobject transference ultimately could be observed and worked through to a termination.

Ms. M revealed through the tragic stories of her involvement with her mother that there were never any moments when she experienced her mother as benevolent or empathic—to the contrary, she experienced her mother always as hateful. Ms. H's situation with her mother, although more bombastic, was of a very different kind. Her mother had episodes of illness, which were followed by periods when she could relate with more interest in her children. She did demonstrate interest in her children's school and social interests when she was not ill, without rancor or signs of depressive behavior. She was unfortunate—as was Ms. M—in the absence of either compensatory or surrogate selfobjects of any magnitude to diminish the impact of her primary self/selfobject bond. Our surmise is that the interminable fixation of Ms. M's archaic self and its selfobject needs reflects the unremitting quality and quantity of the deprivation she experienced in her maternal archaic self/selfobject dyad.

Another surmise is that the constant maternal deprivation experienced by Ms. M extended beyond the critical time in which self-repairs can be effected. Ms. H, on the other hand suffered maternal deprivation that was inconstant, alternating with instances of maternal interest, thus allowing the deprivation to be attenuated. As noted previously, with patients struggling to obtain archaic selfobject supplies of which they—throughout their lives—have been deprived, analysts question whether the process of repetition will be ended. Although the data in the two cases of Ms. H and Ms. M did reveal differences in the primary selfobject, the analytic process was similar in intensity and pervasity of the resistance to the interventions until— and this was momentous—Ms. H "saw" herself entering into the malignant self/selfobject dyad of her past and could then begin to move herself away from this complex. As a result of repeated confrontations and, most important, her capacity to join (ally) with the analyst, the patient could begin to study (self-observe) her experiences rather than live them out. It was then that she revealed the history of her childhood trauma; this event came after some 24 months of our being locked in a transference battle.

The surmise that follows from the finding that a stable self/ selfobject dyad with the analyst was formed in Ms. H's analysis is that Ms. H was able to continue, at least in part, with her self development beyond the dyad she formed with her depriving archaic selfobject, rather than be subject to interminable instances of reliving the past of seeking out selfobject supplies in the ancient, self-demeaning manner. Moreover, as a consequence of her unique experience with her primary selfobject, her appetite for direct bonding (merger), albeit considerably diminished and filled with considerable fear, was not permanently eliminated. Thus, in the case of Ms. H, the analyst could offer himself, the patient ultimately was able to accept. In the case of Ms. M, the analyst offered, but the patient refused permanently. In this instance, the offer was to form a therapeutic bond and thus allow the patient to gain her needed selfobject supplies. In the case of Ms. M, the primary selfobject transference could never be sustained. The patient would not accept freedom from her archaic selfobject dyad of deprivation; her self-growth was permanently arrested at this early stage. From the psychological side, the frozen self of Ms. M could only anticipate from each significant human encounter—albeit through her own unconscious devices—the abuse and neglect of her archaic selfobjects and posture herself appropriately to maintain contact while seeking relief of her emptiness.

In comparing and contrasting these two cases, the analytic observer has uncovered what may be a necessary factor in the understanding of the degrees of fixation in these two cases. The generalizability of the findings in these cases may be of some consequence in future clinical situations. Thus each analysis becomes a research project on the fixation process in *this* person and with *this* analyst, the queries being: Is this patient's fixation to her past permanent? If the fixation is capable of being altered, will the patient respond in a reasonable period of time to the ambience of the analysis and form a therapeutic bond, a self/selfobject transference? If the patient's fixation is intractable, will it be revealed early in the analysis or only in the working-through phase or in the termination period? Has the analyst been able to sustain a neutral tone throughout the analysis with an optimum of his transference and countertransference reactions?

Those patients who have selfobject fixations cannot be recognized prior to the actual operation of analysis. Neither can they be recognized through the techniques of the child researchers. The data that we as analysts gather in our early sessions with patients simply can not inform us of the intensity of the fixations our patients are harboring. Moreover, we cannot predict which of our patients will be able successfully to pass through the working-through phase, and neither can we foresee which patients will master the termination period. To estimate the intensity of the fixation to the archaic selfobject requires that the investigator be able to measure the fear of the loss of the archaic selfobject, which is immeasurable. It is, of course, an experience that is both difficult to predict and difficult to empathize with. It emerges from its buried depths only in reaction to a real or fantasied threat of rupture with the subject's archaic selfobject. The subject cannot inform us—certainly not in his anamnesis—that he possesses this overwhelming disintegration anxiety, and therefore interminable fixation, should his ties with his archaic selfobject be terminated. As the analysis progresses and he becomes connected to his analyst through his selfobject transference, his fears of disengagement with the past, latent until this point, now become activated, and, of a sudden, the patient is once again reliving his archaic self in relationship with his archaic selfobject. In those patients in whom the fear of permanent separation from the archaic self/selfobject dyad is overwhelming—the interminable patient, the patient with the permanent fixations—each time in analysis that the threat to the bond with the archaic selfobject becomes activated, the cycling to the past begins anew.

The child observers have illuminated many of the emerging "senses" of the child as he begins to engage with his world. Preoccupied as these researchers are with understanding and organizing the development of the normal self, they nevertheless have addressed the issue of those caretakers who have had a noxious influence on children's development (Stern, 1985). However, the findings of the developmentalists offer little in the apprehension of those special forces that make for the permanent fixations; one cannot predict from the observations of developing children and their caretakers which selves will become addicted to their archaic selfobject and which will not. The process of fixation is an intrapsychic event and therefore unobservable.

All of our considerations point to this: the analyst must proceed in each analysis as if the ubiquitous self/selfobject fixations he will encounter will be amenable to change. From this vantage point, it seems reasonable that all patients in analysis, all patients struggling to overcome their self/selfobject fixation, be given the opportunity to overcome their inhibitions through illumination of their self/selfobject past, an analysis of their selfobject transferences, leading if possible to the overcoming of their self-deficits. Kohut's contributions (1971, 1982, 1984) in this context are two: (1) the developing self requires vital acquisitions from its surround of objects (selfobject) in order to be cohesive and (2) an analysis of a self deficient in these acquisition has as its major goal the furtherance of development of the self. What Kohut taught was that analysts focus their activities on the establishment of a learning milieu in which the crippled self can grow.

Now our investigation resumes: what has this analysis uncovered that gives us an insight into what made this self/selfobject movable or immovable? Recall that we never can gain awareness into the *actual* experience of the child-self and its fears of separation or violence or whatever from its selfobject—the factors that made for the fixation. We can gain insight at some remove from the actual buried child-self and its concerns that may be of assistance in our continuing search for the experiential factors involved in terminable and interminable self/selfobject fixations. Granted our data base in analysis cannot capture the actual experiences of the infant fear, our transference analyses offer us experiences that have been and will continue to be instrumental in establishing the importance of key factors in our understanding of the fixations and in our therapeutic methods. In this connection, recall Kohut's (1971) findings of the selfobject transferences derived from his analyses with patients with narcissistic deficits.

In one of the most widely known passages in psychoanalytic literature, Freud (1937a) described his version of the so-called bedrock in analytic treatment:

> We often have the impression that with the wish for a penis and the masculine protest we have penetrated through all the psychological

strata and have reached bedrock, and that thus our activities are at an end. This is probably true, since, for the psychical field, the biological field does in fact play the part of the underlying bedrock. The repudiation of femininity can be nothing else than a biological fact, a part of the great riddle of sex. It would be hard to say whether and when we have succeeded in mastering this factor in an analytic treatment [p. 252].

From the selfpsychology viewpoint advanced here, massive self/selfobject fixations represent psychological bedrock, a point beyond which no further impact can be made on the self and its hunger for its original self/selfobject bond. The interminable patient cannot, at least through our techniques, thus far elaborated in analysis, remove himself from the necessity to become immersed in the specific archaic self/selfobject dyad of fixation. Perhaps this is the underlying issue that has urged analysts in the past to initiate psychotherapeutic treatment with these patients whose development is limited. Perhaps these patients represent those cases in which an "emotionally corrective experience" is inadvertently initiated, with the analyst becoming a permanent selfobject-in-function.

In any case, neither our theories nor our techniques yet inform us about what the processes of liberation from many of these interminable fixations would be or of what they consist. Our theories of cure, or, better put, of change, have always held that the patient's self will be able at some point in the analysis to invest "our" relationship with importance sufficient to join us in a therapeutic bond for self-growth and not rush away from us as soon as the patient becomes aware that he has moved away from his major archaic selfobjects. However, it is clear that the study of fixations—the focus on the developmental influences and the therapeutic forces in analysis that are liberating—is best conducted in the clinical setting of a self/selfobject-oriented analysis that offers the unique advantage of observing relevant derivatives of the infant-self's fear of its archaic selfobjects. In this setting we hope to study the major impediments to psychological development in man. It is also only in this setting that we both offer the fixated self of the patient the best opportunity to continue its growth through our ministrations *and* hope to expand our therapeutic knowledge and skills to be of service to those to whom our current efforts are of limited help. Kohut's vision in expanding our clinical horizons should serve as an important model for the elaboration of new therapeutic approaches in the area of fixations. As he (Kohut, 1977) said, speaking of basic elements in clinical psychoanalytic theory, "I would still insist that some future generation of psychoanalytic might discover psychological areas that require a novel conceptual approach . . ." (p. 308).

SUMMARY

The crippled self, unable to be freed from its endless search for the selfobject who will be its savior either in life or in analysis, cannot be recognized as an interminable case prior to the psychoanalytic treatment. The diagnosis of interminability can be made only after a selfobject transference has been unfolded and the analyst has been able to evaluate the intractability of the self/selfobject transference.

Our comments on the genesis of the fixation disorders have stressed a multidetermined view implicating the influences of massive deprivation, the presence or absence of compensatory and surrogate selfobjects, and the limitations imposed by the genetic input into the nervous system.

Freud's (1937a) final comments in his "Analysis Terminable . . ." essay are statements with which we can join by altering his final allusion to "it". The "it" we refer to is the archaic self/selfobject bond: "We can only console ourselves with the certainty that we have given the person analyzed every possible encouragement to reexamine and alter his attitude to it" (p. 253).

REFERENCES

Balint, M. (1937), *Primary Love and Psychoanalytic Technique*. London: Hogarth Press, 1952.

Blum, H. (1987), Analysis terminable and interminable: A half-century retrospective. *Internat. J. Psycho-Anal.*, 68:38–47.

Freud, A. (1936), *The Ego and the Mechanisms of Defense, Writings 2*. New York: International Universities Press, 1966.

Freud, S. (1926), Inhibitions, symptoms and anxiety. *Standard Edition*, 20:87–172. London: Hogarth Press, 1959.

———— (1937), Analysis terminable and interminable. *Standard Edition*, 23:216–253. London: Hogarth Press, 1964.

Furst, S. (1967), *Psychic Trauma*. New York: Basic Books.

Greenacre, P. (1967), The influence of infantile trauma on genetic patterns. In: *Psychic Trauma*, ed. S. Furst. New York: Basic Books, pp. 108–153.

Greenspan, S. I. (1981). *Clinical Infant Reports: No 1. Psychopathology and Adaptation on Infancy*. New York: International Universities Press.

Gutman, S. (1963). On analysis terminable and interminable twenty five years later. *J. Amer. Psychoanal. Assn.*, 11:229–244.

Hartmann, H. (1939), *Ego Psychology and the Problem of Adaptation*. New York: International Universities Press.

Jones, E. (1957). *The Life and Work of Sigmund Freud,* vol. 3, New York: Basic Books.

Kanzer, M. (1975), Panel, Termination: problems and technique. W. Robbins, reporter. *J. Amer. Psychoanal. Assn.,* 23:166–176.

Kohut, H. (1971), *The Analysis of the Self.* New York: International Universities Press.

——— (1977), *The Restoration of the Self.* New York: International Universities Press.

——— (1984), *How Does Analysis Cure?* ed. A. Goldberg and P. Stepansky. Chicago: University of Chicago Press.

Mahler, M. (1971), A study of the separation-individuation process and its possible application to borderline phenomena in the psychoanalytic situation. *The Psychoanalytic Study of the Child,* 26:403–424. New Haven: Yale University Press.

Muslin, H. (1986), On working through in self psychology. In: *Progress in Self Psychology,* Vol. 2, ed. A. Goldberg. New York: Guilford Press, pp. 280–298.

——— (1987), On termination in self psychology (Unpublished manuscript).

Sander, L. W. (1964), Adaptive relationship in early mother-child interaction. *J. Amer. Acad. Child Psychol.* 3:231–264.

Spitz, R. (1959), *A Genetic Field Theory of Ego Formation.* New York: International Universities Press.

Stern, D. (1985), *The Interpersonal World of the Infant.* New York: Basic Books.

Strachey, J. (1964) Editor's note, Analysis terminable & interminable. *Standard Edition,* 23, p. 214.

Tolpin, M. (1971), On the beginning of a cohesive self. *The Psychoanalytic Study of the Child,* 26:316–352. New Haven: Yale University Press.

Winnicott, D. (1965). *The Maturational Processes and the Facilitating Environment.* New York: International Universities Press.

Wolf, E. (1980). On the developmental line in selfobject relation. In: *Advances in Self Psychology,* ed. A. Goldberg. New York: International Universities Press, pp. 117–130.

Chapter 10

Self-Psychological Perspectives on Suicide

Jerald Kay

There is perhaps no more timely yet enigmatic topic in clinical psychiatry than that of suicide. Our attention has been drawn repeatedly to the dramatic fact that suicide among the young in the United States has tripled in the past 30 years (Holden, 1986). In young people aged 15–24, suicide ranks second as cause of death. Not only the young take their own lives; people over 65 constitute 11% of our population yet are responsible for approximately 25% of all suicides. With more than 29,000 suicides, and 300,000 attempted suicides, each year in this country, many persons are significantly affected by the suicide or attempted suicide of someone for whom they care (Hirschfeld and Davidson, 1988).

With a more comprehensive understanding of childhood depression, an increasing number of articles have appeared recently on child as well as adolescent suicide (e.g. Pfeffer, 1986; Klerman, 1986). Adolescent suicide contagion in general and the impact of the media on imitative teen suicide in particular have also received a great deal of scientific attention (Gould and Shaffer, 1986; Phillips and Carstensen, 1986).

Societal values with respect to death and suicide have changed. The recent secularization of death in Western civilization has brought new issues that appear to be influencing and challenging some

The author wishes to thank Drs. Anna Ornstein and Rena Kay for their thoughtful assistance.

traditional beliefs about the sanctity and value of life. Active and passive euthanasia (Bosman, Kay, and Conter, 1987), hospices, living wills, voluntary but possibly fatal organ donation (at times even for financial gain), the physician's role in capital punishment, consent to potentially lethal experimentation, self-sacrificial protests, high-risk exploration and sports, and the prominent British movement of planned death in old age are but a few of the recent developments that signify change in our views about death.

Yet despite new clinical and epidemiological studies, why one takes one's life always taxes the clinician's understanding and empathy. We are confounded in both our scientific prevention and our prediction of suicide. In part, this confusion is a result of our not yet understanding the many significant factors—intrapsychic, sociocultural, and biologic—that determine and predispose to suicide. Despite the lack of clarity, however, new models of understanding suicidal motivation must be entertained. We must not adopt the position that it is impossible to assign "motivation for suicide beyond the misery of depression" (Murphy, 1986, p. 564). In this chapter, we shall present some alternative ways of conceptualizing suicide and suicide attempts (for they are two distinctly separate phenomena), drawn from the recent contributions of self psychology. The focus will be on the richness and experience-near advantage in viewing self-destructive feelings and acts from the viewpoint of selfobject functioning. To set the stage for these contributions, it will be instructive to review some traditional and more recent notions about the biology and psychology of suicide.

Although there is probably no universally accepted definition of suicide, Maris's (1983) definition that suicide is "self-killing deriving from one's inability or refusal to accept the human condition" (p. xviii) is most succinct. While derived in part from a sociological perspective, the clinical appropriateness of this definition will become apparent shortly.

THEORIES OF SUICIDE

Biological/Epidemiological Theories

In examining the biological and epidemiological contributions toward the understanding of suicide, one is impressed with the centrality of the roles of affective disease and alcoholism. Over the last 25 years or so, studies in this country (Robins et al., 1959), England (Barraclough et al., 1974), Sweden (Beskow, 1979), and Australia (Chynoweth,

Tonge, and Armstrong, 1980) have all underscored the importance of mental illness and suicide but especially of depression and subsequent suicide. In these studies, approximately 50% of those suiciding were diagnosed as having depression, 25% as having alcoholism. It remains unclear what distinguishes those depressed persons who commit suicide from those who do not, for in some studies those who killed themselves did not have excessive life stresses, financial or legal difficulties, or interpersonal conflict (Murphy, 1986). However, compared with the general population, they were twice as likely to be living alone, (Murphy and Robins, 1967). It is of course extraordinarily important to ask how a person became isolated, and here the study of psychological autopsies indicates that lifelong patterns of negative interactions may be more significant than mere social isolation (Fawcett, Leff, and Bunney, 1969). A more recent study (Fawcett et al., 1987), revealed that hopelessness, loss of pleasure or interest, and mood cycles predicted suicide in a large group of affectively disturbed people. Murphy and Robins (1967) have pointed out some differences between depressed and alcoholic suicides. Alcoholics were more likely than depressives to have experienced within the year prior to suicide significant object loss (most often through marital dysfunction); this loss occurred within six weeks of death for one third of them.

Recent studies of the Amish (Egland and Sussex, 1985) support the significant relationship between family history of affective disorder and suicide. In that culture, with extraordinary social networking and family emphasis, strong religious prohibitions against suicide, alcoholism and substance abuse, suicide nevertheless occurs in those families with bipolar and unipolar affective illness. That a genetic vulnerability may be present as well has been raised by the data from the Danish adoption study demonstrating that those adoptees who committed suicide were likely to have come from biological families with suicidal histories (Schulsinger et al., 1979). Finally, epidemiological studies have found higher suicide rates among the divorced, single, and the widowed (Murphy, 1988).

Psychoanalytic Theories

Most depth psychological theories about suicide have been psychoanalytically informed. Meissner (1977) has provided a cogent review of the development of Freud's thinking on suicide and traced it back to as early as 1901, when in the "Psychopathology of Everyday Life" Freud described his understanding of the dynamics of some accidents. A comment subsequently appeared in the Rat Man (1909) that indicated Freud's linking the suicidal wish with aggressive impulses toward another person. The development of this line of thought is most clearly elucidated in "Mourning and Melancholia" (1917) and culminated in "Beyond the Pleasure Principle" (1920) in his idea of the universality of a self-destructive tendency, which he called the death instinct. Psychoanalysis has had, and continues to have, a profound impact on our conceptualization of suicide, for it maintains ultimately, as Freud did, that no suicidal person really wishes to die, since all attempts are motivated unconsciously by aggressive impulses toward another person (Clements, Sider, and Perlmutter, 1981). Menninger (1938), Zilboorg (1936, 1937), and Melanie Klein (1934) furthered Freud's view that suicide and aggression are intimately linked, with Klein also noting the possibility that some suicides could be motivated by the wish to be reunited with the internal and external good objects.

There have been, of course, many subsequent psychoanalytic contributions to the understanding of suicide, but a complete review is beyond the scope of this paper. One recent discussion of adolescent suicide however is worth singling out because of the comprehensive view it advocates and its applicability to all suicides. Mack and Hickler (1981), describing the unfortunate suicide of 14-year-old Vivienne, proposed an "architectural model" to consider in a systems approach as many of the important factors as possible. While a person's intrapsychic characteristics are critical, other considerations are necessary and should include: 1) the sociopolitical context; 2) biologic vulnerability (genetic predisposition); 3) earliest developmental influences and experiences; 4) personality structure and self-esteem regulation; 5) object relationships, especially their state prior to suicidal ideation; 6) clinical depression and other psychopathology; 7) ontogeny or developmental relationship to death; and 8) circumstances of the person's life at the time of clinical assessment (Mack, 1986). This model holds promise for integrating much of the significant recent clinical research in suicide while maintaining a focus on the meaning of the event to the suicidal person and others attempting to understand as well.

SOME BASIC CONCEPTS IN SELF PSYCHOLOGY

Empathy and Selfobject Functioning

Central to the discussion of suicide are the concepts of empathy and selfobject functions. One of Kohut's (1977) vital contributions was the redefinition and refinement of empathy within human developmental theory as well as within the therapeutic relationship. For Kohut, empathy defined the field of psychoanalysis and its method. The latter "lies in the scientific observer's protracted empathic immersion into the observed, for the purpose of data-gathering and explanation" (p. 302). Empathy is a tool for accessing the inner life of man. Empathy is "vicarious introspection which reveals what the inner life of man is, what we ourselves and what others think and feel" (p. 306). In the case of suicidal ideation, "it is through the therapist's empathic immersion into the patient's inner life that he will appreciate that another can accept and understand his hopelessness and desperation" (Ornstein and Kay, 1983, p. 333). Kohut (1980) declared empathy to be an objectifiable and "value neutral operation" (p. 483), and he contrasted this position with that of classical psychoanalytic theory and its resultant value system, which stems from the primacy of the drive and drive taming. In his last work (1984) he argued by extension that in relation to suicidal behavior, psychoanalysis created an important, albeit frequently unexamined, morality system having the following characteristics:

1. The therapeutic task is to make the unconscious conscious, and the patient's facing the truth in the therapeutic process is brave and upstanding, while his shrinking from it, as in the suicide's refusal to examine introjected murderous impulses, is cowardly and weak.

2. In harmony with the work ethic that has dominated Western civilization in recent centuries, it is good to work through life's disappointments and losses; not to do so, as in the case of suicide, means failing to do the work and is undesirable.

3. The unconscious knows nothing of time and change or of birth and death. Indeed man is supposedly unwilling to accept the truth about life and death and about the endless succession of generations. These values are especially understandable in the light of the strong feelings of vulnerability and helplessness that are evoked in the therapist treating the severely suicidal patient.

Developmentally, of fundamental importance is the function of the selfobject "as a precursory substitute for the not yet existing psychological structures" (Kohut, 1977, p. 32). Selfobject relations are not in themselves an indicator of psychopathology since they occur in all contexts throughout all phases of the life cycle: "Man lives in a matrix of selfobjects from birth to death. He needs selfobjects for his psychological survival, just as he needs oxygen in his environment throughout his life for physiological survival" (Kohut, 1980, p. 478). Moreover throughout all phases of life, a person's self-selfobject relationships must be such as to enable

certain representatives of his human surroundings as joyfully responding to him, as available to him as sources of idealized strength and
calmness, as being silently present but in essence like him, and, at any
rate, able to grasp his inner life more or less accurately so that their
responses are attuned to his needs and allow him to grasp their inner
life when his is in need of such sustenance [Kohut, 1984, p. 52].

[T]he small child invests other people with narcissistic cathexis and
thus experiences them narcissistically, ie., as selfobjects. The expected
control over such (selfobject) others is then closer to the concept of the
control which a grownup expects to have over his own body and mind
than to the concept of control he expects to have over others [Kohut,
1971, pp. 26–27].

The selfobject then is experienced as part of the self, as a "functional
unity with one's self" (Goldberg, 1977, p. 106).

However, those persons suffering from a defect in psychic structures that promote, regulate, and maintain self esteem frequently
mobilize one or two narcissistic configurations to sustain and solidify
a sense of self-cohesion. This cohesiveness may be accomplished
through merger with a comforting, soothing, and protecting omnipotent object or through an object that consistently mirrors back the
person's own primitive omnipotent, wishful self. In both instances,
such selfobject relationships compensate for absent or defective en-
dopsychic structures that regulate or maintain the sense of self. In
the treatment situation, these defects are expressed in the activation
of either the omnipotent object and its corresponding transference,
the idealizing transference, or the grandiose self and its mirror
transference.

Idealization provides the person who has a self-disorder with a
sense of calming soothing, and protection, much like that a young
child experiences in the presence of the parent he perceives to be all-
powerful. Deidealization, on the other hand, can be exquisitely painful and traumatic. Such traumatic deidealization, it will be argued, is
a helpful way to conceptualize certain suicidal behavior.

In this brief review of suicide theories, those derived exclusively
from a social framework have not been addressed. Here the proto-
type, of course, is Durkheim's (1897) social context theory. Despite
Durkheim's insistence that suicide cannot be successfully explained
from an individual psychological or motivational perspective, but
needs a larger, macroscopic sociological one, Kohut's notion of selfobject functioning is compatible with and explicates further some of
Durkheim's original formulations. Moreover, the selfobject construct
is consistent with many of the biological and epidemiological findings
reviewed earlier, especially those highlighting contributions of inter-

personal unconnectedness. As viewed within the social context, suicide is the product of disrupted ties between the individual and society; the more the disruption, the higher the potential for suicide. Durkheim posited three types of suicide, each related to a distinct relationship between society and the individual. The anomic suicide is the result of a sudden shattering of this relationship because of catastrophe or trauma such as illness, job loss, death of a loved one. Egoistic suicide occurs when a person is unintegrated into a community and has few ties with family or other social groups. Social sanctions or demands to live are ineffective, since the suicidal person is not connected to a caring community and "excessive individualism" takes over. Altruistic suicides are in a sense mandated by society in that customs and traditions require honorable, self-inflicted death (e.g., hara-kiri, suttee, sepuku). In these instances, group values strongly predominate over individual values.

Two fundamental themes run through sociological interpretations of suicide: the connectedness between the individual and the group, and the authority of the social group over the individual. Durkheim and his followers discovered some very important characteristics of suicide but failed to translate these findings into an experience-near and therefore clinically useful form. They especially failed to distinguish social isolation from its most likely causes, repeated unsatisfactory interpersonal relationships and the manner in which individuals interpret and cope with life events. Kohut's (1971) discovery of idealizing and mirror transferences and the explication of narcissistic disturbances in terms of selfobject functioning bring, as we shall see, a richer understanding to these sociologically defined suicide types, because they relate the suicidal motivations to an important interpersonal and intrapsychic theory that can account for these suicidal types within an individual psychological framework.

SELF PSYCHOLOGY AND SUICIDE

Before attempting to forge a point of view of some suicidal motivations and behaviors based on self psychological concepts, we should recognize that there are distinct differences between those who attempt suicide and those who complete it: the former tend to be young and female, responding to some immediate emotional assault but not necessarily wishing to die; the latter more frequently are older and male, more troubled by isolation, job dissatisfaction, alcoholism, illness, and long-standing maladaptive patterns. On a clinically less obvious level, two other categories of suicide are recognizable: one type of suicide appears on the surface to portray aggression, chiefly through motives of revenge, with its fantasied anguish of the survivors. This group is compatible with earlier psychoanalytic explanations. Indeed, from a self-psychological viewpoint, a variant of such aggression may take place when there is an intense affront to an archaic grandiose self that promotes an enactment of narcissistic rage directed against oneself. In the second group, feelings of hopelessness, meaninglessness, and failure predominate. In both groups of patients, the suicidal ideation reflects a dyadic quality, an observation made by Schneidman (1979) from a different theoretical perspective. In a general sense, suicide is the ultimate product of disturbed or deficient selfobject functioning. More specifically, failures in parental empathy, as expressed through faulty mirroring or idealization, produce a defect in the emerging self that leads the child to seek out restitutive or restorative experiences that promote self-cohesion. This compensatory process, of course, is never completely satisfactory, and the child is left with a specific vulnerability that is likely to be reactivated when future selfobject failures occur. Lacking certain psychic structure, the narcissistically vulnerable individual is without the stability and capacity to master disappointments and frustration that challenge his sense of competence. In such persons, significant narcissistic insults may lead to suicidal behaviors.

Even in the case of those suicides that appear to be of the revenge type related to traumatic disappointment in the idealized selfobject, frequently behind the more apparent rage is a wish for some special kind of merger or union. This often is a union in which the suicidal person persists in a life that is less harsh by establishing, or reestablishing, selfobject relations that protect and comfort. At other times, it may take a less specific form through refuge in a highly idealized notion of peaceful respite that may or may not contain attractive religious or philosophical characteristics. (Adolescents in particular are more susceptible to the appeal of certain idealized intellectualizations.) But, above all, there remains a clear, if not always articulated, version of some form of more positive existence. In this regard, perhaps Freud (1915) was right when he argued for our inability to conceptualize nonexistence. Behind these union or reunion fantasies lies a conviction that one will participate in a different or more fulfilling way of life. There is ample clinical experience that those who employ such mental mechanisms are predisposed to suicide owing to significant prior idealizing selfobject failure.

Traumatic Deidealization

As previously reviewed, Kohut described, on the basis of selfobject transferences within the analytic process, certain narcissistically vulnerable people as having suffered significant and specific selfobject failures along dimensions of mirroring and idealization. With respect to idealization, he noted that the young child, in the presence of an empathic parent, is able to experience feelings of protection, soothing, and calm. Consistent interactions of this sort through the process of transmuting internalization permit the child to acquire self-soothing and self-calming abilities. These interactions, moreover, facilitate the child's development through an increasing conviction and security about his values and ideals, which, in conjunction with his successful utilization of innate skills and talents, create a sense of contentment. The self then is experienced as complete. For some, however, such a process is unsatisfactory, leaving them with a particular vulnerability, often witnessed in the constant search for powerful selfobjects to provide the much needed narcissistic balance. A particular type of suicidal behavior will be described that is perhaps best understood from the vantage point of idealization, or more accurately, traumatic deidealization.

There has been resistance to accepting Kohut's highly original ideas on idealization, for they run counter to traditional psychoanalytic views. Idealization has been customarily "regarded as a reaction formation against the hostile aspects of the ambivalence inherent in the object relations of the oedipal child" (Gedo, 1975). Others, like Kernberg (1974), have conceptualized idealization as a defense against a more primitive or primary aggression. In these instances, when idealization is apparent within the transference, it is regarded as a resistance against competitive or hostile feelings, and its defensive aim therefore must be interpreted to gain access to these more central feelings. Differences in the conceptualization of idealization obviously have great implications for its technical management within the treatment situation.

Just as idealization is a normal developmental constituent, so too is deidealization. For the child to develop with realistic abilities to assess and relate to people, he must throughout the school and adolescent years, accrue an increasingly complex yet accurate picture of his parents. In part, gradual deidealization promotes such a process by permitting the child to view his parents with all their shortcomings as well as their strengths. Failure of this process is evident in those parents who for their own self-esteem require that their children see them in an idyllic fashion without blemishes.

Traumatic deidealization, as the term implies, is an experience of a rapid, painfully intense disappointment in the context of an idealizing selfobject relationship. Such an event frequently leaves the person with feelings of emptiness, confusion, lack of direction, and, at times, fragmentation. Such a process may account for one particular constellation of suicide attempts and possibly suicide completion, although the data is lacking to support the latter. Traumatic deidealization may be an especially helpful concept in understanding some, but not all, adolescent suicidal behaviors.

The concept of traumatic deidealization may also shed some light on the frequently observed contagious nature of adolescent suicidal behavior. Phillips and Carstensen (1986) and Gould and Shaffer (1986) have explored in depth the clustering of teenage suicides after both television news stories and movies about suicide. Earlier studies that examined death certificate data discerned that newspaper reports of suicides are associated with a definite increase in suicide in the readership area served by that newspaper (Phillips, 1974). Moreover, the intensity of this effect appears to be proportional to the public visibility or attractiveness of those suiciding and to the extent of the actual news coverage. The clinical question of what constitutes imitative behavior (Bandura, 1974) from a psychodynamic viewpoint is intriguing, especially in view of the importance of the fame of the suicide completer.

Such was the case in Goethe's "The Sorrows of Young Werther," whose protagonist is a young man "gifted with deep, pure sentiment and penetrating intelligence who loses himself in fantastic dreams and undermines himself with speculative thought, until finally, torn by hopeless passions, especially by infinite love, he shoots himself in the head" (quoted in Eisenberg, 1986, p. 705). According to Eisenberg, this book was quite popular and was the subject of great condemnation for promoting suicide in a highly attractive fashion especially to the young. About the novel's criticism, Goethe wrote

> Just as I felt eased and clearer in my mind at having transformed reality into poetry, my friends . . . thought they must transform poetry into reality, imitate a novel like this in real life, and, in any case, shoot themselves; what occurred at first among a few later took place among the general public, so that this book, which had done me so much good, was condemned as being highly dangerous [Eisenberg, 1986, p. 705].

A modern version of this unfortunate case may be found in a Nevada lawsuit against the heavy metal band, Judas Priest, accused of intentionally making music and lyrics that could promote suicide in susceptible youths. Specifically, two teenage boys listened to the band's songs for two hours, then ran to a churchyard, hugged each other and shot themselves (Tucker, 1987). The judge in this case has refused a motion of dismissal of the suit.

The following brief vignette demonstrates a similar phenomenon. Lisa, at the time of her suicide attempt by carbon monoxide asphyxiation, was 16 and an academically failing sophomore in high school. Living at home with a severely alcoholic father and an ineffectual mother, she described herself as "having been a nobody all of my life." She had a history of drug and alcohol abuse and since the age of 10 had been sexually abused periodically by an older brother. Three weeks prior to Lisa's suicide attempt, a highly admired student at her high school had taken her life. When describing why she had chosen to kill herself by running the engine of her family car inside a closed garage, Lisa replied

> In the back of my head, I had this sort of idea that she was so popular, so bright, so good looking, had it all together with everybody . . . that she must have known what she was doing. What she did had to help me . . . What she did could finally give me some peace. In a funny way, it made me feel not so alone. That's why I even tried to do it just like I heard she did—with the car.

Highly romanticized notions about death among youth, as evidenced in Shakespeare and Goethe for example, are not rare. An especially important component of some of these idyllic fantasies may also have highly specific idealizing selfobject characteristics much like those Lisa employed with respect to her schoolmate. It may be helpful to examine the fantasies of suicide attempters for issues of idealization in the hope that such knowledge will prove useful in preventing teen suicide. Parenthetically, it is evident that such idealizing selfobject relationships have essential links with, and grow out of, earlier unempathic parental responses and therefore may ultimately reflect a deep desire for reunion with a parent.

CASE ILLUSTRATION

M. L. is a 33-year-old recently graduated lawyer, who at the time of his suicide attempt was completing a postdoctoral fellowship in a specific area of legal research. Of particular importance was the striking decrease in the patient's symptomatology when in the presence of an idealizing selfobject and the subsequent decline in his functioning with the loss of such a significant selfobject. He was the oldest of three children born to struggling, lower middle-class Jewish parents. His father had long entertained the wish to attend medical school but was drafted into the army shortly after graduating from college. Serving as a medic, he was among the first Americans to liberate one of the more infamous Nazi extermination camps. This experience threw him into an immediate and profound depression. Upon his return to this country, he entered medical school but dropped out within a month because he could not tolerate gross anatomy and the required dissections. During that month he was flooded by intense memories of the cruelties he had witnessed and was unable to sleep or concentrate. He turned to alcohol initially to self-medicate but, as is the case all too frequently, he rapidly progressed into lifelong severe drinking. Thwarted in his desire for professional education, Mr. L's father took a number of low-paying clerical positions, each of which terminated rapidly. Eventually he was taken into a family grocery business, where he remained and was tolerated for the rest of his life. He was for the most part emotionally unavailable to his wife and children, not only because of his nightly drinking to stupor, but also because of the marked personality change he underwent after the war. Whereas prior to his war experiences he had been a reasonably assertive and accomplishing man, soon thereafter his world view changed dramatically. He became timid and frightened and consistently experienced himself as being at the mercy of a hostile and merciless universe. He was especially fearful of anti-Semitism, a fear that was forcefully transmitted to the patient.

The boy entered school with the absolute conviction that he also would be a target for anti-Semitic attacks. Many of Mr. L's early memories are of highly disappointing encounters with his father, two of which illustrate the significance of these experiences. As is frequently the case, the patient was able to compensate partially for his self-defect by depending for adequate psychic functioning on a narrow band of competence and skills chiefly in the academic arena. He received a scholarship to a prestigious college and one of the top law schools in the nation. On neither of these occasions did the father acknowledge these accomplishments despite the patient's having handed the letters of acceptance directly to his father in the desperate hope of some recognition.

As one might suspect, Mr. L experienced himself in many ways like his father. This is consistent with Kohut's (1977) differentiation between gross identification and transmuting internalization, the former referring to a internalization where the features of the "other" remain grossly unaltered in the self and constitute defensive rather than primary structures.

> These defensive psychological structures in the form of gross identifications serve the function of securing a bond, a reliable connection

between the child and the parent, who because of his preoccupation is
unavailable to perceive and respond empathically to the growing child's
legitimate developmental selfobject needs [Ornstein, 1983, p. 138].

Despite his fine academic performance, Mr. L felt undesirable as a
friend and later as a boyfriend. He was the butt of many jokes and
pranks in elementary school and in high school pleaded with girls to
go out and have sex with him so that he "could experience himself as
a man." By his own account he was universally regarded as "pa-
thetic." While in grade school he began compulsively masturbating
and could not fall asleep without soothing himself in this manner, a
practice that continues in times of stress in adulthood.

The painful loneliness of his formative years was punctuated by
some respite, chiefly through two types of events. First, Mr. L was
an avid radio builder and can recall the many nights spent listening
to distant radio stations. This activity took place, for the most part,
in the evening after he had masturbated and as he was falling asleep.
To this day he recalls the fantasies he entertained about the "people
behind the voices." In his mind, he pictured the announcers as
strong, accomplished, and highly popular men unlike his weak,
frightened, ne'er-do-well father. Second, Mr. L consistently established special relationships with older men. Frequently he would
promote an "adoption," as he called it, in which he established
intense relationships with male teachers, scout leaders, or his after-
school employers. He would perform more satisfactorily in all sectors
of his life when engaged in such a relationship. He remembers that
as a high school student he preferred to stay at work with an admired
supervisor rather than return home to witness his father, drunk,
expounding on the need to accept injustices of the world. True to his
radio hobby, he later in treatment referred to some of the relationships with older men as "capacitors" because they allowed him to
feel that he "could store some of the energy these men had." In
college he always had a "favorite professor" and delighted in doing
favors for these men, who in return would sometimes invite him to
their homes or give him tickets to sporting events. What he most
remembered about his college days was not courses he took or the
knowledge he accrued, but rather the important times spent with
special teachers. Indeed, his choice of law as profession had more to
do with who had made the suggestion (a special history teacher) than
with the field itself. So too with law school; in fact, his fellowship was
undertaken under very similar emotional conditions.

During this fellowship Mr. L was remarkably productive, especially in view of his age, and published many fine papers with his

advisor. He enjoyed traveling to conferences and presenting his work with his advisor. It became common knowledge at the law school that the patient held great academic promise and would no doubt be invited to join the faculty after completing the fellowship program. The therapist saw a dramatic complementarity to this advisor-fellow relationship. As strongly as Mr. L needed a competent, understanding, yet giving father, his advisor responded intensely to a need of his own beyond the traditional bounds of a mentoring relationship. This advisor, then, was easily admirable not only for his charisma, brilliance, and well-deserved national reputation, but for the clarity of protective career direction he provided and his remarkable capacity to make our patient feel special among all the students. Under the guidance of this mentor, Mr. L felt more satisfied than he ever had. He virtually stopped drinking alcohol, which he had used in small amounts on an almost regular basis to settle himself in the evenings. Although he was constantly concerned about displeasing or failing his advisor, overall he felt more stable than in any previous period of his life.

Toward the end of the first year of his fellowship, Mr. L was seen in three diagnostic sessions after he became depressed following the breakup of a relationship with a woman. Due to vacations, there was an interruption between the time of the diagnostic sessions and the scheduled starting date of treatment. In the interim, Mr. L was traveling frequently and decided not to pursue treatment at that time. Approximately four months later, the patient recontacted the author for help after he had made a moderately severe suicide attempt by ingesting a large quantity of minor tranquilizers and alcohol. This overdose occurred after Mr. L heard news of substantial charges of unethical behavior against his mentor. He subsequently returned to drinking, compulsive masturbation, and desperate, inappropriate sexual approaches to women.

The patient was shattered by the news of his mentor's tragedy. He felt lost, confused, and overwhelmed. He described some depersonalization experiences and strong feelings of vulnerability, the latter reminding him of how he had felt at a younger age. He could see little future for himself. All of these feelings prompted his overdose. He was experiencing disintegration anxiety (Kohut, 1977).[1]

Early in the treatment, as the meaningfulness of this event was

---

[1]Disintegration anxiety refers to all the anxieties experienced by a precariously established self in anticipation of the deterioration of its very structure. "Thus the term refers not only to the fear of fragmentation of the self but also to the fear of impending loss of its vitality and to the fear of psychological depletion" (Tolpin, 1978, p. 175).

assessed, the patient recalled numerous memories of his father's timidity and cowardice. He traced the impact of his father's fears on his own development. He compared the pervasive insecurity he experienced in his family with the sense of well-being and accomplishment while he was being mentored. True, he frequently was concerned about failing his professor, but for the most part he was reassured by pleasant images of professional success and protection. He enjoyed being recognized as a protegé and experienced an enormous sense of importance while traveling to professional meetings with his mentor. He compared these moments to childhood family trips, which were drained of any enjoyment because of his father's anxiety about the dangers of travel. They also stood in stark contrast to his intense embarrassment about bringing any childhood playmates home after school for fear that father would be inebriated. During the hours, the patient cried frequently over what he termed a wasted and tormented childhood.

His marked disappointment in his professor also ushered in feelings of being adrift and fears that without this special relationship there would be little future for him. Despite his academic accomplishments, the patient felt he was a "hack" and everyone would eventually see that he was without substance. He no longer viewed a highly visible academic post as exciting and affirming but became plagued by fantasies of incompetence. During this time, Mr. L reassessed his relationship with his mentor and was openly critical of aspects of the man's personality that had heretofore been too painful to acknowledge.

Throughout the first two years of treatment, Mr. L remained somewhat symptomatic. New assignments caused high levels of anxiety; he continued to drink in the evenings, repeatedly engaged in potentially career-damaging sexual encounters, and often rescheduled appointments. Initially, despite the importance of the therapist to him, the patient minimized this relationship because he was only partially aware of his dread of repeating another traumatic disappointment. However, a clear idealizing transference subsequently appeared in the therapy and formed the foundation for further examination and psychic growth.

Conclusion

The case of Mr. L illustrates the usefulness of conceptualizing suicidal behavior within a self psychological framework. The underlying self-object needs and relationships in the processes of idealization and traumatic deidealization seem experience-near for both patient and therapist. For example, one might understand aspects of Mr. L's suicidal motivation as aggression toward his disappointing professor (and ultimately toward his unavailable father), that is, idealization as a defense against the traditional hostility and competitive strivings of an oedipally based conflict. However, the clinical material did not support such an interpretation. Rather it was strikingly consistent with a developmental selfobject failure. What was sensed in Mr. L was a pervasive helplessness and hopelessness over the news of the charges against his professor. Later in treatment, it was possible to come to a still more precise understanding of the dread Mr. L was experiencing when he took the overdose. His suicide attempt was not born of revenge, but of a fear that he would once again have to suffer the kind of humiliation and pain that had characterized his formative years. What frightened him most, however, was the "plunge backwards," a fear of being drawn back into a period without meaningful accomplishments and the ability to enjoy them. His mentor had provided him with crucial idealizing selfobject functions, including an empathic milieu of protectiveness and consistent academic affirmation and self-affirmation, which permitted Mr. L to maximally utilize his innate talents and skills.

As was noted earlier, why a person makes a suicide attempt is not always clear to the clinician. To all of the necessary components of the architectural model (Mack, 1986) this paper has, it is hoped, added a different way to view and assess selected aspects of this model, particularly those addressing personality structure and self-esteem regulation and the state of object relationships prior to suicidal ideation.

REFERENCES

Bandura, A. (1977), *Social Learning Theory*. Englewood Cliffs, NJ: Prentice Hall.
Barraclough, B., Bunch, J., Nelson, B. & Sainsbury, P. (1974), A hundred cases of suicide: Clinical aspects. *Brit. J. Psychiat.*, 125:355–373.
Beskow, J. (1979), Suicide and mental disorder in Swedish men. *Acta Psychiat. Scand.*, (Suppl), 277:1–138.
Bosman, H. B., Kay, J. & Conter, E. A. (1987), Geriatric euthanasia: Attitudes and experiences of health professionals. *Soc. Psychiat.*, 22:1–4.
Chynoweth, R., Tonge, J. I. & Armstrong, J. (1980), Suicide in Brisbane—A retrospective psychosocial study. *Aust. NZ J. Psychiat.*, 14:37–45.
Clements, C.D., Sider, R.C. & Perlmutter, R.A. (1981), The ethics of suicide: Act and intervention. In: *Science and Morality*, ed. D. Teichler-Zallen & C. D. Clements. Lexington, MA: Heath, pp. 239–251.
Durkheim E. (1897), *Suicide*. Glencoe, IL: Free Press, 1951.

Egland, J. A. & Sussex, J. N. (1985), Suicide and family loading for affective disorders. *J. Amer. Med. Assn.*, 254:915–918.

Eisenberg, L. (1986), Does bad news about suicide beget bad news? *N. Eng. J. Med.*, 315–705–707.

Fawcett, J., Leff, J. & Bunney, W. E., Jr. (1969), Suicide: Clues from interpersonal communication. *Arch. Gen. Psychiat.*, 21:129–137.

—— Scheftner, W., Clark, D., Hedeker, D., Gibbons, R. & Coryell, W. (1987), Clinical predictors of suicide in patients with major affective disorders: A controlled prospective study. *Amer. J. Psychiat.*, 144:35–40.

Freud, S. (1901), The psychopathology of everyday life. *Standard Edition*, 6. London: Hogarth Press, 1960.

—— (1909), Notes upon a case of obsessional neurosis. *Standard Edition* 10:153–318. London: Hogarth Press, 1955.

—— (1915), Thoughts for the times on war and death. *Standard Edition*, 14:275–300. London: Hogarth Press, 1957.

—— (1917), Mourning and melancholia. *Standard Edition* 14:237–260. London: Hogarth Press, 1957.

—— (1920), Beyond the pleasure principle. *Standard Edition* 18:3–66. London: Hogarth Press, 1955.

Gedo, J. (1975), Forms of idealization in the analytic transference. *J. Amer. Psychoanal. Assn.* 23:485–505.

Goldberg, A. (1977), Some countertransference phenomena in the analysis of perversion. *The Annual of Psychoanalysis*, 5:105–119. New York: International Universities Press.

Gould, M. S. & Shaffer, D. (1986), The impact of suicide in television movies: Evidence of imitation. *N. Eng. J. Med.*, 315:690–694.

Hirschfeld, R.M.A. & Davidson, L. (1988), Risk factors for suicide. In: *Review of Psychiatry*, Vol. 7, ed. A. J. Frances & R. E. Hales. Washington, DC: American Psychiatric Press, pp. 307–333.

Holden, C. (1986), Youth suicide: New research focus on a growing social problem. *Science*, 233:839–841.

Kernberg, O. (1974), Contrasting viewpoints regarding the nature and psychoanalytic treatment of narcissistic personalities: A preliminary communication. *J. Amer. Psychoanal. Assn.*, 22:255–267.

Klein, M. (1964), *A Contribution to the Psychogenesis of Manic-Depressive States.* New York: McGraw-Hill.

Klerman, O. L. (1986), *Suicide and Depression among Adolescents and Young Adults.* Washington, DC: American Psychiatric Press.

Kohut, H. (1971), *The Analysis of the Self.* New York: International Universities Press.

—— (1977), *The Restoration of the Self.* New York: International Universities Press.

—— (1980), Reflections on advances in self psychology. In: *Advances in Self Psychology*, ed. A. Goldberg. New York: International Universities Press, pp. 473–554.

—— (1984), *How Does Analysis Cure?* ed. A. Goldberg & P. E. Stepansky. Chicago: University of Chicago Press.

Mack, J. E. (1986), Adolescent suicide: An architectural model. In: *Suicide and Depression Among Adolescents and Young Adults*, ed. G. L. Klerman. Washington, DC: American Psychiatric Press.

—— & Hickler, H. V. (1981), *The Life and Suicide of an Adolescent Girl.* Boston, MA: Little, Brown.

Maris, R. W. (1981), *Pathways to Suicide.* Baltimore, MD: Johns Hopkins University Press.

Meissner, W. W. (1977), Psychoanalytic notes on suicide. *Internat. J. Psychoanal. Psychother.* 6:415–447.

Menninger, K. A. (1938), *Man Against Himself.* New York: Harcourt Brace.

Murphy, G. E. (1986), Suicide and attempted suicide. In: *The Medical Basis of Psychiatry,* ed. G. Winokur & P. Clayton. Philadelphia, PA: Saunders, pp. 562–579.

——— (1988, Prevention of suicide. In: *Review of Psychiatry,* Vol. 7, ed. A. J. Frances & R. E. Hales. Washington, DC: American Psychiatric Press, pp. 403–421.

——— & Robins, E. (1967), Social factors in suicide. *J. Amer. Med. Assn.,* 199:303–308.

Ornstein, A. (1983), An idealizing transference of the oedipal phase. In: *Reflections on Self Psychology,* ed. J. D. Lichtenberg & S. Kaplan. Hillsdale, NJ: The Analytic Press, pp. 135–148.

Ornstein, P. H. & Kay, J. (1983), Ethical problems in the psychotherapy of the suicidal patient. *Psychiat. Ann.,* 13:322–340.

Pfeffer, C. R., *The Suicidal Child.* New York: Guilford Press.

Phillips, D. P. (1974), The influence of suggestion on suicide: Substantive and theoretical implications of the Werther effect. *Amer. Sociol. Rev.,* 39:340–354.

——— & Carstensen, M. S. (1986), Clustering of teenage suicides after television news stories about suicide. *N. Eng. J. Med.,* 315–685–689.

Robins, E., Murphy, G. E., Wilkinson, R. H., Gassner, S. & Kayes, J. (1959), Some clinical considerations in the prevention of suicide based on a study of 134 successful suicides. *Amer. J. Pub. Health,* 49:888–899.

Schneidman, E. S. (1979), An overview: Personality, motivation, and behavior. In: *Theories in Suicide,* ed. L. D. Hankoff & M. S. Einsidler. Littleton, MA: PSG, pp. 143–163.

Schulsinger, F., Kety, S. S., Rosenthal, D. & Wender, P. H. (1979), A family study of suicide. In: *Origin, Prevention, and Treatment of Affective Disorders,* ed. M. Schou & E. Stromgen. New York: Academic Press, pp. 278–287.

Tolpin, M. (1978), Self objects and oedipal objects: A crucial developmental distinction. *The Psychoanalytic Study of the Child* 33:157–184. New Haven, CT: Yale University Press.

Tucker, M. E. (1987), Nev. jury to rule whether heavy metal rock music can entice teens to attempt suicide. *Clin. Psychiat. News,* 15:3.

Zilboorg, G. (1936), Suicide among civilized and primitive races. *Amer. J. Psychiat.,* 92:1347–1369.

———, (1937), Considerations on suicide with particular reference to that of the young. *Amer. J. Orthopsychiat.,* 7:15–31.

Applied

Chapter 11

The Self in Jung and Kohut

Lionel Corbett
Paul K. Kugler

The concepts of the self found in the work of Jung and Kohut differ conceptually, ontologically and morphogenetically. While at times Jung and Kohut use the term "self" to refer to very similar clinical phenomena, on other occasions their use of the term refers to strikingly different aspects and functions of the psyche.

This essay proposes that the work of these two psychologists, while different, is complementary and that Jung's earlier concept of the self can provide a useful backdrop against which to understand the later formulations of Kohut. To illustrate this relationship more precisely, let us begin with a brief summary of the self concept in the work of these two theorists, followed by a discussion of ways the two concepts may usefully be interrelated.

KOHUT'S SELF PSYCHOLOGY

Kohut's (1971, 1977, 1984) self psychology is both an intrapsychic and an interpersonal theory. The child's psychological life is determined by, and, in a sense, composed of, the result of the interaction of the young child's early relationships with his or her caregivers and certain innate, "nuclear" narcissistic determinants. These determinants are the infantile potentials for mature self-esteem and a cohesive sense of self. They consist of the archaic, grandiose self, that pole of the infantile nuclear self which eventually leads to the development of ambition and self-assertion, and the image of an idealized parent, which leads to the development of personal goals and values. The tension between these two poles is bridged by a third factor, the individual's innate abilities. For Kohut, the development of a self is synonymous with the maturation and vicissitudes of these narcissistic concerns. In his later work, Kohut moved from positing two separate lines of development (the narcissistic and object relational) to a single line of self-development.

Without true boundaries between self and others, the childhood self consists of selfobjects (objects experienced emotionally as if they were parts of the child), which provide the adhesive necessary for the personality to develop structural integrity. Depending on the quality of the relationship between the child and his selfobjects in infancy, the adult self develops psychic integrity varying from cohesiveness to fragmentation; its level of vitality varies from vigor to enfeeblement, and it may be more or less internally harmonious or chaotic. A structurally firm self allows the personality to tolerate loss, failure, disappointment, or triumph without excessive fluctuations of self-esteem. Affects, impulses, object relationships, perception, and cognition and then integrated into an experience of the subjective unity of the personality. In other theoretical systems many of these functions are considered to be related to the ego; in fact, Kohut's use of the term "self" is similar to the early use of the word "ego," before this was used to designate a set of psychological operations. Self psychology is clearly distinct from object relations theory, since the object is considered to build organization and intrapsychic structure, and not simply to be the object of drives.

Self-disturbances may vary from psychoses and borderline states to narcissistic character disorders. These disturbances, according to Kohut, are not due to conflict in relation to the parents, but are structural deficits that occur when early selfobjects fail to respond empathically (that is, with adequate effective attunement) to the child. Such failure leads to painful childhood experiences of being fragmented, empty, depleted, unreal, or hopeless. Many symptoms, at all levels of disturbance, including addictions, overeating, and sexual perversions, which were formerly thought to be secondary to intrapsychic conflict, can in this light be seen as attempts to counteract the sense of internal emptiness, fragmentation, or depletion produced by a selfobject milieu that was chronically emotionally deficient (Tolpin and Kohut, 1980). Failure of parental empathy, in Kohut's psychology, leads to the experience of emotional deficit, resulting in a self requiring restoration. Where Freud views man as suffering primarily from guilt and conflict, Kohut views the primary cause of emotional suffering to be *incompleteness*—a concept also found throughout Jung's work.

Historically, Kohut's immediate intellectual precursors are Hartmann (1964) and Aichhorn (1936). In attempting to clarify the difference between ego and self, Hartmann defined narcissism as the libidinal cathexis of the self, then understood as an intrapsychic representation. Kohut differs from Hartmann in several important respects: 1) Kohut initially conceptualized "narcissistic libido" as primary, distinct from sexual libido, and thus having its own developmental course. Eventually, he abandoned the concept of narcissistic libido, along with the drive-defense model of psychopathology. 2) Hartmann's self is a self-representation, not the superordinate structure it later became for Kohut. 3) Kohut conceives of the self as a purely narcissistic structure, derived from primary narcissistic determinants. Healthy narcissism is synonymous with normal self development.

Kohut was influenced by Aichorn in two ways. First, Aichorn was Kohut's personal analyst in Vienna; and, second, Kohut's theory of the development of the self was influenced by Aichorn's work with delinquents. According to Kohut, Aichorn's therapy with juvenile delinquents had safely mobilized an idealizing transference, which his patients deeply longed for. In terms of classical theory, Aichorn's therapy with adolescents illustrates the transformation of infantile narcissism into an ego ideal (Havens, 1986).

Kohut's (1971) early theory of the self (in the "narrower" sense) permitted the analysis of patients who could not be analyzed using classical techniques. In this work, Kohut describes the self as a mental structure that has self-representations within the id, ego, and superego. The self is conceived of as a content of the mental apparatus, but not as one of the agencies of the mind. "Agency" here refers to id, ego, and superego in the sense that these putative mental systems carry out groups of related functions. The self is not simply a set of mental operations related to a common function but is "the way a person experiences himself as himself"—a permanent mental structure consisting of a collection of feelings, memories, and behaviors that are subjectively experienced as being continuous in time and as being "me." The self is also a "felt center of independent initiative," and an "independent recipient of impressions." Kohut's (1977) self is the center of the individual's psychological universe. He asserts, however, that he has not precisely defined the term, nor does he feel that this is a necessary prerequisite for its theoretical usefulness.

In this later work, Kohut developed the concept of the self in a "broader" sense, conceiving the drives themselves to be constituents of the self. This reformulation allowed the tripartite model to be bypassed and set the stage for his notion of the bipolar self.

Kohut describes a group of patients who spontaneously develop a mirror or an idealizing transference, or a mixture of the two. The quality of the transference is determined by the extent to which the establishment of the patient's self is incomplete. These transferences are fundamentally different from those of patients with a cohesive self, but who suffer from unconscious intrapsychic conflicts. In the latter case, the analyst is experienced as a current version of the parents, toward whom libidinal and aggressive drives are directed. However, in the case of the developmentally earlier transference, the analyst is experienced not as a separate individual, but as a selfobject, functioning either as part of the self or in the service of the self. Because early childhood needs for mirroring or idealizing were frustrated, the injured self, with its specific needs, is reactivated. When archaic grandiosity is involved, the resultant mirror transference revives the need for a mirroring and affirming selfobject, whereas the idealizing transference revives the childhood need for an idealized, powerful, and omnipotent selfobject. Such transferences occur either when the development of the patient's self has been arrested or in order to restore its vitality and consolidate its cohesiveness.

The successful working through of the mirror transference in therapy leads to the acquisition of mature self-assertion and ambition, while the working through of the idealizing transference culminates in the acquisition of internalized ideals and values. The person's innate talents and abilities, which bridge these two poles, may then be used in the service of ambition and ideals whose forerunners exist in the nuclear self of childhood.

Kohut postulated the existence of a separate line of development for narcissism, distinct from the development of object love and hate. Through this new formulation, he could explain why early narcissism was not transformed into object love and, therefore, why classical psychoanalysis was not successful in the treatment of narcissistic disorders through the attempt at resolution of oedipal conflicts. Thus, in a radical departure from Freud, narcissism was no longer seen as pathological, and its appearance in treatment was not considered defensive. This idea represented a major step away from a purely linear, unimodal, sexual theory of neurosis toward a superordinate psychology of the self. Although Kohut's self remains monomodal, it is unclear why he conceives of the self in terms of these particular "poles," since there are other conceptual models available. Various authors (for example, Meissner, 1986) have taken issue with the concept of the self as reducible to purely narcissistic concerns, but this theoretical debate may be more of a semantic problem arising from how one defines the terms "self" and "narcissism," rather than a fundamental difference in clinical observation.

JUNG'S CONCEPT OF THE SELF

Jung's (1969a) concept paradoxically refers both to the regulating center and the contents of the total personality. It cannot be described in any singular, unitary way. We have, therefore, collected Jung's various uses of the term in the following four sections.

The Self as the Principle of Order and Totality, and Its Symbolic Representation

The self is the principle of structure and order within the psyche. It motivates the personality toward the realization of its potential wholeness through the process of individuation. For Jung (1969a) individuation means the gradual unfolding of the self throughout the life span. The self is also conceived of as the totality of the conscious and unconscious psyche, and its ultimate purpose is the integration of the personality. For Jung, the psyche is viewed as a self-regulating system that attempts to maintain equilibrium just as the body equilibrates its metabolism. The organizing center from which this regulating effect arises is the self. For example, if the conscious attitude becomes too onesided or unbalanced, the self readjusts psychic equilibrium by producing compensations in the unconscious in the form of symptoms, dreams, or fantasies. The compensations are not simply illusory wish fulfillments, but actual psychic facts that become even more actual the more they are defended against. For example, the more we ignore eating, the more hungry we become. Failure to integrate the self-motivated compensations simply maintains the conscious attitude that prompted the compensatory symptoms in the first place.

Consider for a moment Jung's views on how the self is symbolized, or self-represented. It is axiomatic in Jungian psychology that the self depicts its own processes through the production of specific imagery. Use of the term "image" or "imago" in analytical psychology does not refer to a merely empirical representation of an outer object, but to the result of an interaction between the outer environmental influences (contents of perception) and the specific psychic reactions of the individual. An imago of mother, for example, does not simply represent mother but is the result of the interaction of the actual mother with the child's unique emotional reactions and unconscious fantasies. The mental image, therefore, reflects the historical event or object with very considerable qualifications. But, more important, the imago is a distinct psychological entity existing independently of any historical referent. Even when the parents have long been dead, their imagos still are somehow present and lead a shadowy but nonetheless potent existence in the child's mind. The continued existence of the imago is autonomous, independent of the agents responsible for its creation. Just here, we can sense the therapeutic significance of differentiating the imago from its objective referent. As long as the imago is identified with the actual behavior of the object in the outer world, for example, the erotically excited father imago identified with the actual father, the presence of the imago as a distinct psychological entity within the personality will remain unconscious. Psychic reality will be fused with physical reality; the finger pointing toward the moon will be confused with the moon itself. In contemporary painting, the distinction between object and imago has been ingeniously portrayed by Rene Magritte in his painting of a green Meershaum pipe. Magritte entitled this work (English translation), "This is Not a Pipe" (see Kugler, 1987).

By attributing "objectivity" to the psyche's imagos, Jung takes a philosophical position midway between empiricism and idealism. The empiricist position, on one hand, focuses on "natural," objective "things," untouched by the human psyche; whereas the idealist position insists that we never "know" the objective world directly, but only through subjective, innate ideas, a priori categories, or projective horizons. Jung, however, views the imago as ontologically primary, more fundamental than either objective things or subjective ideas (the ego's images). The imagos of "things" constitute psychic reality and are as autonomous as the things themselves. They are experienced just as objectively and autonomously as objects in the outer world. These imagos constitute Jung's "objective psyche" and provide us with a sense of interiority, otherness, and psychic reality. Imagos are not simply what we see, but the way in which we become conscious of our inner life in relation to the outer world.

Self-imagos are no exception. They arise from a conjunction of outer environmental influences (selfobjects) with the specific reactions of the individual. Let us be more specific about what this conjunction implies. For Jung, the self image is "determined as to its content only when it has become conscious and is therefore filled out with the material of conscious experience. Its form, however, . . . might perhaps be compared to the axial system of a crystal which as it were, preforms the crystalline structure in the mother liquid although it has no material existence of its own" (Jung, 1969a, pp. 79–80).

Jung applied this structural notion to the problematics of perception and apperception, suggesting that the individual's unconscious and conscious experiences are organized according to psychological laws—archetypes. The archetypes constitute a microscale of laws of the personality, analogous to individuals within a society where the self as "governing" principle emerges out of the consensual interaction of these archetypal elements. The self contributes the emergent macroscale structuralization within the personality.

Images of the self appear in various forms, ranging from the most abstract to the most human, depending on which aspect of the self is being stressed. The psychic factor being emphasized in the image usually compensates for whichever aspect of the personality is being ignored by ego consciousness. For Jung, psychic images function as symbols that bridge conscious perceptions with unconscious apperceptions and heal through a reconciliation of these apparent opposites within the psyche.

Empirically, self-symbols often possess a numinous character and are experienced as awe inspiring, powerful, attractive, and mysterious. Historically, this numinous quality has often led to their religious characterization culturally. The unconscious, for Jung, functions autonomously from the point of view of consciousness and thus seems to behave objectively (as if independent of the subjective will). In contrast to Freud's concept of the repressed unconscious, Jung believed that the unconscious is the original psychological matrix out of which the experience of individual, self-reflexive, conditioned consciousness arises. Jung is very clear about this transcendant or transpersonal aspect of the self, which might be related to the concept of the Atman in Vedic philosophy (Jung, 1969a). Jung's self, therefore, also corresponds to the traditional religious idea that the core of the self is in fact eternal and related to the divine (psyche in its original sense of soul). The psychic blueprint is a preexistent given, not simply a byproduct of developmental processes. Addressing the issue of whether his approach to the psyche is essentially religious, Jung (1967) writes that he tried to "strip things of their metaphysical wrappings in order to make them objects of psychology" (p. 49). Through this procedure he attempted to discover primary psychological facts that had been obscured by theological elaboration and dogmatic literalizing.

In Kohut's terms, Jung's self is both experience-distant as a metapsychological concept, but also experience-near when experienced as immanent through a personal symbolic experience. Such experiences may take several forms, occurring in dreams, in fantasies, or in projection onto figures in the world. Typical symbols that mediate the experience of the self include:

1) Geometric figures suggesting symmetry, wholeness, and completion, particularly forms such as the circle or square (and their derivatives such as cities and wheels), or motifs containing quarternities, a number traditionally expressing completeness.

2) Human figures that are idealized or transcendant, such as those of royalty, the priesthood, savior figures (Christ, Buddha), or any human being who is sufficiently admired to warrant carrying such projections.

3) Figures representing a union of opposites, for the self is a "complexio oppositorum" (Jung, 1971) [a complex of opposites] with a "paradoxical, antinomial character" (Jung 1968a, p. 225) Kohut's self is also structured as a pair of opposites in the sense that grandiosity implies that the greatest value lies within the person, whereas idealization locates this within another individual. However, for Jung, many other pairs of intrapsychic opposites can also be found within the self. For instance, in dreams the self may be represented by a king and queen, a marriage pair, a hermaphrodite, an elderly wisdom figure accompanied by a child, and the like. These images of unity transcend oppositions such as self and other, male and female, age and youth, the developmental past and the future potential. Thus they attempt to heal the fragmentation that occurs when consciousness identifies with only one side of the image.

4) The self may also be symbolized as an awe-inspiring natural phenomenon, such as an animal, mountain, lake, or tree. It is commonly (some Jungians would say always) the true subject of religions, mythology, and fairy tales, where it may be referred to as "the treasure hard to attain," the "pearl of great price," or the "panacea."

Jung's (1968b) research into the phenomenology of the self led to his interest in arcane subjects such as alchemy. He felt that depth psychology needed an outside system of reference with which to compare itself and that the tradition of alchemy provided just such an opportunity to study a record of the structure and dynamics of the psyche in projected form. For instance, the "gold" (the "aurora apprehensio," golden understanding) which the alchemists worked toward extracting out of their states of "chaos," psychologically represented the achievement of an inner sense of value, understanding, coherence, and permanence. This result was brought about by a gradual process of becoming conscious of intrapsychic processes experienced as chaotic or depressed in their original "leaden" state. The true goal of the alchemical opus was the production of a coherent experience of the self. Jung considered alchemy to be an example of the projection of internal psychic states onto the material operations of the laboratory. Thus, the alchemical opus represented a self-motivated process toward individuation. Alchemical texts are precise records in symbolic language of unconscious processes projected onto physical substances. Their symbolic work focused partially on those psychic contents that were not consciously being integrated by the dominant system of consciousness of the time, namely, Christianity. Their work illustrated attempts to integrate the unconscious aspects of the culture in which they were immersed.

The Self as Center, and Its Relationship to Ego

At the same time as the self is a totality, it is also the true center of the whole personality, just as the ego is the felt center of consciousness. In Jung's psychology, "ego" does not mean a set of mental operations but rather is used in practice as though it were roughly synonymous with the experience of personal identity. But Jung (1970) also regarded the ego as "a highly complex affair full of unfathomable obscurities . . . as a relatively constant personification of the unconscious itself, or as the Schopenhauerian mirror in which the unconscious becomes aware of its own face" (p. 107). The difference between ego and self is essentially one of standpoint (p. 110). Thus, the idea of the self as center implies a "deeper" or more fundamental center of the psyche than can be experienced by ego-consciousness. It is a virtual midpoint that acts as a psychological center of gravity (Jung, 1966) pointing to a level of the psyche that is ultimately unknowable. The "ego" is that aspect of the self which is experienced as personal and self-reflexive. According to Jung (1966), through the process of individuation, the ego increasingly experiences itself as an object of a superordinate subject. The ego stands to the self as the moved to the mover (Jung, 1969). Thus, the self is the preexistent matrix from which consciousness arises. In refusing to reduce the psyche to an epiphenomenon of the brain or derive consciousness from brain physiology, Jung, following in the tradition of Plato and Kant, accounts for the origin of the unconscious—or the self—by positing a priori categories (archetypes) of the psyche. These structures represent Jung's ontological ground and are irreducible to any more fundamental phenomenon. Continual interaction between the ego and its ontological ground, the self, is essential for mental health.

Without ego consciousness, the self could not be realized in the outer world; and without the self, the ego has no depth, meaning, or source of integration. What Kohut (1971) refers to as the experience of a cohesive self, Jung frequently describes as the experience of the internal unity or integration of the personality.

The Self as an Image of the Highest Value Within the Psyche

The self throughout history has been projected onto images of the divine. For Jung (1968b) the self functions as an intrapsychic god image, a symbol of the highest value and hierarchical dominant within the psyche. While Jung (1969c) acknowledges the psychological reality of god images, he makes *no* metaphysical or theological claims as to the existence of an extrapsychic god. This point is widely misunderstood. Clarifying the issue, Jung (1969b) writes, "It must be remembered that the image (of God) and the statement (the *Bible*) are psychic processes which are different from their transcendental object" (p. 363). Jung's focus is on the phenomenology of self-images in religious systems, not on making metaphysical assertions about transcendental objects. Different religions and mythological systems document the evolution and vicissitudes of self images, and as such are valuable sources of information about human psychology quite apart from considerations of historical or theological "truth." In modern times, for instance, self-images have also been projected onto secular "religions," such as science, money, political systems, and even psychoanalytic schools of thought and their founders. For example, Jung or Kohut may function as projection carriers for the self-image of some of their followers.

The Self and the Intrapsychic Problem of Morality

The self is psychic totality; therefore, the self-image, with its light and dark, "good" and "bad" aspects, is not entirely benign. If the self is the totality of the psyche and evil exists as a psychological reality, then evil must be an essential aspect of the intrapsychic god image. This realization led Jung (1964) into an exploration of the problem of evil and opened him to the inevitable criticism this position would provoke from theologians committed to the belief that evil is simply the absence of good *privatio boni*. Consequently, the individual is confronted with the moral problem of mediating the tension between the intrapsychic opposites of good and evil inherent in human nature. Morality for Jung thereby became an inherent intrapsychic problem, not only a societal function of imposing a superego on an individual. For Jung, each person must make moral judgments based on the tension between ego consciousness and the superordinate demands of the self. A conscious attitude that ignores the strivings of the self is immoral. One function of the self is to reconcile dialecticallly through symbols the opposition between good and evil within the personality.

Thus, the self is paradoxically conceived of as both the matrix of awareness and also as a goal, simultaneously a point of view and the end point of conscious development (Jung 1966, p. 239–240). Furthermore, it is both a totality and a center, possessing immanent and transcendent characteristics.

Of all Jung's theoretical formulations, the self is the most central and, until recently, the least debated. In the past decade, a variety of publications have appeared discussing the differences and similarities in theory and description between the classical Jungian self and the Kohutian self.

THE INTERFACE OF JUNG AND KOHUT

The question of the relationship between the concepts of the self in the work of Jung and Kohut has been debated by various Jungian analysts (for example, Jacoby, 1981; Schwartz-Salant, 1982; Redfearn, 1983; Samuels, 1985; Corbett, 1989). Jung's self-concept seems to have been largely ignored by self psychologists with one exception. Oremland (1985) equates Jung's self with the cosmos and suggests that Jungian therapy tends toward "mystical purpose." His essay presents a distorted view of Jung's self concept and Jungian therapy. Oremland believes that to compare Kohut and Jung would provide ammunition for Kohut's detractors. While Oremland is critical of interrelating Jung and Kohut, most other authors of comparative essays have focused constructively on the similarities and differences.

Jacoby (1981) for example, points out the following parallels between the two theorists. Kohut (1977) sees the self as the center of the psychological universe, in contrast to the more traditional Freudian view of the self as a content of the mental apparatus (that is, as a representation). This formulation is close to Jung's definition of the self. Kohut, again, bears a striking resemblance to Jung when he writes that man's ultimate goal might be "the realization, through his actions, of the blueprint for his life that had been laid down in his nuclear self" (p. 133). Further, when Kohut states that "our transient individuality also possesses a significance that extends beyond the borders of our life" (p. 180) and describes "cosmic narcissism" that transcends the boundaries of the individual (Kohut, 1966), he seems to be referring to the phenomenon Jung describes as the transpersonal/transcendant aspects of the self. This is further reflected in Kohut's view of the cognitive inpenetrability of the self per se. For Kohut (1977) only "its introspectively or empathically perceived psychological manifestations are open to us" (p. 311). Gordon (1980) also notes how Kohut (1977), while discussing Kafka and O'Neill, emphasizes man's search for wholeness and meaning, and thus is very close to Jung's association of the experience of the self with the discovery of meaning.

Schwartz-Salant (1982) believes that Kohut is attractive to Jungians because his approach his similar to Jung's synthetic or purposive attitude toward therapy. Because of Jung's opposition to the idea of psychic determinism, he characteristically adopts a "final" perspective in which the self is conceived of not simply as the sum or outcome of causal sequences and antecedent connections in the past, but also as prospective and purposive, apparently possessing a sense of future direction and intention. Hence, it cannot be analyzed purely historically. Jung (1971) maintained that no psychological fact about an individual can be explained in terms of causality alone. For many Jungians, the idea that the self points toward future development frees one from the tyranny of a psychology based purely on developmental vicissitudes. Kohut's (1966) description of the narcissistic transference, for example, is reminiscent of Jung's (1969c) insistence that the transference be understood not only in terms of its historical antecedents, but also in terms of its purposefulness.

A variety of theoretical differences also exist between Jung and Kohut. For example, one of the major differences between the two authors lies in their different theories of the origin of intrapsychic structure. For Kohut (1971) structuralization of the child's inner world is the result of the parental selfobject's empathic responsiveness to the child's innate needs, whose origin is not specified. Jung, on the other hand, postulates that the child is born with an a priori psychological matrix, out of which personal consciousness will emerge. This matrix is structured in characteristic ways (archetypes) that provide the potential for particular forms of experience, whose content is determined by the child's interaction with his specific environment. The image[1] that Kohut uses to illustrate the creation of intrapsychic

[1]When speaking about the unconscious, we can only speak metaphorically. All discussions about the unconscious become caught up in and are tropologically structured by our figures of speech. These metaphors will unconsciously structure our

structure is that of eating and assimilating food, which is digested to become part of the person. For Kohut, if we eat hamburger, we do not become hamburger, because the substance of the empathic interaction is assimilated in a unique way. This process of digestion creates the building blocks that eventuate in the development of a self. To continue within this metaphor, for Jung the unconscious contains specifically configured "enzymes" that digest the person's psychic substances (experiences) taken in during the course of the person's life, resulting in the subjective experience of personal identity. These "enzymes" are given with the person's psychic anatomy and are not simply the product of the person's interacting with his selfobjects, although the quality of this interaction is important in modifying their effects on the growth of the person.

Other theoretical differences have been noted by various authors. Jacoby (1981), for example, points out that one major difference between the two theorists is in their focus on the "location" of self-experiences. Jung provides a wealth of intrapsychic symbolic descriptions of the self, while Kohut focuses more on the transference manifestations of the self, although it is clear that these are all intrapsychic phenomena for the person. Schwartz-Salant (1982) also highlights certain differences, noting how Kohut's references to the cosmic qualities of the self are "only metaphors of little significance," not referring to the transpersonal realm of Jung's self. Further, Schwartz-Salant believes Kohut's characterization of negative affects, such as rage, as disintegration products of the self, differs significantly from Jung's idea that the self intrinsically contains both dark and light aspects. (Kohut is, however, clear that a cohesive self may experience rage as a primary expression of itself rather than as a disintegration product.) Samuels (1985) points out that Kohut's self is created during psychic development, and this notion is antithetical to Jung's concept of the self as a priori, especially when Kohut indicates that the self forms at a point in time. Samuels compares Kohut's theory of a self that gradually coalesces from smaller units to the

perception of the patient's psychology, highlighting certain aspects and filtering out others. The unconscious functioning like "digestive enzymes" is only one of many images of the unconscious used to account for the interrelation between structure and substance. Other images that have been used to depict this interaction are the relationship between architecture and building materials, the relation between syntax and lexical units, and the relation between a crystalline structure and the mother liquid. If we forget that these are only figures of speech, then the privileged metaphors in the theories we are committed to will begin to unconsciously structure our way of psychologically thinking, speaking and practicing. When this happens, the rhetorical structures in our theories will begin producing unconsciousness in our clinical practice.

theory developed by Fordham (1976, 1985), a developmentally oriented Jungian who describes the baby as possessing an initially integrated self unit that unfolds or "deintegrates" because of the interaction of its innate organizing ability with environmental experiences. Fordham is clearly presenting Jung's view, as for example, when Jung (1966) writes that the "meaning and purpose (of self-realization) is the realization in all its aspects, of the personality originally hidden away in the embryonic germ-plasm, the production and unfolding of the original potential wholeness" (p. 110). Jung's and Fordham's idea of the unfolding of innate potential, like Kohut's concept of the blueprint, raises several important questions about the origin of the self: Is the self solely the result of developmental processes with no a priori structures? Is the self given a priori with the birth of the individual? Is the self the result of innate structures interacting over time with the environment? These questions will be taken up in the next section.

THE ORIGIN AND EVOLUTION OF THE SELF

This section focuses on the problem of how a self self-organizes. Both Jung (1966) and Kohut (1977) assume that the infant is born with a nuclear blueprint of a self. This position presents certain problems. For example, to account for the origin of the blueprint of the self, these theories presuppose a designer, an agent more complex than the phenomenon being explained. Kohut, for example, posits two originary needs (mirroring and idealizing) and poles (the idealized and the grandiose), which set in motion an intrapsychic dialectic creating the self. This, however, sidesteps the problem of explaining how a self self-organizes out of simpler components. Either Kohut believes the origin and evolution of the self can be accounted for by the reduction of psychological development to brain mechanisms (the two poles of the self originate in physiology, which, in turn, is structured through another "blueprint" posited outside the field of psychology in genetics), or he assumes psychic organizing principles that are independent of the physiological structures embodying the mental properties (Yates and Kugler, 1984). Kohut's position here is not clear, although some self psychologists seem inclined to reduce the "blueprint" to a more ontologically primary physiological substratum.

Jung (1969) approaches the problem of self-organization differently, positing archetypes as self-organizing psychic principles. He still begs the question of morphogenesis, but at least Jung keeps psychology's first principles *within* their own realm of discourse, broadening our empirical base of observation, rather than projecting the "source" of self-organization onto the environment, the cerebral cortex, or the genetic code.

The problem of accounting for "the apparent intentionality of living systems without *without reaching outside the frame of the system itself* to get the answer" confronts all natural sciences (Kugler, 1986, italics added). Explaining the complex organization of the personality without appealing to structuring principles outside the system is the challenge. Important in this respect is differentiating between microscopic and macroscopic descriptions of the same system. There has been, for example, a tradition in physiologically based psychology to look for "smart" microscopic cells ("grandmother" cells) to explain macroscopic psychological events. Explaining the old mind-body problem in this way has never been successful because the model inevitably regresses into either genetics, the physical environment, or innate metaphysical first principles, without ever accounting for their structurality. The question confronting the attempt to understand self-organization is how macroscopic psychic regularities can emerge out of microscopic physiological elements such that the psychological regularities exhibit autonomy and sovereignty. The psychological cannot be reduced to the physiological because psychic events have their own regularity, describable by laws. The regularities of the personality form the basis for Jung's archetypes, which behave like intrapsychic laws, just as biological regularities form the basis for the laws of physiology and, on yet a more microscopic level, physical regularities form the basis for the laws of physics. The essential point is that at each level (psychological, biological, physical) the laws are autonomous of the other levels (Kugler and Turvey, 1987). Furthermore, laws, by definition, are *nonembodied*. Whereas rules run into the problems of representationalism and the regress problem of embodiment, laws avoid this dilemma. The laws of the self (archetypes) are not embodied in genes, the cerebral cortex, the physical environment or the metaphysical, but simply are lawful consequences of the boundary conditions of physiology, which is in turn governed by the lawful consequences of the boundary conditions of the physical world.

Jung's concept of a self-organizing objective psyche is analogous to the biological theory of morphogenetic fields. In embryology, for example, morphogenetic field is currently being used to explain the development of more complex from less complex living forms where the whole becomes more than the sum of its parts. This is also true in psychology. The emergent properties of the self as an organizing psychic system are more complex than the sum of its parts and may account for the purposeful and prospective aspect of the self. The idea of an objective psyche is in accord with a process that has also taken place within other sciences, namely, the relativizing of man in relation to nature. In physics and biology we are not longer quite as anthropocentric as we were.

Jung's emphasis on an original wholeness that is experienced as fragmented and requires reuniting parallels physicist David Bohm's (1980) theory of implicate and explicate order. Implicate order refers to an original holographiclike unity, as opposed to classical physics' perception of reality as separated into discrete parts, as if viewed through a lens. The implicate order includes the whole of reality;[2] when unfolded, this is experienced as fragmented or explicate. Bohm believes that the implicate order applies to consciousness as well as matter, and in the unbroken wholeness of the implicate order, consciousness cannot be separated from matter. In modern physics, reality is conceived of as an inseparable whole structured into dynamic patterns that cannot be disembedded from their context without destroying its self-organization. Analogously, it is not possible to study microscopic intrapsychic events and structures as if they were building blocks from which the whole could be understood.

Freud's world view was based on 19th-century mechanistic physics, committed to studying reality by breaking it down into its component parts. Jung (1969c), on the other hand, was deeply influenced by his collaboration with physicist Wolfgang Pauli, a pioneer in the study of quantum mechanics and the physics of consciousness. Jung was one of the first analysts to extend Heisenberg's theory of the interdependency of the observer and the object of observation to the realm of psychology, noting that the analyst-observer significantly influences what is clinically observed in the patient's unconscious. Since the psyche is not particulate and clearly does not obey the Neutonian model, we cannot yet say what, if any, physical model is applicable to it.

According to Jung, the human psyche is "composed of" consciousness, an irreducible quality, containing an information matrix to allow the development of the personality. Jung's self is an original whole, or undifferentiated source of consciousness. While it initially lacks the capacity for self-reflection, it might be conceived of as the source

---

[2]This corresponds to Jung's concept of the "unus mundus," a level of reality characterized by the interrelatedness or oneness of all things. It has been suggested that Jung developed this concept as a defense against the threat of disintegration of his personal self. It is unlikely that modern subatomic particle physicists also suffer from disintegration anxiety.

of the blueprint for Kohut's self, with its archetypal components (the laws of the psyche) functioning as the morphogenetic determinants of its development.

It is not surprising that Kohut's two major narcissistic determinants are also found in Jung's phenomenology of the self. Kohut's infantile grandiosity appears in Jungian psychology in various ways. First, as the state prior to ego-self differentiation. This condition reappears whenever the ego becomes identified with the self, producing a sense of grandiosity. Kohut's idealized parent imago, on the other hand, is understood in analytical psychology to result from the "projection" of the experience of the self onto the parent.

While Jung does not present elaborate descriptions of these experiences as they occur interpsychically within the context of transference and countertransference, he does extensively discuss their various intrapsychic representations. These two archetypal aspects of the self, infantile grandiosity and the idealized parental imago, Jung describes phenomenologically as the archetypes of the "divine child" and "the great mother" (idealized mother imago). The image of the divine child, with its combination of helplessness, unusual power, and capacity for miraculous deeds, reflects Kohut's archaic infantile grandiosity. For Jung, mythologies express psychological truths, or the dynamics of the self; the tension between the grandiose and the idealized pole, the divine child and the idealized "great mother," is found as the principal theme in many of the great mythologies: the stories of Jesus, Zeus, Horus, Krishna, Dionysius, Hermes, and so on. According to Jung, the image and theme of the divine child in dreams, fantasies, and myths reflect futurity, beginning and end, invincibility, and potential for growth, as the personality flows into the future, paving the way for future change, anticipating the synthesis of conscious and unconscious elements. Neumann (1934), a colleague of Jung's, describes the fateful psychic interrelation between the divine child and the idealized mother: "Even for the youthful god, the Great Mother is fate. How much more, for the child, whose nature it is to be an appendage of her body" (p. 43). Neumann amplifies the mythologies of the mother goddess and her divine son-lover, demonstrating how myths such as those of Attis, Adonis, Tammuz and Osiris reflect the need of the developing child to differentiate itself from containment within the mother. Kohut's self psychology, with its emphasis on the child's need to differentiate consciousness through the experience of frustration, mirrors such mythic dynamics. Neumann's pioneering work emphasizes the importance of mirroring in infancy and its function in differentiating the mother-child dyad (Samuels, 1985). For Neumann, the mother "carries" the image of the child's self in unconscious projection, functioning "as" the baby's self. Neumann further observes that the infant experiences a self only in relation to mother and her maternal capacity to mirror back the child's selfhood.[3] The child's development is dependent on both the mother's capacity to mirror and the infant's innate capacity meaningfully to structure such an experience. That aspect of the child's psyche which structures this experience, the archetype of the mother, represents the transpersonal quality of the self evoked in the human relationship. Just as the structuring laws of physics (gravity, the speed of light) are experienced as superordinate to matter, so, too, are the organizing laws of the self experienced as superordinate to the personal relationship. The apperception of an underlying organizing principle contributes a sense of numinosity to the child's experience of his mother. She is idealized and related to "as if" she were the Great Mother goddess. This idealization is repeated in the idealizing transference relationship, when the self is projected onto the analyst and the patient therapeutically lives out the missing relationship to the idealized other. In Jung's (1966) work, this form of the transference is referred to as an archetypal transference, since the patient is projecting mythological rather than purely personal material, and these contents tend to behave autonomously (see also Corbett, 1989).

Jung (1973), in response to a letter from a student concerning how technically to handle a difficult patient, wrote the following:

> In some such cases, it is always advisable not to analyze too actively, and that means letting the transference run its course quietly and listening sympathetically. . . . No technical-analytic attitude, please, but an essentially human one. The patient needs you in order to unite her dissociated (internally split) personality in your unity, calm and security. For the present, you must only stand by without too many therapeutic intentions. The patient will get out of you what she needs [p. xxxiii].

This comment by Jung about the correct therapeutic attitude and the curative function of the transference, bears a certain resemblance to Kohut's.

SUMMARY

Jung's theory of the self, emphasizing its intrapsychic phenomenology, is significantly complemented by Kohut's self psychology, with

---

[3]Modern observations of infant development have cast doubt on this notion, (e.g., Stern, 1985). The post-Jungian writer Fordham (1976) also disagrees and stresses the existence of a primary self in the child not dependent on the mother.

its view on the vicissitudes of the self in particular transference/ countertransference relationships. Jung's and Kohut's theories provide important contributions to our understanding of the function of the self in the organization of the psyche, the generation of psychopathology and the production of intra and inter-personal dynamics.

Finally, we would like to emphasize the need for more integrative attempts between the various branches of depth psychology. Those of us involved with particular schools of thought started around charismatic leaders know how difficult it is to resolve an idealizing transference to such an individual and his theories and how powerful is the twinship transference that needs the affirming sameness of one's colleagues. There is, however, no need for analysts to perpetuate the personal heritage of father-son difficulties that Freud and Jung transmitted to some of their followers.

REFERENCES

Aichhorn, A. (1936), The narcissistic transference of the "Juvenile Impostor." In: *Delinquency and Child Guidance*, ed. O. Fleischmann, P. Kramer & H. Ross. New York: International Universities Press, 1964, pp. 174–191.

Bohm, D. (1980), *Wholeness and the Implicate Order*. London: Routledge & Kegan Paul.

Corbett, L. (1989), Kohut and Jung: A comparison of theory and therapy. In: *Self Psychology: Comparisons and Contrasts*, ed. D. Detrick & S. Detrick. Hillsdale, NJ: The Analytic Press.

Fordham, M. (1985), *Explorations into the Self*. London: Academic Press.

———— (1976), *The Self and Autism*. London: Heinemann Medical Books.

Gordon, R. (1980), Narcissism and the self. *J. Anal. Psychol.* 25:247–264.

Hartmann, H. (1964), *Essays on Ego Psychology*. New York: International Universities Press.

Havens, L. (1986). A theoretical basis for the concepts of self and authentic self. *J. Amer. Psychoanal. Assn.*, 34:365–000.

Jacoby, M. (1981), Reflections on Heintz Kohut's concepts of narcissism. *J. Anal. Psychol.*, 26:107–110.

Jung, C. G. (1964), Civilization in transition. In: *The Collected Works of C. G. Jung*, Vol. 10. Princeton, NJ: Princeton University Press/Bollingen Series XX.

———— (1966), Two essays on analytic psychology. In: *The Collected Works of C. G. Jung*, Vol. 7. Princeton, NJ: Princeton University Press/Bollingen Series XX.

———— (1967). Commentary on the secret of the golden flower. Alchemical studies. In: *The Collected Works of C. G. Jung*, Vol. 13. Princeton, NJ: Princeton University Press/ Bollingen Series XX.

———— (1968a), Aion. In: *The Collected Works of C. G. Jung*, Vol. 9, pt. 2. Princeton, NJ: Princeton University Press/Bollingen Series XX.

———— (1968b), Psychology and alchemy. In: *The Collected Works of C. G. Jung*, Vol. 12. Princeton, NJ: Princeton University Press/Bollingen Series XX.

———— (1969a), The archetypes and the collective unconscious. *The Collected Works of C. G. Jung*, Vol. 9, pt. 1. Princeton, NJ: Princeton University Press/Bollingen Series XX.

—— (1969b), Psychology and religion. In: *The Collected Works of C. G. Jung*, Vol. 11. Princeton, NJ: Princeton University Press/Bollingen Series XX.

—— (1969c). The structure and dynamics of the psyche. In: *The Collected Works of C. G. Jung*, Vol. 8. Princeton, NJ: Princeton University Press/Bollingen Series XX.

—— (1970), Mysterium coniunctionis. In: *The Collected Works of C. G. Jung*, Vol. 14. Princeton, NJ: Princeton University Press/Bollingen Series XX.

—— (1971), Psychological types. In: *The Collected Works of C. G. Jung*, Vol. 6. Princeton: Princeton University Press/Bollingen Series XX.

—— (1973), *Letters*, Vol. 2, ed. G. Adler. Princeton, NJ: Princeton University Press.

Kohut, H. (1966), Forms and transformations of narcissism. *J. Amer. Psychoanal. Assn.*, 14:243–272.

—— (1971), *The Analysis of the Self*. New York: International Universities Press.

—— (1977), *The Restoration of the Self*. New York: International Universities Press.

—— (1984), *How Does Analysis Cure?* ed. A. Goldberg & P. Stepansky. Chicago: University of Chicago Press.

Kugler, P. (1987), Childhood seduction: Physical and emotional. *Spring*, Spring, pp. 4–68.

—— & Turvey, M. (1987), *Information, Natural Law and the Self Assembly of Rhythmic Movements*. Hillsdale, NJ: Lawrence Erlbaum Associates.

Meissner, W. W. (1986), Can psychoanalysis find its self? *J. Amer. Psychoanal. Assn.*, 34:379–400.

Neumann, E. (1954). *The Origin and History of Consciousness*. Princeton, NJ: Princeton University Press.

Oremland, J. D. (1985), Kohut's reformulations of defense and resistance as applied in therapeutic psychoanalysis. In: *Progress in Self Psychology*, Vol. 1, ed. A. Goldberg. New York: Guilford Press.

Redfearn, J. W. T. (1983), Ego and self terminology. *J. Anal. Psychol.*, 28:91–106.

Samuels, A. (1985), *Jung and the Post Jungians*. London: Routledge & Kegan Paul.

Schwartz-Salant, N. (1982), *Narcissism and Character Transformation*. Toronto: Inner City Books.

Stern, D. (1985), *The Interpersonal World of the Infant*. New York: Basic Books.

Tolpin, M. & Kohut, H. (1980), The disorders of the self: The psychopathology of the first years of life. In: *The Course of Life*, Vol. 1, ed. S. I. Greenspan & G. H. Pollock. Washington, DC: NIMH.

Yates, F. E. & Kugler, P. N. (1984), Signs, singularities and significance: A physical model for semiotics. *Semiotica*, 52:49–77.

Chapter 12

The Myth of the Repetition Compulsion and the Negative Therapeutic Reaction: An Evolutionary Biological Analysis

Daniel Kriegman
Malcolm Owen Slavin

PSYCHOANALYSIS AND EVOLUTIONARY BIOLOGY

Evolutionary Analysis versus Biological Reductionism and Genetic Determinism

Elsewhere (Kriegman, 1988; Slavin, 1985; Slavin and Kriegman, 1988a,b) we have tried to demonstrate that an evolutionary biological analysis yields a unique perspective on some of the central controversies in psychoanalytic theory. In this paper we will extend our evolutionary biological approach directly to the clinical situation.

Many analysts, especially self psychologists, have difficulty with biological approaches to psychoanalysis, because our associations to the term "biology" are unnecessarily narrow. Biology in the narrow sense conveys the somatic, the physiological, the biochemical—the study of the physical substrate of life phenomena. Kohut (1982) was correct in saying that psychoanalysis ought to be a "psychology through and through," true to the data of vicarious introspection, not *derivative* of psychophysiological concepts. As the science of complex mental states, it should divorce itself from biology in the narrow sense. However, biology in the broad sense embraces all that the scientific study of life entails. In this sense, psychoanalysis lies within the domain of biology. It thus becomes a matter of whether we are informed and explicit about our biological assumptions, or

209

whether we tuck them in, so to speak, implicitly in unquestioned assumptions about the human condition and human nature (see Kriegman, 1988; Slavin, 1988). More about this later.

Evolutionary biological analysis is the study of how life was shaped by natural selection. Figure 1 illustrates that evolutionary biological analysis is an attempt to understand the *distal* or ultimate causes, that is the selective pressures in the evolutionary history of species (the left hand column). These are the historical and functional pressures that shaped the phenotypes we see today.

The right hand column of Figure 1 lists the *proximal* mechanisms, in other words, the current structures and processes that mediate the ongoing expression of the phenotype. Evolutionary biological analysis is basically an attempt to find the *distal causes* (or ultimate functional rationales) for *proximal mechanisms*. (This relationship is represented by the solid arrow in Figure 1.) This is not an attempt to reduce the psychological to the somatic.

Kohut (1959, 1977, 1980, 1982) presented us with the psychoanalytic arguments for the "reductionist barrier." It is not a *psychoanalytic* enterprise to try to reduce psychology to somatic biology; mixing this nonanalytic enterprise with psychoanalysis tends to obscure and

THE QUESTION OF "REDUCTIONISM" IN EVOLUTIONARY EXPLANATIONS *

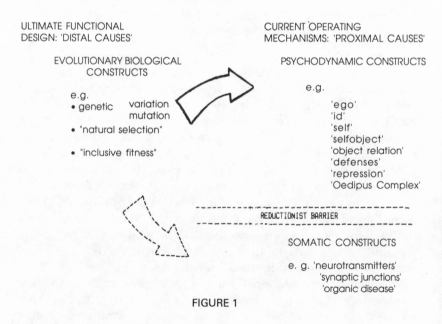

ULTIMATE FUNCTIONAL
DESIGN: 'DISTAL CAUSES'

CURRENT OPERATING
MECHANISMS: 'PROXIMAL CAUSES'

EVOLUTIONARY BIOLOGICAL
CONSTRUCTS

PSYCHODYNAMIC CONSTRUCTS

e.g.
• genetic   variation
           mutation

• "natural selection"

• "inclusive fitness"

e.g.

'ego'
'id'
'self'
'selfobject'
'object relation'
'defenses'
'repression'
'Oedipus Complex'

REDUCTIONIST BARRIER

SOMATIC CONSTRUCTS

e. g. 'neurotransmitters'
'synaptic junctions'
'organic disease'

FIGURE 1

*Adapted from Kriegman (1988)

distort the data obtained through vicarious introspection. The solid arrow in Figure 1 represents the nonreductionist relationship between evolutionary biology and "pure" psychological constructs.

What we present here is not a simplistic "evolutionism" in which every human trait is seen as an unfolding of prerecorded genetic instructions. Such deterministic attempts to explain the psyche in terms of genes (e.g., aspects of the sociobiology of Wilson, 1975) have been critiqued from many points of view (see Gould, 1977; Kitcher, 1985). What is critical for our purposes is that they tend to bypass the construct of mind and eliminate psychodynamics. In so doing they add little of interest or utility to a psychoanalytic psychology of human inner life and, especially, little of clinical interest.

Approached differently, however, evolutionary biology can provide a perspective on the nature of the world in which the basic functional design of the psyche was shaped over evolutionary time. Thus, evolution theory can help us understand the relationship of the psyche to the environment in which it evolved and must function. A more fully elaborated and accurate understanding of the functional design of the human psyche can allow us to evaluate and compare different psychoanalytic paradigms, each of which contains specific assumptions about the nature of the object world to which the human psyche is adapted.

Clearly, an evolutionary biological analysis is at such a level of theoretical remoteness from the inner workings of the psyche that it cannot, by itself, generate a psychology. The development of a model of the psyche is the proper province of psychoanalysis. Figure 2 illustrates how we can conceptualize psychodynamic "deep structure" as the crucial set of proximal mechanisms that mediate between genes and inner experience.

We are saying that psychological constructs can stand as a "pure psychology" and still be subjected to an evolutionary analysis that is, after all, our only scientific theory of creation. For example, we can speak of the adaptive pressures that led to the natural selection of the opposable thumb (a physical feature of human form) just as we can speak of the adaptive advantages of intelligent thought, a nonsomatic psychological construct. Although this psychological construct surely has physiological correlates (for example, enlarged frontal lobes), we can speak of its adaptive advantages without reference to its physiology. Similarly, we can speak of the evolutionary adaptive value of a highly developed self (Kriegman, 1988), of repression (Slavin, 1985), of drive pressures or wishes (Slavin, 1988), without reducing these psychological constructs to somatic constructs. You may wonder how this can apply even to constructs such as drives, since we are so accustomed to the highly somatic metaphors of the classical metapsy-

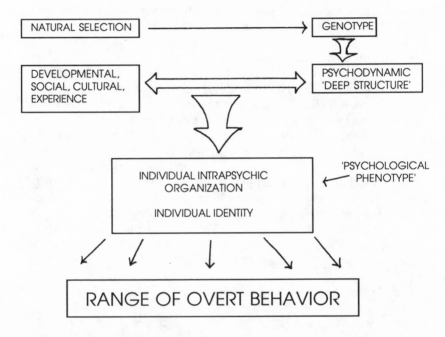

**THE QUESTION OF DETERMINISM IN
EVOLUTIONARY EXPLANATIONS**

RANGE OF OVERT BEHAVIOR

chology as the only real basis for the drives. We shall treat this matter
later on.

The Relevance of Evolutionary Biology
to Psychoanalysis

From Freud to Kohut, almost all psychoanalysts have made an evolutionary biological pitch in support of their theories. Freud was emphatically clear about the need to develop psychoanalysis within an
evolutionary context, but there were significant limitations in his
understanding of evolution (Sulloway, 1979; Slavin and Kriegman,
1988). Others have been less clear about this commitment, less
conscious in their attempt to use an evolutionary framework, but
have nonetheless appealed to the "evolutionary court" for support of
their theoretical positions.

A typical example is Kohut's (1982) attempt to understand parental
devotion to offspring. His logic was consistent with Freud's appropriate insistence that we must not exclude ourselves from the animal
kingdom even though, as we know, Kohut was extremely

wary of a certain type of reductive biologizing. Thus, Kohut implicitly argued that, as in all species whose young must receive significant parental care, the human psyche must contain an inherent tendency to act altruistically toward offspring. Kohut described this congruent fit between the needs of the child and the innate emotional response of the parent as "man's deepest and most central joy, that of being a link in the chain of generations" (p. 403).

Despite his biological disclaimers, Kohut was appropriately following an evolutionary biological line of reasoning when he applied to his own conception of intergenerational relations King's (1945) notion of normal healthy functioning: that "man's deepest and most central joy" was seen as adaptive and healthy, representing an organism functioning *"in accordance with its design"* (1945). Thus, Kohut was employing a line of thought that lies at the heart of evolutionary biology: our most basic innate pleasures motivate crucial, adaptive behavior.

In this view of normal functioning there are implicit assumptions about the nature of the *relational world*. As can be seen in Kohut's reasoning, the assumptions about human nature that underlie psychoanalytic viewpoints are frequently supported by brief appeals to the logic of functional design. This is an almost universal feature of psychoanalytic theorizing—for example, the adaptive views of Hartmann (1939), A. Freud (1936), Loewald (1965), Erikson (1964), Mahler, Pine, and Bergman (1975), Winnicott (1965), and many others. We suggest that it is an appropriate feature, yet it is rarely spelled out clearly; and the evolutionary assumptions involved are usually very simplistic or poorly understood.

Thus, every psychoanalytic position entails implicit assumptions about human nature that are, in turn, based on assumptions about the nature of the relational world in which we function. The key contribution of the evolutionary perspective is a *clarification of central aspects of the relational world to which the design of our psyche may well represent a critical adaptation.* In addition, evolution theory insists that the *psyche (and virtually all important and necessary organismic features) can properly be considered an adaptation to the environment in which an organism must survive and reproduce.*[1] Thus, as we noted earlier, evolutionary theory does not, by itself, provide us with a specific model of the psyche. This is the province of a psychology such as psychoanal-

---

[1]We will discuss the limits on this adaptationist perspective (e.g., the cautions of Stephen J. Gould) shortly. Another question has to do with the evolutionary time frame during which natural selection could have shaped the human psyche: Has natural selection had enough time to shape the human psyche?

ysis. Evolutionary theory clarifies our assumptions about the nature of the relational world and provides a set of criteria for generating and evaluating the adaptive validity of different models of the mind.

Since every psychological theory has its own implicit views about the relational world, with assumptions about how the psyche is designed to fit within—or represents an adaptation to—that reality, we need a way to disentangle different views of the relational world from their underlying ideological biases. We need a different, more objective vantage point from which to compare and evaluate psychological models. We believe that evolution theory provides such an anchor in a reality that takes account of the long history of our psyche and what it shares with the rest of nature.

There are certain features of the intra- and interorganismic world that are universal for all life forms. Unless we try to restrict our

For example, take a quick look at two versions of a trait that offers almost no visible selective advantage or disadvantage. If those who possessed version A averaged 1.2 successful, healthy offspring, while those with version B averaged 1.2001 successful, healthy offspring, then even a careful observer would be unable to measure a difference in adaptive success given modern methodology. However, in just 99 generations, individuals with version B would average 692,981 more descendants than version A individuals, in a situation where version A has an eight thousandths of one percent selective disadvantage. In situations where the selective pressure is more significant— that is, measureable using available methodology, as many selection pressures are— the time necessary for evolutionary change is well within that which has been available.

> In humans . . . it takes 10,000 years for a trait with a 1% selective disadvantage to go from 99% of the population to less than one percent. . . . Yet 10,000 years is but the blink of an eye in evolutionary time. . . . The best evidence suggests that we are at least 5 million years separated from a common ancestor with the chimpanzees. The traits that differentiate us from chimpanzees have passed through at least 200,000 generations of selection [Trivers, 1985, p. 29].

We have had about 5 million years of selection since the beginning of technology (tool use); 30 million years (3 million generations) of selection since the beginning of adaptation to living in social groups; more than 50 million years (10 million generations) of adaptation to living in small face-to-face groups of kin, "friends," and dominants (Trivers, 1985).

Thus, the evolution of social patterns has had a 50 million year history for our ancestral line. Since divergence from the ancestral line we share with our nearest living primate relatives, another 200,000 generations have passed. This is more than enough phylogenetic history for the further shaping and refining of inner processes and structures for regulating interactional patterns—for the shaping of a significant part of human nature and the human psyche—part of which were shaped during a period of history when our line was coincident with other species, and part of which is a result of our unique human history. In fact, there is reason to believe that the rapid increase in brain size may have resulted from the selective pressures that result from the *social* context, specifically from living in an extended family and larger social environment, with its enormous complexities. It is currently assumed by most paleontologists that this "social selection" may account for far more of our increase in brain size than tool use, hunting skills, or the like (see Kriegman, 1988; Trivers, 1971).

vantage point to one that avoids or excludes the "blow to human narcissism" inherent in evolution theory (Freud, 1917, p. 140) we must accept these features as being part of the human world. Assumptions about reality that do not conform to these universal features need to be questioned. For our purposes here, the most important examples of these universal features are: 1) that the understanding of important central features of a species may be enhanced when adaptive/functional analyses of the features are carried out; and 2) that the genetic distinctness of all individuals in sexually reproducing species (that is, nonclones) implies that the self-interest of one individual is never the same as another's, though there may be significant overlap. The hypotheses generated in this way can then be evaluated according to how well they help to explain psychoanalytic observations. We shall use this evolutionary "anchor" to help us sort through various views of repetition and the negative therapeutic reaction.

The approach we are using differs radically, both philosophically and technically, from the aspects of Freudian biological thinking that have historically been applied to psychoanalysis, often to its detriment. Freud's earlier (1895) biological thinking and the whole classical metapsychology was a biology of proximal mechanisms (instincts and defenses) divorced from any ultimate or evolutionary functional rationale. Indeed, his biology often was precisely the somatic biology of proximal mechanisms, not the functional biology of ultimate causes. Freud's later (1913, 1915) attempts to find such an evolutionary rationale were based on an inaccurate and incomplete understanding of modern evolutionary theory (Slavin and Kriegman, 1988). Thus, although our historical experience of the application of evolutionary biology to psychoanalysis has, indeed, been rife with problems, that we have been "burned" once by an unproductive form of biologizing, should not lead us—in a phobic manner—to throw the baby out with the bathwater.

THE REPETITION COMPULSION AND THE NEGATIVE THERAPEUTIC REACTION: DEFINITIONS AND DIFFERENT CONCEPTUALIZATIONS

Beyond the Pleasure Principle: The Repetition Compulsion Based on the Death Instinct

Prior to his formulation of the death instinct and the repetition compulsion proper, Freud (1914) speaks of a compulsion to repeat.

Freud (1920) again speaks of the persistence of the unconscious in its striving towards expression. As Fenichel (1945) later clarified, such a persistence would tend to create a *pattern* of repetition as opposed to a *compulsion* to repeat. In this type of repetition, the work of analysis aids the repetitive reexpression of the instinctual material by loosening the repression.

However, Freud was a psychological, observational scientist and therefore felt obliged to face the fact that this "compulsion to repeat also recalls from the past experiences which include no possibility of pleasure, and which can never, even long ago, have brought satisfaction even to instinctual impulses which have since been repressed" (1920, p. 20). Thus began Freud's journey "beyond the pleasure principle."

As Freud develops his view that *"an instinct is an urge inherent in organic life to restore an earlier state of things"* (p. 36), he begins to use a form of Aristotelian teleological logic (Mayr, 1982). Freud's conception of the beginning of all life was, given our current state of knowledge, somewhat accurate. He saw the first life forms (which we now believe were viruslike DNA-spiral precursors to the living cell) as fragile and quickly dying. In current evolutionary theory, random variation eventually produced forms that were less fragile and could replicate their patterns. They became more frequent as natural selection and the process of evolution began.

Slowly, newer and more complex forms evolved and the fragile, short-lived first forms of life began to be replaced by more stable organisms that could survive until replication was possible. New patterns, structures, and strategies arose that made these forms more viable and successful. Out of random variation, natural selection favored more durable and reproductively successful patterns. Freud came to view this evolutionary development as merely the creation of a circuitous route to death. In Aristotelian teleological logic, things fall to earth because that is were they belong. Similarly, for Freud *"the aim of all life is death"* (1920, p. 38).

The attributes of life were at sometime evoked in inanimate manner by the action of a force. . . . The tension which then arose in what had hitherto been an inanimate substance endeavored to cancel itself out. In this way the first instinct came into being: the instinct to return to the inanimate state. It was still an easy matter at that time for a living substance to die; the course of its life was probably only a brief one, whose direction was determined by the chemical structure of the young life. For a long time, perhaps, living substance was thus being constantly created afresh and easily dying, till decisive external influences altered in such a way as to oblige the still surviving substance to diverge ever more widely from its original course of life and to make ever more complicated *detours* before reaching its aim of death [pp. 38–39].

There is a fundamental principle of nature that parallels Freud's death instinct: the Second Law of Thermodynamics governs all matter in its relentless movement toward a maximum state of entropy. However, this is not a biological principle and certainly not an instinct. Biological forces as shaped by natural selection, have found a way of *opposing* this natural tendency of matter. They form a matter eddy wherein the forces of nature are organized. Of course, they do not operate outside of the Second Law, but the degree to which an organism is favored by natural selection is *precisely* the degree to which it can *stave off* entropic disintegration (maximum entropy in its own body) long enough to pass on the principles of organization (genes) to other viable new organisms (offspring).

Freud apparently confused a fundamental law of nature (the Second Law of Thermodynamics, which governs inanimate matter) for which "purpose" and "function" are inappropriate terms, with biological processes, for which an adaptive functional analysis is necessary (Mayr, 1982). This confusion led to a conceptualization of repetitions based on the death instinct that has no clear current motivational or situational basis. Thus, the tendency to repeat becomes its own motivation, an irreducible inherent quality of all instincts.

Freud felt that the concept of the death instinct as the ultimate explanation for repetition resolved certain theoretical inconsistencies. Yet, in this process he left the biological realm. Even he appeared to recognize that this view did not make adaptive biological sense. As Freud (1926) said himself, "This view of instincts strikes us as strange because we have become used to see in them a factor impelling towards change and development, whereas we are now asked to recognize in them the precise contrary . . ." (p. 36).

In Freud's later writings this *compulsion to repeat* became reified, taking on a life of its own, an existence independent of the metaphysical death instinct and the search for quiescence. For example, in speaking of the repressed impulse that due to repression, is free from control by the ego, Freud (1926) wonders what will occur if

the danger-situation changes so that the ego has no reason for fending off a new instinctual impulse analogous to the repressed one. . . . The new impulse will run its course under an automatic influence—or, as I should prefer to say, under the influence of the compulsion to repeat. It will follow the same path as the earlier, repressed impulse, as though the danger-situation that had been overcome still existed. The fixating factor in repression, then, is the unconscious id's compulsion to repeat—a compulsion which in normal circumstances is only done away with by the freely mobile function of the ego. The ego may occasionally manage to break down the barriers of repression which it has itself put up and to recover its influence over the instinctual impulse and direct the course of the new impulse in accordance with the changed danger-situation. But in point of fact the ego very seldom succeeds in doing this: it cannot undo its repressions. . . . The regressive attraction exerted by the repressed impulse and the strength of the repression are so great that the new impulse has no choice but to obey the compulsion to repeat [pp. 153–154].

In some manner the compulsion to repeat has become a primary feature of the id, of instincts. Freud had several functional/adaptive explanations for repetitions (for example, mastery of traumatic instinctual pressures), but he felt they were inadequate to explain fully the whole range of pain-inducing repetitions. Freud did not hypothesize the death instinct in *opposition* to the pleasure principle. In going "beyond the pleasure principle," he found a supraordinate, more fundamental explanation for it. The seeking of quiescence, or of a tension-reducing return to inactivity, was always the *modus operandi* of the drives. This principle was in turn further reduced to a new tensional urge: the seeking of a return to an inorganic state, death. As can be seen in the foregoing quotation, in his clinical attempt to explain neurotic symptoms, Freud does not need to speak of a death instinct. He does start to speak of this compulsion to repeat as being a regular primary feature of the instincts.

The dual theory of life and death instincts, along with the concept of the compulsion to repeat, became essential concepts to Freud (Jones, 1953). However, the compulsion to repeat appears increasingly in Freud's writings, without constant reference to the death instinct.

Outside analysis, too, something similar can be observed. There are people in whose lives the same reactions are perpetually being repeated uncorrected, to their own detriment, or others who seem to be pursued by a relentless fate, though closer investigation teaches us that they are unwittingly bringing this fate on themselves. In such cases we attribute a "daemonic" character to the compulsion to repeat [Freud, 1933, pp. 106–107].

Following such usage by Freud, in later psychoanalytic writings by others, this primary feature of human mental activity, and especially of the id, is accepted without reliance on the death instinct. Relatively lengthy discussions of the repetition compulsion occur under the assumption that the reader has accepted this conception as a basic feature of human mental life, for example, Hartmann, 1939 (pp. 95–99); Bibring, (1943); and Glover, 1955 (pp. 80–86).

Again, removed from its metaphysical base (without the death instinct), we see the reified repetition compulsion in a dialogue between Joseph Sandler and Anna Freud:

> Anna Freud: What I take up . . . is the overwhelming urge to re-peat. . . .
> Joseph Sandler: Would you say that the repetition compulsion, then, as an urge to repeat, applies equally to the ego in all aspects of its functioning? . . .
> Anna Freud: The concept was first applied to the drives, but I think that now . . . we would apply it equally to the urge to repeat early modes of functioning. . . .
> Joseph Sandler: . . . Of course, the question of the repetition compulsion being truly a compulsion is always questioned, and I do not know whether there is a problem of translation here. It is more a *tendency* to repeat.
> Anna Freud: It is called *Wiederholungszwang* in German. It really refers to an urge, a compulsion in the sense of an urge [Sandler, 1985, pp. 62–63].

In clinical theory, as we will see more fully later, the concept of a compulsion to repeat is frequently cited as a given with no explanation as to why it should exist once the death instinct has been removed. As Kohut (1984) pointed out, without the death instinct, certain aspects of classical analytic theory ultimately lose their cohesion and internal consistency. This loss is reflected in the efforts of many analysts to explain the repetition compulsion without following Freud in his move "beyond the pleasure principle."

The Return to the Pleasure Principle for Explanations of Repetition

Some authors have attempted to find a clear rationale for repetitive patterns in concepts unrelated to the death instinct. For example, Fenichel (1945) sees no need to question the pleasure principle's adequacy in explaining observed repetitions. He accepts Freud's initial formulations of the forces underlying repetitions but stops short of following him through to what he considers Freud's "metaphysical" death instinct. He sees no need to go beyond the pleasure principle and ends up finding no real *compulsion* to repeat but, rather, patterns of repetition. He sees three different categories in which actions and patterns are repeated. The first category is rooted in the "periodicity of instincts." This is a simple type of repetition as exemplified by hunger, which recurs following satiation. The second major category—the one that Fenichel (1945) finds at the heart of most neuroses—is "repetition . . . due to the tendency of the repressed to find an outlet" (p. 542).

> What happens is that a repressed impulse tries to find its gratification in spite of its repression; but whenever the repressed wish comes to the surface, the anxiety that first brought about the repression is mobilized again and creates, together with the repetition of the impulse, a repetition of the anti-instinctual measures. Neurotic repetitions of this kind contain no metaphysical element [p. 542].

Fenichel's final category of repetitions contains those repetitions "of traumatic events for the purpose of achieving a belated mastery" (p. 542). This became the cornerstone of the ego analytic conception of repetition. Thus, in an early, important ego analytic work we are presented with an internally consistent view of psychodynamics with repetitions, but with no *compulsion to repeat*, per se. In this aspect of Fenichel's view, the repetition, which is clearly a result of other motivational forces, is identified as a means toward other, presumably adaptive, ends.

In the work of Fenichel we see the rejection of the death instinct and of the repetition compulsion, whereas what Fenichel retained from Freud's original thinking about repetition is a more clinically useful way of understanding patterns of repetition. Fenichel sees neurotic patients as striving to express something within themselves and as, repeatedly, reaching the same dead end. Traumatized patients are seen as attempting to master overwhelming experiences by turning the passively experienced trauma into a controlled, assimilated event by reliving it in memory and dreams. Combined with the "periodicity of the instincts" and the presumed "tendency of the repressed to find an outlet," patterns of repetition emerge. But do these explanations really address and explain those universal, apparently maladaptive, and painful repetitions that originally forced Freud to go "beyond the pleasure principle"?

There are two major limitations in Fenichel's view: 1) "the tendency of the repressed to find an outlet" is a mechanistic, somatic notion that is not itself understood in an adaptive context, that is, a context that shows how such a presumed universal "tendency" might serve adaptive ends; 2) his more ego-psychological conception of "mastering trauma," following Freud, is rather narrowly defined in terms of the dynamics of intrapsychic drive mastery. What needs to be mastered is virtually never conceived of as aspects of external reality; the focus is almost exclusively on inner, instinctual oversti-mulation. This tends to leave out the broad range of early relational experiences that may have a maladaptive impact on development. Features of the environment are thus typically overlooked as sources of trauma and, more important, as the objects of repeated attempts at revision.

Fenichel depicts the compulsion to repeat as the result of more basic structural/libidinal dynamics, not as a global tendency with a life of its own, so to speak, that derives from a supraordinate death instinct. Freud's belief, on the other hand, was that the libidinal/structural dynamics of the pleasure principle could not be stretched this far. A broader, supraordinate principle that at times may run counter to the pleasure–unpleasure continuum was necessary to explain the power and universality of repetition in the human condi-tion. By not accepting the death instinct, Fenichel dispensed with a nonbiological encumbrance on the theory without, however, satisfy-ing the need for a broader, supraordinate rationale for repetitions that appear motivated by forces and geared to ultimate ends that go beyond the dynamics of libido and instinctual mastery.

Fenichel's notions may thus be seen as consistent with self-psycho-logical views of an organism trying to protect itself from fragmenta-tion. That his views did not include a supraordinate principle to replace the death instinct and supplement the libidinal/structural model left a large gap in the theory. This lack has permitted more global notions of an inherent compulsion to repeat to remain within the classical paradigm. Clinically, as Stolorow, Brandchaft, and At-wood (1983) point out, the repetition compulsion in a moralistic, "blaming the victim" form continues to characterize much analytic work.

Beyond the Pleasure Principle: Other Psychoanalytic Views of Repetition

Object relations theorists have added what we might call a fourth source of repetition, which in its own way does go "beyond the pleasure principle." Fairbairn's (1952) concept of libido as object seeking rather than pleasure seeking leads to a view in which painful object ties are retained because they represent an alternative to loss. The fifth explanation for repetition can be found in self psychology.

These explanations will be discussed more fully later. This, we believe, constitutes a brief summary of the major conceptualizations of repetition.

The Negative Therapeutic Reaction

In many ways the idea of the negative therapeutic reaction can be seen as the clinical translation of the repetition compulsion or as the negative effects of the repetition compulsion in the transference. The literature on the negative therapeutic reaction consists of a set of explanations, the logic of which closely parallels the attempt to explain the more general phemonena of maladaptive repetitions. As Freud noted (1920), it is difficult to explain maladaptive repetitions. In the clinical context, explanation becomes even more difficult because repetition challenges the analyst's self-esteem, and thus explanations are liable to take on a particularly moralizing, self-righteous, and self-justifying tone. Thus an atmosphere is created that makes it especially difficult to perceive and evaluate the functional and adaptive aspects of apparently maladaptive repetition—which can be quite painful for both parties—in the clinical setting.

While Brandchaft (1983) suggests that the negative therapeutic reaction defines the limits of psychoanalytic success, we feel that this position makes the concept too general and that other factors must be considered when defining clinical limitations. We, therefore, use a restricted definition of the negative therapeutic reaction. We apply the term to a negative reaction—anger, dysphoria, worsening of symptoms, premature termination of treatment by the patient—that occurs in response to an essentially correct interpretation,[2] in response to an opportunity to make use of insight to act differently, or in the face of feeling good.

Glover (1955) engages in a lengthy analysis of the repetition compulsion as id-resistance. Although he distinguishes it from the superego resistance of the negative therapeutic reaction, his description of a patient engaged in id-resistance is a classic description of a negative therapeutic reaction:

> Now it is partly true that sooner or later the patient behaves like a perverse child. . . . He may experience the impulse to yell and scream,

---

[2]We are aware that the "correctness" of an interpretation is relative. What is correct to the analyst (and perhaps his colleagues) is not correct in any absolute sense and is certainly not necessarily experienced as correct by the patient. But the expression "essentially correct interpretation" is retained to highlight the crucial point that there can be a marked disparity between the general *accuracy* of the therapist's comments and the patient's *reactions* to them.

to throw things about, to gnash his teeth, to say 'shant't' when encouraged to associate. . . . Sooner or later we find that some situations cannot be reduced [by interpretation]. . . . We give what seems a valid interpretation, but the effect seems to be either minimal or transient or entirely nil . . . [interpretations along numerous lines are tried] . . . But the situation does not alter . . . we are faced with the bare fact that a set of presentations is being repeated before us again and again. That is . . . a clue to the . . . situation . . . [T]he nearer we get to seemingly blind repetition, the nearer we are to a characteristic of instinctual excitation . . . we seem to have given a fillip to the repetition-compulsion [pp. 80–81].

Note that Glover never uses the term death instinct and never explains why the "Id-resistance presents the repetitive characteristics of instinctual excitations" (p. 82). This is simply accepted as a given. However, this now poorly defined resistance is seen by Glover to lie at the heart of the negative therapeutic reaction (as we defined it earlier) and determines the limits of psychoanalysis: "No case should be recommended for analysis without making a careful estimate of the chances of striking an intractable Id-resistance" (p. 85). In Glover's schema, the only way to identify an id-resistance is to see if it yields to interpretations: "the existence of Id-resistances is generally arrived at by a process of exclusion, and in practice it is prudent to do so [in order to avoid overlooking other sources of resistance]" (p. 85). Therefore, we can define each instance of psychoanalytic failure as an inherent resistance to cure.

In fairness to Glover, it should be noted that he does warn against blaming the patient for countertransference problems (Glover, 1955, 1956). However, by his definition of the process that leads to the identification of an intractable id-resistance, failure to achieve a cure is always due to id-resistance, never to a deficit in technique or theory. This is so because if one is using proper (ego-analytic) technique, and if the analyst is not acting out countertransference, then *by Glover's definition*, a failure to achieve therapeutic results is due to an id-resistance.

Masochism: The Drive/Structure Linkage Between the Repetition Compulsion and the Negative Therapeutic Reaction

In fact, it was Freud (1937) who laid the groundwork for future analysts to separate the repetition compulsion from his notions of a death instinct and to attach it to conceptualizations regarding a primary masochism as he developed the concept of the "negative therapeutic reaction."

> In yet another group of cases the distinguishing characteristics of the ego, which are to be held responsible as sources of resistance against analytic treatment and as impediments to therapeutic success, may spring from different and deeper roots. . . . No stronger impression arises from the resistances during the work of analysis than of there being a force which is defending itself by every possible means against recovery and which is absolutely resolved to hold on to illness and suffering. . . . If we take into consideration the total picture made up of the phenomena of masochism immanent in so many people, the negative therapeutic reaction and a sense of guilt found in so many neurotics, we shall no longer be able to adhere to the belief that mental events are exclusively governed by the desire for pleasure. These phenomena are unmistakable indications of the presence of a power in mental life . . . which we trace back to the original death instinct of living matter. . . . For the moment we must bow to the superiority of the forces against which we see our efforts come to nothing [pp. 242–243].

Though, again, we see that for Freud the negative therapeutic reaction was firmly rooted in the death instinct, modern analysts have relatively easily rejected the death instinct because Freud had also developed the related concept of primary masochism, which—without the death instinct—is simply one of the nonteleological primary instincts, aggression, turned on the self.

> If one is prepared to overlook a little inexactitude, it may be said that the death instinct which is operative in the organism—primal sadism— is identical with masochism. . . . Let us . . . consider . . . the extreme and unmistakably pathological form of this masochism. . . . I [have] pointed out the sign by which such people can be recognized (a "negative therapeutic reaction") and I did not conceal the fact that the strength of such an impulse constitutes one of the most serious resistances and the greatest danger to the success of our medical or educative aims. The satisfaction of this unconscious sense of guilt is perhaps the most powerful bastion in the subject's . . . gain from illness—in the sum of forces which struggle against his recovery and refuse to surrender his state of illness [Freud, 1924, pp. 164–166].

Using this concept, one could then place responsibility for the failure of the analytic work on the patient's masochism. Note how, by the use of masochism, our most difficult patients can be described without reference to the death instinct:

[They] exhibit what is known as a "negative therapeutic reaction." There is no doubt that there is something in these people that sets itself against their recovery, and its approach is dreaded as though it were a danger. . . . In the end we come to see that we are dealing with what may be called a "moral" factor, a sense of guilt, which is finding its satisfaction in the illness and refuses to give up the punishment of suffering [Freud, 1923, p. 49].

Modern analysts have taken the role of guilt in the negative therapeutic reaction and reworked it to make it compatible with the structural theory of intrasystemic conflict and superego guilt.

There are also complex explanations of repetitions due to *characterological*, or highly structuralized, ego syntonic masochism. This theme is especially salient in modern attempts to combine ego-psychological and object-relational approaches in which the Kleinian emphasis on innate sources of destructive envy plays a prominent role. For example, in talking about the "negative therapeutic reaction" Kernberg (1975) states:

I am referring here exclusively to those cases in which the need to destroy the helpful aspects of the psychotherapy or psychoanalysis clearly predominate in the patients impulse-defense configuration. . . . Many patients with depressive-masochistic character structures do present this type of resistance [p. 126].

There is a sense that, for these types of patients, we have reached a form of psychological bedrock in our failure to be able to truly alter their narcissistic resistances, that is, their sadomasochism:

However, there are cases in which the narcissistic resistances cannot be worked through, and the patient after lengthy periods of stalemate prefers to terminate the treatment, or the analyst feels that he cannot help the patient any further. Under these conditions, a shift into a more supportive approach of the kind which in my opinion is implied (although not intended) in Kohut's work may be very helpful. . . . There are also patients with intense negative therapeutic reactions who can accept certain improvement only at the cost of simultaneously defeating the analyst in his purpose to bring about further change. In many cases of this kind, the treatment may have to shift at some point, into a supportive tolerance of the narcissistic constellation in combination with the preparation for the termination of the treatment [Kernberg, 1975, pp. 289–290].

Kernberg is suggesting that one must accept substantial limitations or failures in work with such patients. What one sees in approaches such as Kernberg's is that even after the death instinct has been left behind, its corollary of basic destructive forces continues to live on in a major emphasis on certain patients' tendencies to repeat and seek out suffering and failure, as well as in their tendency to destroy positive relationships. Treatment failures can certainly be left at the door of such an edifice.

More adaptive views of such treatment struggles have been developed in psychoanalytic theory. In each case they add something new to the explanatory schema as they attempt to make sense out of repetitive, self-defeating, patterns in terms that ultimately are more compatible with evolutionary adaptive logic.

Adaptive Views of Repetition in the Transference

Loewald (1969) focuses on preoedipal object relations in an attempt to explicate the negative therapeutic reaction. His discussion is fused with speculations about the death instinct that we find untenable. However, his discussion of the repetition compulsion (Loewald, 1965) has a feature that, at its heart, is an adaptive notion. First, he sees repetition as a feature of life. Second, he distinguishes passive from active repetition in a manner reminiscent of, but significantly different from, Freud's notions of turning passive to active in an attempt to gain mastery over trauma. He speaks of "re-creative repetition" as opposed to simple repetition, which is "reproductive repetition." In re-creative repetition there is a tendency to repeat in order to have a chance for further growth and novel development, as the second (or third, fourth, fifth) time around there is an opportunity to find new ways of expressing old impulses and conflicts.

Fairbairn (1952) took his own step "beyond the pleasure principle" when he reconceptualized libido as object seeking, not pleasure seeking. Thus, Fairbairn's views on repetition and the death instinct provide a thorough reworking of Freudian metapsychology that in some ways prefigures the self-psychological viewpoint (Greenberg and Mitchell, 1983). Fairbairn's use of the term "ego" was actually closer to the concept of the self than to the traditional concept of the ego in the tripartite structural system. In Fairbairn's system, libido is "object directed"; because the person needs others, obstinate attachments form in which the patient may be willing to play a masochistic role if that protects the all-important relationship to others.

For Fairbairn, the ego has three parts, each attached to an internal representation of an aspect of experience with important objects. The gratifying object has attached to it the central ego, which is available for real relationships with real objects in the world. Attached to internal representations of the "enticing" object and the "rejecting" object are the libidinal and antilibidinal egos. The libidinal ego repeatedly attaches to enticing but unavailable objects, while the antilibidinal ego is full of rage at all enticing objects and at the libidinal ego itself. Thus, repetitions occur as the ever-searching libido pursues its object-directed course, colored and distorted by previous experience in the form of the libidinal and anti-libidinal egos. The adaptive quality of this arrangement was dramatically illustrated in Robertson's (1952) film, "A Two-Year-Old Goes to the Hospital."

> In this movie we see a two-and-a-half year old girl who is separated from her mother for the first time. She is traumatically bewildered as mother leaves her alone in the strange hospital. She cries herself into spent, blank, staring, exhaustion. After a long while she accepts the attention of the hospital staff and begins to respond to them. When mother returns, after a brief hesitation, she re-engages joyfully with her, only to be re-traumatized when mother leaves at the end of visiting hours (this movie was made when hospital rules did not allow parents to remain with their children). As this is repeated over the next few days, we witness the little girl begin to turn *away* upon mother's arrival. By the end of the week, mother must work to re-engage the petulant rejecting (!) child who stares away, as if disinterested.

It is almost like sped-up-action photography; one can actually watch the development of Fairbairn's antilibidinal ego, tied to the frustrating internalized object, angry at mother. The adaptive significance? Clearly, such a mechanism protects us from overwhelming trauma by making us more cautious about whom we allow ourselves to depend on. It was if the antilibidinal ego were protecting the child's interest by saying, "Oh, yeah. You again. Well I'm not going to fall for it this time." This pattern is, of course, frequently encountered in analysis and is a significant part of many, if not all, negative therapeutic reactions.

Self psychology moves "beyond the pleasure principle" as it reconceptualizes primary motivational forces in self-structural relational terms. As with Fairbairn, the pendulum has swung all the way in the opposite direction from nonrelational drive/structure to relational/ structure theorizing (Greenberg and Mitchell, 1983). Brandchaft (1983) has presented a careful self-psychological analysis of the negative therapeutic reaction. His views are similar in some ways to those of Fairbairn, who saw the masochistic tie to bad objects as expressing the central human need for object relatedness: a tie to a bad object is better than no tie at all. For Brandchaft, "the need of a patient with a vulnerable self to maintain a tie with an analyst experienced as a relentlessly failing archaic selfobject lies at the root of the negative therapeutic reaction" (p. 336).

Contrasting his own views with those of Olinick (1964), who felt that the analyst should interpret how the patient's negativity forces the analyst to introject something and end up feeling guilty and helpless, Brandchaft (1983) felt it was crucial to understand the patient's subjective experience and "recognize the kernel of truth within the patient's complaint" (p. 343). He felt that the negative therapeutic reaction

> arises within two contexts: (1) as an initial and sometimes continuing defense against the mobilization of the archaic selfobject longings . . . and (2) in response to a persistent negativism in the patient's subjective experience of the analyst in response to some aspect of the patient's nuclear self—its strivings or demands, angry assertiveness or complaints, necessary protective structure or autonomous developmental step [p. 343].

Note again the similarity between Fairbairn's antilibidinal ego in its relationship to the libidinal ego and the enticing object, and Brandchaft's negative defense against the mobilization of the archaic longings. What is most important, from an evolutionary standpoint, is the inherently adaptive conceptualization that characterizes the self psychological view:

> These were not the intrinsic intrapsychic energies and agencies, but rather the insistent supraordination of the pathological selfobject needs of his objects . . . to the *legitimate* selfobject needs remaining from childhood to define an authentic self and to initiate its own intrinsic pattern of development within a supporting and confirming setting [p. 352].

What do patients seek when they enter analysis? Our common assumption is that they seek some form of cure, growth, relief, increased control over their lives. All of these have an adaptive function, as does Ornstein's (1984) self-psychological notion of a "curative fantasy" with which patients enter treatment in hopes of completing arrested self development; in the hope of using a selfobject relationship "for 'a new beginning' and an activation of [their] 'thwarted need to grow' " (p. 180).

In Freud's (1920) struggle to understand the painful repetitions he saw in his patients, he postulated the existence of a universal, supraordinate "compulsion" to repeat that stands in marked contradistinction to an inherently adaptive notion such as the "curative fantasy." Rather than seeing the repetitions that occur in the transference as representing and signaling the patient's strivings toward growth, or the patient's seeking something that was not obtained earlier, Freud ascribed the repetition of painful experiences to a compulsion within the patient, with no intrinsic functional goal, healthy striving, or adaptive functioning. While Fenichel, Fairbairn, and others may have developed revised views of the motivational dynamics involved in repetition, self psychology is the only psychoanalytic model that offers a new supraordinate functional concept (the self) that (1) supplants the death instinct in generality and scope; and (2) represents the person's self-interest. Self psychology is thus consistent in interpreting motivation in reference to the organism's long-range self-interest, with the evolutionary biological emphasis on functional design in the organization of the psyche.

One characteristic of both the repetition compulsion and the negative therapeutic reaction, when they appear in most non-self-psychological viewpoints, is that they describe inherently *maladaptive* processes. That is, they are based on universal tendencies that have no clearly advantageous function and, as their operation is described, almost always function to the detriment of the person. Such a feature has *no selective value;* it would not have been favored by natural selection and is unlikely to have become a regular part of our species equipment. We can find adaptive aspects of repetition (see Fenichel, 1945) or of aspects of the negative therapeutic reaction. But, as classically defined, these concepts are essentially maladaptive processes. That is, the concepts are used when other explanations fail, and they describe blind repetition and self-defeating patterns. Further, these maladaptive features are attributed to some inherent, universal characteristics of the human psyche.

We are not claiming that our patients do not repeat destructive patterns. And we can see a "correct" interpretation as being descriptively accurate, for example:

> You are afraid of the intensity of your longings (sexual, idealizing, fears of positive transference, merger, fusion, vulnerability, etc.) so you denigrate me. You do this with others and you evoke hurt feelings in people who then leave or attack you and thus you live in a self-fulfilling prophecy. You repeatedly set up the same end result: everyone does abandon you or abuse you.

Yet, as can be seen, some analysts use the "stubbornness" of the repetitive pattern to argue for *intent*, thus for masochism: if patients stubbornly repeat painful patterns, despite an accurate interpretation, then intent to suffer must exist even if it is unconscious.

Freud (1920) saw this intent to seek self-frustration and pain as the repetition compulsion based on the death instinct. Those who followed Freud in seeing "intent" had three options: 1) accept the death instinct as Freud did, 2) reject the death instinct and use the repetition compulsion concept without clearly defining one's terms or attempting to make metapsychological sense, or 3) reject the death instinct and replace it with the aggressive instinct with either primary or secondary (guilt based) masochism. In all three cases, a central feature of the patient's motivational system becomes the conscious or unconscious intent to repeat blindly, self-destruct, or relish self-inflicted pain. From an evolutionary, adaptive perspective, we must move beyond all these theoretical strategies to one in which a *new supraordinate motivational principle* has a central role.

THE EVOLUTIONARY PERSPECTIVE ON THE OBJECT WORLD: THE HUMAN PSYCHE AS AN ADAPTIVE "ORGAN"

Beyond the Pleasure Principle: The Principle of Adaptation

The evolutionary perspective insists that we ask, "What adaptive function could be served by a tendency to repeat, or by self-defeating behavior?" We must show that the constructs we are using to explain the human psyche are consistent with what we assume must be an overall adaptive design. In cases of common, almost universal, pathology, we must be able to elucidate the related adaptive functions that have somehow gone awry. This simple evolutionary concept alone disposes us to seriously question maladaptive views of repetition based on a primary death instinct or primary masochism.

At this point we turn briefly to deal with an objection that readers who are aware of current debates in evolutionary theory may raise. Gould (1980), Mayr (1982), and others have repeatedly emphasized that it is scientifically unsound to take every organismic feature and assume that a specific adaptive, evolutionary explanation can be derived to explain its current role and functions. Any given feature may be a part of another feature or larger adaptive organismic system; thus, it may not have been selected because it, in itself, was adaptive. Or the feature may be an accidental creation—that is, one fortuitously connected to some other adaptive feature—that persists in the genotype because it does not seriously impair the organism's functioning. These considerations comprise important caveats. However, as Mayr

(1983) points out, "The adaptationist question, 'What is the function of a given structure or organ?' has been for centuries the basis for every advance in physiology" (p. 328). In other words, the adaptationist question is the source of our most fruitful hypotheses. This question has also, of course, been the source of many incorrect hypotheses. What is crucial is that the logical structure of adaptationist hypotheses, combined with a dedication to empirical investigation, has enabled us to sort out the difference.[3] For this reason Mayr concludes that, contrary to what is claimed by the adaptationist program's more radical critics, when it is carried out in a fashion that correctly identifies the level of organization on which selection has operated, "it would seem obvious that little is wrong with the adaptationist program as such, contrary to what is claimed by Gould . . ." (p. 332). Mayr goes on to argue for the attempt to identify as "adaptations" those structures which truly play a central role in the organization of the person, not incidental or secondary aspects of the "whole."

We are in agreement with Mayr and believe that it is psychodynamic structure that represents precisely this correct level of organization. Thus, we believe that the concerns of well-intentioned critics such as Gould are probably far less applicable to a *psychoanalytic* use of the concept of adaptation than to what is essentially the naive behaviorism of certain proponents of "sociobiology." All too commonly, sociobiologists isolate specific, discrete behaviors out of the context of the whole organism and its psyche as the focus of adaptive hypotheses in which specific gene = behavior links are assumed to exist. We, however, are looking at the fundamental nature of the psyche, as a deep structure, so to speak, that underlies myriad specific individual, social, and cultural variations and values. This essential human inner organization and propensity to follow certain developmental paths is not a minor feature that could be accidental. We are examining the basic organization of the psyche and its major psychological components. Certainly such universal features (for example, the self, major motivational themes, and the mix of selfobject needs with other motivations to pursue narrower individual interests) that seem to underlie human behavior, and often can mean the difference between a successful life and abject failure (even death), are unlikely to be accidental features of the organism that lie outside the ken of the adaptationist hypothesis. Only an antianalytic

---

[3]For psychoanalysis, using the adaptationist's logic, we may now achieve new insights into our clinical observations—always remembering that, in the final analysis, it is the clinical data to which we must return.

approach would dismiss these dynamic features as being unessential aspects of our psychological equipment. Whether or not one wishes to pursue any specific biological analysis of these features, the effort to understand then from an adaptive perspective cannot be ruled out.

Returning now to our presentation of the evolutionary perspective, we note that simply applying the adaptive viewpoint may be helpful in starting to evaluate the logic underlying different explanations of the tendency to repeat and self-defeating action. However, modern evolutionary theory provides us with a far more powerful and sophisticated perspective from which to view different psychoanalytic views of motivation in general and repetition in particular. We will return to the psychoanalytic views of repetition after we present this evolutionary perspective.

The Principle of Inclusive Fitness

Evolutionary theory not only gives us an overarching, generalized insistence on analysis in terms of adaptive design, but goes further to provide a clear definition of "adaptation." *Inclusive fitness* is the modern biological term that defines the concept of adaptation. It is different from the more familiar, narrow, Darwinian notion of "fitness." Inclusive fitness does not refer to the *individual's* fitness, but rather to the survival and successful reproduction of the genetic material carried by the individual. In other words, inclusive fitness includes the success of one's relatives, especially offspring.

Important universal psychological features that currently exist were favored by natural selection because they represented functional designs that in evolutionary time were advantageous; that is, they increased the *inclusive* fitness of individuals who possessed such psychological organization. The distinction between fitness in the narrow sense and inclusive fitness has broad and important implications for psychoanalysis; we shall turn to these later. Evolution theory not only tells us that all life forms are designed to maximize their own *self-interest*, it also defines self-interest as *the maximization of one's inclusive fitness*. Thus, self-interest is no longer defined in the narrower sense that was used in Freud's day as the maximization of personal fitness or the survival of the individual organism. Rather, inclusive fitness is defined as the maximization of the representation of one's genes in the future gene pool of the species (Hamilton, 1964; Trivers, 1985).[4]

[4]The principle of inclusive fitness, as distinguished from the older, narrower notion of personal fitness, enabled evolutionists to solve an age-old problem for evolutionary

Kin Ties and Reciprocal Ties: The Principle of Overlap and Distinctness

Figure 3a presents a model of an individual in relationship to others. Humans are inherently social creatures, and we can diagram relationships with connecting lines: the shorter lines indicate close relationships, the longer lines indicate weak ties. Figure 3a represents the socially observed, or *apparent*, level of relatedness. The overlapping circles and lines in Figure 3b show a more accurate and complete picture of relatedness from an evolutionary perspective. Parts of the individual genotype are shared with related others. In a real (evolutionary) sense, then, self-boundaries may well include parts of other individuals!

This blurring of self/other boundaries may sound a bit like a psychotic view of reality. What does it actually mean? Remembering our definition of the all-important concept of inclusive fitness, from

theory: the problem of altrusim. Conflict between individuals can be easily explained using the individualistic "survival of the fittest" conception of natural selection. The problem, however, lies in the evolution of patterns of behavior that are patently dangerous or costly to the individual who performs them, such as the widespread self-sacrifice and altruism observed in many species. More commonly, how does one explain the enormous amount of cooperation and compassion that social species, such as we, demonstrate some of the time?

Freud's (1915a, b, 1921, 1930) solution was to see such phenomena as reaction formations built around aim-inhibited impulses, anaclitic attachments, and essentially learned identifications. Thus, he was able to explain behaviors that seemed to contradict basically self-centered drives (consistent with selfish survival of the fittest, in the narrow sense) by developing a system in which these drives are repressed, disguised, and transformed by the internalized, oppositional pressure of civilization embodied in the superego.

The pre-Hamilton (1964) evolutionary view explained behavior that was costly to the individual, yet benefited others, as having evolved for the good of the "group" or, often, for the good of the species as a whole. Thus, penguins control their birthrate, having fewer offspring under overcrowded conditions, because this benefits all penguins. Groups of penguins that do not control their birthrates are less successful than those which do. This is the notion of "group selection" (Wynne-Edwards, 1962).

Yet, how could the altruist, the innate cooperator, the self-sacrificer, be more successful at replicating his of her genes (surviving and leaving more viable offspring) than other, more selfish competitors? Would not the competitors regularly have the evolutionary advantage? Hamilton (1964) proved that this was not the case when the altruist lived and operated in a largely kin setting. The shared genotypes in such conditions mean that helping (related) others actually enhances one's own inclusive fitness enough to frequently offset the cost of such actions. Trivers (1971) then went on to demonstrate that, in long-lived, social species, significant amounts of self-sacrifice could be selected for even among unrelated individuals if inner dynamics had evolved to guarantee that such prosocial behavior was likely to be *reciprocated*. Using these evolutionary advances, "for the good of the species" notions have largely been discarded (Kriegman, 1988).

THE "SELF": PHENOTYPIC AND GENOTYPIC PERSPECTIVES

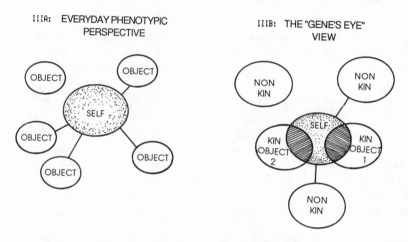

FIGURE 3

an evolutionary perspective we can not look at individuals as separate and distinct creatures. At the same time, no two individuals are genetically the same—the inclusive fitness (or self-interest) of any two individuals (aside from identical twins) is to some degree always different. Both the fundamental overlap and the inevitable distinctness have clear and powerful implications for all social species.

An Evolutionary View of the Object World

Using advances in modern evolutionary theory, Kriegman (1988) has shown that relational needs such as altruism, cooperation, a need for a self-selfobject milieu, are inherently adaptive. Evolutionary theorizing—specifically social evolution theories of kinship and reciprocal altruism (Hamilton, 1964; Trivers, 1971, 1974, 1985; Axelrod and Hamilton, 1981)—along with the clinical data, forces us to go beyond drive/structure theorizing and acknowledge the importance of relational/structure theorizing, as found in self psychology. In classical metapsychology these relational needs are seen as anaclitic attachments or as ultimately representing reactions against the drives. In either case they are reduced to the vicissitudes of the two drives that are assumed to be the basic, irreducible motivating forces of a *self-interested* organism (Greenberg and Mitchell, 1983). The evolutionist can show that relational needs, including altruism and compassion, *directly serve a self-interested individual* by maximizing individual inclusive fitness (Kriegman, 1988). However, the evolutionist would go on to conclude that without certain built-in motivations, e.g., drives, that are inherently *asocial*, the individual's social motives would actually allow a bias to form in favor of *others'* interests. The logic is as follows.

Imagine a socially oriented species without some inherently selfish motives. An instinctually selfish mutation introduced into such a population would quickly take advantage of the social orientation of the others and outcompete them. After a number of generations, the selfish, asocial (driven) gene would dominate. Thus, social creatures with no innate method of protecting their self-interest from the influence and self-interest of others would be rapidly replaced by those who were equipped to take advantage of them.[5]

Evolutionary theory tells us that even the most responsive, attuned, facilitative, mutually regulated social environment (including the intimate interactions between devoted parent and child) will inevitably be characterized by a degree of *interpersonal conflict* (Slavin, 1985). These are intersubjective conflicts in which all parties are inherently biased toward seeing reality and dealing with others in terms of their own unique individual interests. These conflicts, the evolutionist tells us, characterize the normal, natural, universal state of object relations. They *must* constitute the fundamental reality of a relational world that is composed of *genetically distinct, evolved, naturally selected/shaped*) organisms. This is so because the inclusive fitness of any two genetically distinct organisms can never be identical, even though there may be some overlap. Consequently, all individual organisms, while they may be innately disposed toward mutually cooperative interactions with others, must be equipped to have guaranteed access to some sources of motivation that are, in a sense, totally dedicated to the promotion of their individual interests. Such motivations serve as a guard against having one's genetic self-interest usurped by the social influence of important others, notably, those functioning in the powerful, influential selfobject role (see Kriegman and Solomon, 1985a,b for the extremes this can reach).

Elsewhere Slavin (1985, 1988) has tried to show how it is possible to translate certain essential aspects of classical drive theory, to redefine the drives in functional terms, as the ultimate guardians of individual self-interest. Freed from the trappings of classical metapsychology, drives can therefore be understood as the source of certain

---

[5]This is essentially the same logic that has relegated "group selection" to a minor role in evolution (see footnote 4). Those who operated for the good of the group would rapidly be outcompeted by more selfish individuals.

relatively egocentric, selfish individual aims and goals that will, to some degree, inevitably conflict with the goals of even closely related others.

Thus, we find ourselves accepting drives and *internal conflict* as inherently necessary *adaptive* features of human psychology. This is because the psyche is an adaptation to a relational world in which interpersonal, intersubjective conflict is an intrinsic feature. The organism *must be in conflict* between its *driven* self-protective, self-sustaining, and self-enhancing asocial motivations, and its *social* self-protective, self-sustaining, and self-enhancing relational needs. Clearly, this is not a retreat to the drive/structure paradigm of Freud. But, rather, it is an attempt to find a balance between two inherent and necessary aspects of what is adaptive and functional in human nature and to place these part functions within a supraordinate structure—the self. In part, it is the task of this overarching structure to find a balanced expression of these needs, a balanced expression that maximizes inclusive fitness.

This framework is one in which the realities of the relational environment include both the existence of some degree of inevitable competition and the enormous benefit resulting from inclusion in the social network. As a result of the realities—the selection pressures—of this environment, we have evolved an internal experience of reality that is *semisocial;* the deep structure of the psyche is semisocial. Unlike the classical metapsychology in which drive gratification and structure based on drives is seen as an end in itself, our reconceptualization holds that the drives are a means operating within this larger functional organization of the aims of the individual.

SOME GENERAL THEORETICAL IMPLICATIONS OF THE EVOLUTIONARY PERSPECTIVE REGARDING REPETITION AND THE NEGATIVE THERAPEUTIC REACTION

Table 1 presents an historical summary of the concepts of the repetition compulsion and the negative therapeutic reaction, organized within an adaptive perspective.

The Death Instinct and Id Resistance: Prebiological Concepts

Although at first Freud (1920) used adaptive/functional conceptions in his attempt to understand repetition, he finally settled on the

TABLE 1
An Hierarchical Adaptive View of Repetition in Psychoanalytic Theory

		Repetition Compulsion	Negative Therapeutic Reaction
NON	ADAPTIVE	1. THE DEATH INSTINCT: a prebiological concept with no possible shaping selective pressures	1. ID RESISTANCE A: an inherent id feature which when based on the death instinct is also pre-biological
ADAPTIVE COMPLEXITY INCREASES	FUNCTIONAL UTILITY INCREASES	2. PERIODICITY OF THE INSTINCTS & "STICKY" LIBIDO: simple adaptive concepts	2. ID RESISTANCE B: partially adaptive concept of fixation and character
		3. MASTERY A: a nonrelational notion of ego mastery of trauma and internal overstimulation	3. MORAL MASOCHISM A: superego resistance as an outgrowth of the functional need to control drives
		4. MASTERY B: relational concept—goal is to maintain an old object tie to avoid the trauma of loss	4. MORAL MASOCHISM B: based on the belief that selfpunishment is a necessary prerequisite for relatedness
		5. THE SELF: aim is to find (or to induce others to provide) what was needed; goal is to build structure	5. CURATIVE FANTASY A: seeking selfobjects; activity organized by the "overarching" self
		6. THE SELF OF INCLUSIVE FITNESS: the self seeks to resolve inherent conflicts *and* realize its nuclear program	6. CURATIVE FANTASY B: the self struggles to use selfobjects to resolve conflict *and* build structure

237

death instinct as the most fundamental source of repetition, and as the source of inherent id resistance and direct (primary) masochistic self-punishment in the transference. As we noted earlier, Freud confused two levels of analysis and applied Laws of Nature appropriate to the discussion of rules governing inanimate matter (in which "purpose" and "function" are inappropriate concepts) to biological processes. Thus, the death instinct—a concept that in some ways is similar to the Second Law of Thermodynamics—is a biologically untenable notion that is preadaptive in our conceptual scheme. We suggest that what is "beyond the pleasure principle" is *adaptation*. The organism is not designed to maximize pleasure (or minimize pain); it is designed to maximize its inclusive fitness.

Some of the other concepts that Freud and many later analysts used to understand repetition may, however, have adaptive consequences. These mechanisms are derivative of the "pleasure principle" or the principles of "object seeking" or "attachment" found in some object relational frameworks (e.g., Fairbairn, Bowlby). As *parts* of the organismic whole—as subsidiary adaptive mechanisms—they can be seen to fit into the adaptive hierarchy outlined in Table 1. These are numbered two through four.

Periodicity of the Instincts, "Sticky Libido," and Character: Simple Adaptive Concepts

At the lowest level of adaptive complexity we have what have traditionally been called instincts or drives. These drives insure that, despite other powerful influences (e.g., the threat of the loss of selfobjects if, in certain conflict situations, one's self-interest is not subordinated to the self-interest of the selfobject) there is some mechanism to motivate various activities necessary for the survival and reproduction of the individual. In the classical model, drives became the tail wagging the dog. As Brandchaft (1983) has pointed out, when they are used as the whole story, the patient can justly accuse the analyst of holding up one corner "of my personality . . . with the implication that the corner was me" (p. 349).

Taking away the trappings of classical metapsychology, our translation of drive theory motivation into *nonrelational aims that serve as an endogenous check on social influence* have some place within the whole. We define drives in *functional* terms within the framework of a *supraordinate self theory*. Thus, we can envision endogenous urges that like the repetitive "tendency of the repressed to find an outlet" noted by Fenichel (1945), can lead to repetitions in relationships, including the analytic situation.

Slightly more sophisticated as an adaptive mechanism is the notion of "adhesive libido," which is related to character types based on fixations. The adaptive function of sticky libido was never clarified, although there are clearly adaptive consequences of character. Character organizes fairly complex psychological events into semiautomatic processes. One need not deal afresh with each new situation if there is a characterological response. At a more complex level, character has adaptive features in interpersonal relationships as it allows us to predict the behavior of others. However, the notion of adaptive characterological repetitions based solely on adhesive libido (fixations) is a simple concept with limited explanatory utility.

Drive Mastery: Gaining Control Over Instinct

At the next higher level of functional explanation, we have the first of the mastery concepts: *nonrelational* mastery of internal conflict. In this conception, the adaptation is the ego's attempt to overcome traumatically overwhelming instinctual demands (Freud, 1920). As Bibring (1943) noted, the goal is to make an internal "homeostatic adjustment" or return to the "pretraumatic state," not to effect a change in the environment. Inasmuch as inclusive fitness must be maximized through interactions with the environment, a mechanism that leads to purely internal adjustments can provide only limited functional utility for the organism. As an overall explanatory construct, such a notion is of limited scope.

Relational Mastery: Maintaining Object Ties

At the next higher level of the adaptive hierarchy, we have the more complex notions of *relational* mastery. In these conceptions, our patients are trying to reenact experiences of childhood—old object relational patterns—in order to sustain old object ties. Patients for whom apparently intractable repetitive patterns seem to reaffirm that a bad object is better than none, so to speak, are seen quite frequently. They seem to feel a need to maintain a self-punishing stance in order to preserve archaic object ties (or crucial introjects) for fear that their relinquishment may leave an inner void or a sense of helplessness (disintegration anxiety). The adaptive goal is to avoid the more extreme trauma of the loss of an internal object tie or of a selfobject.

The avoidance of traumatic loss can be seen as a part of a larger system of attachment-maintaining behaviors that—as Bowlby (1969) has argued—are compatible with an evolutionary biological perspective. But concepts such as "trauma avoidance" or "attachment main-tenance" are relatively static and do not include strivings that are designed to produce adaptive internal or external *changes*. Our crite-rion of adaptation—inclusive fitness—suggests that psychological functions and behavior patterns must be structured at still higher levels of organization.

In a related schema, e.g., Racker's (1968) use of projective identifi-cation, there is an adaptive function played by the patient's actively attempting to manipulate the other to play the role of the punishing parent. Rather than seeing this as a manipulation in the service of maladaptive masochistic gratification—or simply a case of a bad object being better than none—we suggest that this is *adaptive mis-trust*. That is, the patient actively attempts to provoke the therapist because he or she has valid reason to expect a punishing response from parental objects. In such a circumstance, before making the self vulnerable and allowing the powerful selfobject longings to be remo-bilized, it is adaptive to test the analyst to see if he or she will respond like the punishing parent. We see such patients as actively exploring the self-object environment in order to determine the risks and benefits of opening up for renegotiation intricately structured char-acterlogical solutions—solutions that cover painful vulnerability—to the problem of knowing, maintaining, and promoting one's inclusive self interest.

Self-Structuralization: An Overarching Adaptive Concept

At a still more comprehensive level of adaptive analysis in existing psychoanalytic theory, we have certain self-psychological concepts. Patients repeat because they are still seeking what was developmen-tally missing; they attempt to influence others to *be* what was missing, to fill the role of the missing selfobject. The goal is to finish building self-structure. In this conception, there is an overriding adaptive organizational system. Patients do not enter treatment to repeat trauma or actively resist; rather they seek a selfobject that can help them realize the nuclear program for the self.

Patients may exercise extreme caution when they are reluctant to become vulnerably dependent on the analyst—to remobilize archaic longings for a selfobject—until they have ascertained that the relation-ship is safe, that is, that the analyst's empathic capacity and motiva-tions make it reasonably certain that a reliable selfobject is available. This caution and the defense against the remobilization of the archaic selfobject needs vis à vis the analyst—a narcissistic transference—can appear to be stubborness or resistance. A negative therapeutic reaction then ensues if the analyst fails to recognize this and instead attempts to interpret this reaction as a defense against instinctual wishes or, even worse, if the analyst attempts to cajole the patient into a more trusting openness.

As we have noted, most important, from an evolutionary standpoint, is the inherently adaptive conceptualization that characterizes the self-psychological view. For example, when faced with a negative therapeutic reaction, Brandchaft (1983) does not look for drive-dominated masochism, but instead emphasizes "the *legitimate* selfobject needs remaining from childhood" (p. 352). Self psychology is the only psychoanalytic perspective that has consistently interpreted motivation with reference to the organism's long-range self-interest, thus emphasizing functional design in the organization of the psyche.

The Fully Adapted Self: Repetition and the Self of Inclusive Fitness

Our evolutionary perspective forces us, however, to modify the self-psychological view of the adaptive self. The modification consists of what could be called the *innately conflicted supraordinate self of inclusive fitness*. In this view, the self is the overarching concept that must organize inherently disparate self-aims, cope with internal conflict, and maximize the actualization of the person's nuclear program for the self. The disparate self-aims are related to some of the partial adaptive concepts already discussed. All of these partial adaptations (for example, the tendency of the repressed to find an outlet, belated attempts to master trauma) can be seen as part-functions, integral elements in a larger adaptive process. These part-functions are orchestrated in ways that are basically designed to maximize the chance for the successful operation of the curative fantasy.

CLINICAL IMPLICATIONS OF THE EVOLUTIONARY PERSPECTIVE

Conflict in the Self-Selfobject Milieu

In self-psychological theory and clinical interpretation, parental failure is seen as a result of pathological narcissism or other parental inadequacies. In our evolutionary view, this failure is only partly based on parental inadequacy. It is also inherent in the differing goals of parents and children. Their inclusive fitness overlaps but is not identical; at times, parents' interests will be in conflict with their children's interests. Thus, the parents' *healthy* narcissism, their actively seeking to maximize their *own* inclusive fitness, may lead to their "failure" as selfobjects for their children.

Innate Resistance: The Analyst as Pseudo-Kin

Our evolutionary vantage point further enriches our understanding of certain aspects of self-functioning as we examine a powerful innate source of resistance that, as far as we can tell, has never been mentioned in the psychoanalytic literature. The evolutionary biologist shows us two primary types of human ties: *kin* ties and *reciprocal* ties (in Figure 3, overlapping circles designate kin ties and lines represent reciprocal ties). Kin ties are based on the fact that relatives share a significant amount of genetic material, and therefore their success increases our own genetic success. This overlap of interests lies at the heart of all family ties, but especially parental care of offspring.

In reciprocal ties, relationships are based on reciprocity. The success of one person does not automatically benefit the inclusive fitness of the other; there must be an exchange of care, goods, support, and the like. Part of the goal of treatment is related to the crucial maturational goal of any species that has a long period of infantile/childhood dependency: separation from parents is necessary so that the successful creation of one's own family can be negotiated in the world. The goal is to move from primary dependency on kin ties to primary dependency on reciprocal ties (marriage, work, friendships).

A significant part of treatment, then, is the wearing of our patients from pathological kin ties to newer and potentially more adaptive reciprocal ties. Yet our patients are *designed to resist!* That is, they are designed to expect unrelated others to have no inherently overlapping self-interest with them. As much as they may seriously fail as selfobjects, parents still have far greater overlapping interests with their child than does their child's analyst. Parents will often provide concrete signs of this overlapping interest even when they are unable to function as psychological selfobjects. They may provide tangible investments such as money, goods, or shelter. The analyst, on the other hand, asks the patient to pay (dearly) for a relatively small (though perhaps crucial) investment!

This overlapping self-interest with kin should lead to a profound preference for retaining old patterns of attachments. Patients enter treatment innately somewhat more suspicious of reciprocal ties than of close kin. They are then presented with powerful role expectations: "Though I give you nothing tangible in return—and, in fact, insist that you pay me—I expect you to trust me and open yourself up to my (essentially pseudo-parental) influence that I imply will be good for you and of great value." Thus, the analyst is asking the patient to assume that there is an overlap between the patient's self-interest and the motives of the analyst, that is, *the patient is asked to react as if the analyst were kin, even though the analyst is not.* This "setup" should make the patient suspicious: the analyst creates a setting designed to mobilize the persuasive power of kin ties without the reality behind it, that is, to elicit a transference relationship. In such a setting, patients are asked to allow themselves to become reinvolved with the emotional experience of the kin ties (transference). This reinvolvement, however, represents the very emotional experiences that caused the problem in the first place!

Herein lies the unique mixture of opportunities and dangers of the analytic situation. Because the analyst is in fact not kin, he or she can have a vantage point that can potentially be free of the inherent biases that exist in the kin tie. What has not been appreciated is that, at some level, it is deeply known by both parties that the analyst cannot have those kinds of altruistic motivations that are exclusively the province of kin ties; therefore, this type of resistance has an innately *adaptive* basis.

One may object that the weight given to the analyst's non-kin status does not make sense, that parents often are untrustworthy and unrelated others are often far more willing and able to treat our patients with kindness and concern than are their families of origin. Yet, the extent of this investment by unrelated others is generally far more limited, certainly when the other is the analyst.

The basic knowledge of these universal rules of kinship is typically possessed by our patients, the more "primitive" of whom will insist that we, too, acknowledge it. Consider the following:

A borderline patient regresses in response to hearing that his male analyst just had a first child added to his life. The analyst presents a "zero-sum life view" interpretation, "You think that there is a limit to the amount of love and concern available in the world and that if I give to my son I will have less available for you." As an interpretation, there is an implicit suggestion that the patient's experience is a pathological carry over from childhood, e.g., an enactment in the transference of sibling or oedipal rivalry.

Following this, the patient regresses further. Finally, when the analyst acknowledges the inherent, current-day *truth* in the patient's feelings—that, of course, the analyst's life energies will be somewhat absorbed by a child of his flesh, leaving somewhat less of a capacity to be thoroughly concerned with his patient—the patient is able to begin to recover and even to expect that the analyst's experience nurturing his own child may have some beneficial impact on the treatment.

One way to view Brandchaft's (1983) concept of a defense against the mobilization of archaic selfobject longings is that our patients *should* be cautious about trusting strangers—who do not make themselves vulnerable and whom our patients have to pay for highly ritualized and structured relating—before making themselves vulnerable. This is an innate, healthy resistance that should be identified and acknowledged, but not necessarily interpreted. Our experience shows that, as in the brief clinical example just presented, this acknowledgment is experienced by the patient as an empathic statement and, as such, can partly allay the patient's normal mistrust of the non-kin analyst.

Thus, we therapists have to prove, by our actions—being a reliable selfobject, recognizing our failure to be selfobjects, not acting in anger, and not misusing the relationship for self-aggrandizement (see Kriegman and Solomon, 1985a, b for discussions of this last issue)—that we are, indeed, trustworthy selfobjects. Only then can our patients tentatively take their first, cautious steps into a trusting relationship. They must allow themselves, however tentatively, to be weaned from kin relationships, which, although perhaps destructive in some aspects, are based on deep, overlapping self-interests, with concomitant deep emotional attachments. Kin relationships are to be replaced, in part, by potentially more rewarding reciprocal relationships in which the patients will *never* be loved simply for being—they will always have to give something in exchange.

Innate Resistance: The Analyst as Pseudo-Friend

In the powerfully socially oriented psychological/motivational system of the human social animal, certain evolved features maximize self-interest. When looking at non-kin relationships, the person must have a way to ascertain those who will reciprocate in exchanges of goods and selfobject support and those who are inclined to cheat (Trivers, 1971). Trivers has even argued that this selective pressure was in significant part responsible for the rapid enhancement of human intelligence (see Kriegman, 1988).

When patients view their analysts, they see someone acting interested and involved in their inner experience. The degree of interest and the degree to which the analyst's goals are put aside produce a powerful experience in the analysand. In no way can the patient construe the analyst's stance as neutral (Kohut, 1984). The analyst engages in an empathic immersion in the analysand's psyche that is simply not a neutral experience for the patient. This is highly unusual behavior that the evolved emotional system of the patient is designed to interpret as a high degree of investment, caring, or love. Despite the fact that money is exchanged for this investment, it is easy to lose sight of the importance of payment in the ongoing, minute-by-minute experience of the therapy: the patient has the disturbing experience of feeling that the analyst cares deeply—for the analyst acts as no one would in our evolutionary past except for a best, most trusted friend—while simultaneously being aware that the investment is extremely limited.

Thus, the patient's emotional system has been designed to be deeply moved by the analytic work while simultaneously doubting the appropriateness of the patient's own internal emotional response. A basic aspect of this conflict should be acknowledged and interpreted without necessarily being seen as a resistance based on the patient's past experience.

Further Clinical Implications of the Evolutionary Biological View

Because conflict and drive interpretations have historically been seen as being in opposition to the patient's resistance to facing certain truths, they are often not offered in the spirit of self-psychological interpretations and are often experienced as assaults, and the assaultive experience is repeated over and over until the patient finds some way to demonstrate acceptance of the interpretation. This clinical derivative has led self psychologists away from the tripartite model and the biological concept of drive. However, the model of the self of inclusive fitness can hold for explanations presented to the patient regarding drives (embedded in the self or in relation to the supraordinate self) and conflicting self-aims. It is not drive or conflict content of an interpretation that leads to a narcissistic injury. It is the sense that one's experience is being ignored. In this case, either the interpretation is wrong—thus the analyst's insistence (that the patient's refusal to face the truth is the patient's resistance) repeatedly abandons and assaults the patient—or the interpretation of drive/conflict may miss its true experiential meaning: its embeddedness within or impact on the supraordinate self. These are the dynamics that underlie many "negative therapeutic reactions."

It is clear that nonbiological concepts such as the death instinct, blind repetition, and self-defeating masochism cannot be inherent, evolved features of biological organisms that have been shaped to survive and reproduce. We believe that the adaptive function of negative patterns and stubborn repetitions becomes clear if analysts ally themselves with the patient's self-interest and attempt to perceive the situation as an observer viewing the situation from such a vantage point. This essentially adaptive view of resistance renders meaningful, in an evolutionary sense, a universal feature of human functioning:

> [T]he so-called defense-resistances are neither defenses or resistances. Rather, they constitute valuable moves to safeguard the self, however weak and defensive it may be, against destruction and invasion. . . . The patient protects the defective self so that it will be ready to grow again in the future, to continue to develop from the point in time at which its development had been interrupted. And it is this recognition, deeply understood by the analyst who essentially sees the world through his patient's eyes while he analyzes him, that best prepares the soil for the developmental move forward that the stunted self of the analysand actively craves [Kohut, 1984, p. 141].

We believe that this view of Kohut's conveys a sense of the central adaptive organization of the psyche as the evolved "organ" that defines, promotes, and safeguards the inclusive self-interest of the individual. However, we also believe that while it is both theoretically and clinically crucial to maintain this overall perspective on the psyche in general and the phenomena of repetition and negative therapeutic reaction in particular, it is also necessary to recognize some corollaries to the central evolutionary concept of inclusive fitness: 1) an innately divided psyche represents a necessary, important, and functional adaptation to an intrinsically conflictual relational world; and 2) such a divided psyche must, indeed, operate simultaneously to resist and defend against the awareness (or revelation to others) of certain profound inner tensions between its basic social, mutualistic aims, and its equally natural and ultimately functional selfish, egocentric strivings that conflict with the self-interest of others.

In the self-psychological approach, with its emphasis on the field-defining empathic stance, the analyst would experience "himself . . . not as the target, but as the subject of the patient's wishes, needs, demands, and fantasies" (Ornstein, 1979, p. 102; Schwaber, 1979). The alternative to perceiving oneself as the object of the patient's drives is to experience oneself, along with the patient, as the subject of the drive (or wish or need) and to reflect back to the patient the inherently healthy and adaptive function that the drive (or wish) serves for the supraordinate self.

Thus, the clinician can be equipped with a functional understanding of the nature of certain drives and desires that may be the only way to account for the inherent conflict in the human psyche, conflict that is thus seen as adaptive, that is, of value to the patient's inclusive fitness. Such a conception maintains a view of the drives as a distinct, but nonetheless integral part of the adaptive aims of the psyche as a whole. Unlike the classical model, e.g., A. Freud (1936), this model does not view the individual as somehow "saddled" with a drive endowment that must be tamed because it is somehow antagonistic to the presumably adaptive aims of the ego. At the same time, however, the drives promote and safeguard individuality in the face of the enormous pressures and enticements of even the "good enough" and devoted social world (Slavin, 1988).

Clinically, even if drives (or wishes) are expressed in our patients' lives in a manner that appears to be maladaptive, their existence and expression should be seen as essentially adaptive. Either our patients are attempting to express an important aspect of inclusive fitness that has been blocked and has no appropriate outlet (basically similar to Fenichel's (1945) notion of the persistence of the repressed in seeking an outlet), or their exaggerated preoccupation with drive experiences and sensuality can be seen as an attempt to avoid further fragmentation and to maintain self-cohesion—to preserve the self so that future opportunities for self-growth or enhancement can be utilized. In either case, consistent with an evolutionary view, common features of the human psyche are seen in an adaptive framework that was lost in the classical, particularly ego psychological, perspective.

Clinical discussions and attitudes in the classical tradition frequently reflect a sense that there is an inherent, infantile compulsion to repeat that serves no adaptive function and is stubbornly held on to by the patient, and that this must be brought into the patient's awareness, along with a challenge to act more maturely and to force oneself to abandon the regressive repetitions. "Working through," defined by Freud as necessitated by stubborn id resistances due to the repetition compulsion/death instinct, is a dangerously misleading concept, even when separated from the death instinct. When working through is directed at an id resistance—without id-resistance seen in the larger functional context in which it may play a role in adaptively safeguarding certain self-aims against harmful influences—it can become an aggressive attempt on the part of the therapist to convince the patient that an interpretation is correct. That is, it can become an attempt to convince the patient that the interpretation being made, the analyst, and the analyst's viewpoint (psychoanalytic theory) are idealizable or can be put in the place of the analysand's ego ideal. As such, it is a process against which "the rules of analysis are diametrically opposed" (Freud, 1923, p. 50)!

While modern clinicians usually do not follow Freud's conclusions regarding the death instinct, they can frequently remain close to the spirit of a drive/structure psychology in which the patient is seen as refusing to let go of primitive drive gratifications. Thus, it becomes the role of the therapist to confront the patient's refusal and failure to take responsibility for the repetitive patterns.

Actually Freud was pointing out the problem with this very notion, for patients repeat traumas without gaining drive gratifications. Rather they experience greater discomfort and tension. Freud explained this with his teleological notion of a compulsion to repeat. What we all too often see in current clinical practice going under the name of Freud's "repetition compulsion" is at root an accusatory exhortation, the underlying message of which is, "You are repeating because of an infantile refusal to stop repeating, not because I have failed to help you."

The data of repetition have never been disputed by self-psychology: clinical data confront us with the fact that people repeat the same patterns. The reaction of the self psychologist is quite different. The self-psychological stance is fundamentally different from the classical, confrontational clinical approach of making the ego aware of the unconscious drives despite the ego's inherent resistance and the inherent human tendency to repeat. Rather than "support" being seen as a nonanalytic stance (see Kernberg, 1975), in the self psychological approach it can be essential:

> [E]arly deficits in the development of healthy narcissism cannot be *corrected* by insight . . . *alone*, but require actual support from the therapist in the form of affirmation and acceptance of the patient's total personality. [This should not be] confused with the gratification of instinctual drives; it is supportive in the name of a reconstruction of the patient's self [Menaker, 1981, p. 305].

CONCLUSION

Nonbiological concepts such as the death instinct, blind repetition, and primary masochism cannot refer to inherent, evolved features of biological organisms that have been shaped to survive. Such features have no selective value; they would not have been favored by natural selection and are unlikely to have become regular, universal parts of our species equipment. The repetition compulsion and negative therapeutic reaction as they have usually been defined may, in fact, not exist, though certain kinds of repetitions—even driven repetitions—may well exist as means toward adaptive growth and restructuring of the self. On the other hand, persistent and powerful sources of resistance can also be found in the adaptive biology of our very selfobject strivings. Unlike the notion of the negative therapeutic reaction, an understanding of these innate warnings about the potential for bias in the analyst's motives can potentially enhance our insight into, and our capacity to empathically reflect, certain conflicts and dilemmas experienced by our patients in the analytic situation.

Clinically, when mythical, maladaptive features are attributed to some inherent characteristic in the individual, this can result in a pejorative assault on the patient, who is blamed for the failure to improve. The extreme that this can reach was described by Schmideberg (1970), who reported knowing "of two patients treated by leading analysts for twelve and twenty years respectively, who eventually were sent by their analyst for lobotomy" (p. 199).[6]

The adaptive function of negative patterns and stubborn repetitions becomes clear if analysts ally themselves with the patient's self-interest. The self psychological view conveys a sense of the central adaptive organization of the psyche as the evolved "organ" that defines, promotes, and safeguards the inclusive self-interest of the individual. However, while it is both theoretically and clinically crucial to maintain this overall perspective on the psyche, it is also necessary to recognize some corollaries of the central evolutionary concept of inclusive fitness: 1) an innately *divided* psyche represents a necessary, important, and functional adaptation to an *intrinsically conflictual relational* world; 2) such a divided psyche operates simultaneously to resist and defend against the awareness (or revelation to others) of the profound inner tensions between basic social, mutualistic aims, and selfish, egocentric strivings that, to some degree, inevitably conflict with the self-interest of others.

While our evolutionary analysis suggests some significant modifications of self-psychological assumptions about human nature (and therefore some changes in the content of certain interpretations), both evolutionary biology and self psychology reject the myth of an inherent compulsion to repeat that serves no adaptive function. Consistent with a self-psychological approach, the patient's central

---

[6]For a detailed account of a psychoanalytic failure (focused on an autobiographical account of a failed training analysis), see Strupp (1982). Strupp, Hadley, and Gomes-Schwartz (1977) offer one of the most thorough discussions of the general problem of negative effects in psychotherapy.

strivings are seen as predominantly in search of growth and the utilization of selfobjects for further self-development, organized in terms of a curative (developmental) fantasy. This self-psychological clinical viewpoint finds support in evolution theory. "Negative therapeutic reactions"—distinct from *other* powerful sources of resistance—are basically explainable in terms of analysts' failures to ally themselves convincingly with the self-interest of the patient.

The maladaptive compulsion to repeat found in classical psychoanalysis is replaced by a picture of repetition in which patients strive to overcome earlier traumatic selfobject failures in later relationships that often cannot provide the necessary emotional response. The complex, continuing, and often persistent attempts to use relationships in this manner exemplify the underlying adaptive strivings of biological organisms.

REFERENCES

Axelrod, R. & Hamilton, W. D. (1981), The evolution of cooperation. *Science*, 211:1390–1396.

Bibring, E. (1943), The conception of the repetition compulsion. *Psychoanaly. Quart.*, 12:486–519.

Bowlby, J. (1969), *Attachment and Loss*, vol. 1. New York: Basic Books.

Brandchaft, B. (1983), The negativism of the negative therapeutic reaction and the psychology of the self. In: *The Future of Psychoanalysis*, ed. A. Goldberg. New York: International Universities Press.

Erikson, E. (1964), *Insight and Responsibility*. New York: Norton.

Fairbairn, W. R. D. (1952), *An Object Relations Theory of the Personality*. New York: Basic Books.

Fenichel, O. (1945), *The Psychoanalytic Theory of Neurosis*. New York: Norton.

Freud, A. (1936), *The Ego and the Mechanisms of Defense*. New York: International Universities Press.

Freud, S. (1895), Project for a scientific scientology. *Standard Edition*, 1:295–397. London: Hogarth Press, 1966.

―――― (1913), Totem and taboo. *Standard Edition*, 13,1–161. London: Hogarth Press, 1953.

―――― (1914), Remembering, repeating and working through. *Standard Edition*, 12:145–156. London: Hogarth Press, 1958.

―――― (1915a), Instincts and their vicissitudes. *Standard Edition*, 14:117–140. London: Hogarth Press, 1957.

―――― (1915b), Thoughts for the times on war and death. *Standard Edition*, 14:273–302. London: Hogarth Press, 1957.

―――― (1915c), *A Phylogenetic Fantasy*. Cambridge, MA: Belknap Press, Harvard, 1987.

―――― (1917), A difficulty in the path of psycho-analysis. *Standard Edition*, 17:136–144. London: Hogarth Press, 1955.

―――― (1920), Beyond the pleasure principle. *Standard Edition*, 19:3–64. London: Hogarth Press, 1961.

—— (1921), Group psychology and the analysis of the ego. *Standard Edition*, 18:65–143. London: Hogarth Press, 1955.

—— (1923), The ego and the id. *Standard Edition*, 19:1–66. London: Hogarth Press, 1961.

—— (1924), The economic problem of masochism. *Standard Edition*, 19:155–170. London: Hogarth Press, 1961.

—— (1926). Inhibitions, symptoms and anxiety. *Standard Edition*, 20:75–175. London: Hogarth Press, 1959.

—— (1930), Civilization and its discontents. *Standard Edition*, 21:59–145. London: Hogarth Press, 1961.

—— (1933), New introductory Lectures on Psycho-analysis. *Standard Edition*, 22:1–182. London: Hogarth Press, 1964.

—— (1937), Analysis terminable and interminable. *Standard Edition*, 23:216–254. London: Hogarth Press, 1964.

Glover, E. (1955), *The Technique of Psychoanalysis*. New York: International Universities Press.

—— (1956). *On the Early Development of Mind*. New York: International Universities Press.

Gould, S. J. (1977), *Ever Since Darwin*. New York: Norton, 251–259.

—— (1980), *The Panda's Thumb*. New York: Norton.

Greenberg, J. R. & Mitchell, S. A. (1983), *Object Relations in Psychoanalytic Theory*. Cambridge, MA: Harvard University Press.

Hamilton, W. D. (1964), The genetical evolution of social behavior. *J. Theor. Biol.*, 7:1–52.

Hartmann, H. (1939) *Ego Psychology and the Problem of Adaptation*. New York: International Universities Press, 1958.

Jones, E. (1953), *The Life and Work of Sigmund Freud*, Vol. I. London: Hogarth Press.

Kernberg, O. (1975), *Borderline Conditions and Pathological Narcissism*. New York: Aronson.

King, D. (1945), The meaning of normal. *Yale J. Biolog. Med.*, 17:493–501.

Kitcher, P. (1985), *Vaulting Ambition*. Cambridge, MA: MIT Press.

Kohut, H. (1959), Introspection, empathy, and psychoanalysis. *J. Amer. Psychoanal. Assn.*, 7:459–483.

—— (1977), *The Restoration of the Self*. New York: International Universities Press.

—— (1980), Reflections. In: *Advances in Self Psychology*, ed. A. Goldberg. New York: International Universities Press.

—— (1982), Introspection, empathy, and the semi-circle of mental health. *Internat. J. Psycho-Anal.*, 63:395–407.

—— (1984), *How Does Analysis Cure?* ed. A. Goldberg & P. E. Stepansky. Chicago, IL: University of Chicago Press.

Kriegman, D. (1988), Self psychology from the perspective of evolutionary biology: Toward a biological foundation for self psychology. In: *Frontiers in Self Psychology*, ed., A. Goldberg. Hillsdale, NJ: The Analytic Press, pp. 253–274.

Kriegman, D. & Solomon, L. (1985a), Psychotherapy and the "new religions": Are they the same? *Cultic Studies J.*, 2:2–16.

—— (1985b), Cult groups and the narcissistic personality: the offer to heal defects in the self. *Internat. J. Group Psychother.*, 35:239–261.

Loewald, H. (1965), Some considerations on repetition and repetition compulsion. In: *Papers on Psychoanalysis*. New Haven, CT: Yale University Press, 1980.

—— (1969), Freud's conception of the negative therapeutic reaction, with comments on instinct theory. In: *Papers on Psychoanalysis*. New Haven, CT: Yale University Press, 1980.

Mahler, M., Pine, F. & Bergman, A. (1975), *The Psychological Birth of the Human Infant.* New York: Basic Books.

Mayr, E. (1982), *The Growth of Biological Thought.* Cambridge, MA: Belknap Press, Harvard.

———— (1983), How to carry out the adaptationist program. *Amer. Naturalist,* 121:324–334.

Menaker, E. (1981), Self-psychology illustrated on the issue of moral masochism: Clinical implications. *Amer. J. Psychoanal.,* 41:297–305.

Olinick, S. L. (1964), The negative therapeutic reaction. *Internat. J. Psycho-Anal.,* 45:540–548.

Ornstein, A. (1984), Psychoanalytic psychotherapy: A contemporary perspective. In: *Kohut's Legacy,* ed. P. E. Stepansky & A. Goldberg, Hillsdale, NJ: The Analytic Press, pp. 171–181.

Ornstein, P. (1979), Remarks on the central position of empathy in psychoanalysis. *Bull. Assn. Psychoanal. Med.,* 18:95–108.

Racker, H. (1968), *Transference and Countertransference.* New York: International Universities Press.

Robertson, J. (1952), "A Two-Year-Old Goes to the Hospital." London: Tavistock Child Development Research Unit; New York: New York University Film Library.

Sandler, J. (with A. Freud) (1985), *The Analysis of Defense,* New York: International Universities Press.

Schmideberg, M. (1970), Psychotherapy with failures of psychoanalysis. *Brit. J. Psychiat.,* 116:195–200.

Schwaber, E. (1979), On the "self" within the matrix of analytic theory—some clinical reflections and reconsiderations. *Internat. J. Psycho-Anal.,* 60:467–479.

Slavin, M. O. (1985), The origins of psychic conflict and the adaptive function of repression: An evolutionary biological view. *Psychoanal. Contemp. Thought,* 8:407–440.

———— (1988), The biology of parent-offspring conflict and the dual meaning of repression in psychoanalysis. Presented meeting of American Academy of Psychoanalysis, Montreal, May 6.

Slavin, M. O. & Kriegman, D. (1988a). Freud, biology, and sociobiology. *Amer. Psychol.,* 43:658–661.

———— (1988b), Psychoanalysis, biological reductionism, and the evolution of human psychodynamics. Unpublished.

Stolorow, R., Brandchaft, B., & Atwood, G. (1983), Intersubjectivity in psychoanalytic treatment: With special reference to archaic states. *Bull. Menn. Clin.,* 47:117–128.

Strupp, H. (1982), Psychoanalytic failure. *Contemp. Psychoanal.,* 18:235–250.

Strupp. H., Hadley, S. & Gomes-Schwartz, B. (1977), *Psychotherapy for Better or Worse.* New York: Aronson.

Sulloway, F. (1979), *Freud, Biologist of the Mind.* New York: Basic Books.

Trivers, R. L. (1971), The evolution of reciprocal altruism. *Quart. Rev. Biol.,* 46:35–57.

———— (1974), Parent-offspring conflict. *Amer. Zool.,* 14:249–264.

———— (1985), *Social Evolution.* Boston: Addison-Wesley.

Wilson, E. O. (1975), *Sociobiology.* Cambridge, MA: Belknap Press, Harvard.

Winnicott, D. W. (1965), *The Maturational Process and the Facilitating Environment.* New York: International Universities Press.

Wynne-Edwards, V. C. (1962), *Animal Dispersion in Relation to Social Behavior.* Edinburgh, Scot: Oliver & Boyd.

Chapter 13

The Search for the Self of the Future Analyst

Charles Kligerman

In the wide range of Heinz Kohut's rich and seminal contributions, one particular aspect has received only scant attention. This was his lively interest in the problem of the evaluation of applicants for psychoanalytic training. Indeed, I believe this activity constituted his major scientific effort within the framework of the International Psychoanalytic Association, culminating in his chairmanship of the 2nd Pre-Congress Conference on training in Copenhagen in 1967— more than 20 years ago—in which this theme was addressed. There are probably two reasons for the seeming neglect: (1) the conference was followed by a period of extraordinarily creative activity in the development of the psychology of the self, of which the work on candidate evaluation was but one small facet of applied analysis, and (2) it dealt with a topic ordinarily relegated to the administrative halls of psychoanalytic institutes, usually in an atmosphere of hushed confidentiality.

Yet, this subject has always been a matter of deep concern to anyone who ever aspired to be an analyst and to those who had to make the decisions of selection. In spite of a fairly large literature in this area, ubiquitous discussions in institute committees, ambitious research projects, period follow-up studies, a sense of disquietude persists about the success of our efforts, a less than optimistic feeling about our ability to judge in advance who would make a good analyst. If psychoanalysis is an impossible profession, the task of selecting future analysts is even more impossible, if you will forgive the oxymoronic extension.

The candidate evaluation problem is closely related to another: who is a good analyst anyway? On what basis does one make this decision? I well remember how in my own candidate days, some of us played the game "find the ideal analyst"—whom do we admire the most and wish to emulate? Naturally, the choice was usually (though not always) one's own analyst. But the second and third choices, on which there was a good deal of consensus, were significant. How these evaluations were made was not quite clear, but I will return to that later.

This game was predicated on the assumption that somewhere there was an ideal analyst—the very model of a *homo psychoanalyticus*. But, of course, there is no such thing; there are many different kinds of very good analysts, with diverse theoretical persuasions, personality types, self-structures, special assets, psychopathology, creativity, lack of creativity. Kohut (1968a) laid strong emphasis on this variety in his introductory talk to the Pre-Congress, stressing that it was important to determine if each applicant had the potential to develop into *his* kind of analyst. Thus Kohut heralded his work on the nuclear self and nuclear program.

In the face of such bewildering diversity, the logical step would be to isolate those qualities and configurations that are optimal, perhaps mandatory, for any good analyst, regardless of the surrounding matrix. And here I am referring to qualities long described and familiar to all: intelligence, motivation, psychic stability, psychological mindedness, ability for self-observation, propensity for caretaking, capacity to be objective and nonjudgmental, empathy, analyzability (the list is long), compassion, passion for truth. *Passion for truth*?

I pause because Kohut's (1984) critique of Freud's culture boundness, as well as Freud's personal reasons for adhering to this *summum bonum*, might be construed by some as a devaluation of the truth standard, although Kohut specifically denied this. Here I would like to refer to the final portion of his compelling and eloquent introductory statement to the participants of the 1967 Pre-Congress. He (Kohut, 1968a) quoted a simple and charming letter of reply by Anna Freud to a 14-year-old boy who, with Kohut's encouragement, had written her to ask, in effect, what it takes to become an analyst. Miss Freud wrote:

Dear John,
    You asked me what I consider essential personal qualification in a future psychoanalyst. The answer is comparatively simple. If you want to be a real psychoanalyst you have to have a great love of the truth, scientific truth as well as personal truth, and you have to place this

appreciation of truth higher than any discomfort at meeting unpleasant facts, whether they belong to the world outside or to your own inner person [p. 474].

Miss Freud briefly outlined some other criteria, such as broad interests, then closed with the statement, "In the great literary figures you will find people who know at least as much of human nature as the psychiatrists and psychologists try to do" (p. 474).

Kohut, on his part, concluded his statement as follows: "Yet whenever the discussions should reach an external or internal impasse during the meetings, it behooves us to recall one sentence from her letter: 'If you want to be a real psychoanalyst, you must have a great love of the truth' " (p. 475). I do not think Kohut ever seriously retreated from that position. He simply wanted equal time for the criteria of empathy and certain others. Actually, one might argue that the love of truth criterion is universal in any science but that empathy is specific to psychoanalysis—not empathy alone, but at least empathy.

Following the introductory session, the Pre-Congress broke up into small discussion groups. I was privileged to join one that included Miss Freud. The course of this discussion fell into a pattern that has been uncannily repeated in nearly every group of this kind I have ever witnessed.

1) The attempt to formulate positive criteria becomes bogged down in complexity.

2) Someone proposes that it would simplify our task if we could agree on factors that are outright disqualifying.

3) At once, homosexuality is brought up, and the battle is joined. In 1967, virtually no institute would knowingly accept a homosexual candidate; but after some debate in our group, it was agreed in principle that the decision would depend on the kind and degree of the homosexuality and the role it played in the total psychic economy, particularly in regard to narcissism and the so-called analytic function. Yet at the end of this phase of the discussion, there was an uneasy feeling that might be expressed by the question, Would you send your son to a homosexual analyst? It might not be exactly bedrock, but castration anxiety is far from dead.

The discussion of homosexuality and perversion led to the considseration of the degree and kinds of other psychopathology that would be unacceptable and, short of overt psychosis or low intelligence, this proved to be a most difficult issue. At one point, Anna Freud observed with dry gentility, "Be sure we don't select ourselves out," reminding us that some of the greatest early analysts had high degrees of psychopathology.

When the 1967 Pre-Congress ended, on Kohut's initiative an ongoing Study Commission on the Evaluation of Applicants was appointed, with Kohut as chairman and me as secretary. This was the first, and to date only, such ongoing study group in the International Psychoanalytic Association. In 1975, Paul Ornstein became a valued member. After a number of years, Kohut withdrew because of the increasing pressure of his creative work.

At some future date, some of the findings will be published. I am not at liberty to discuss them now, but I can tell you that one of the most important results was the depth of insight each member felt he had developed from his internal experience alone in addressing this important problem.

One approach that did not come up in our group could be called a "nonapproach"—namely abdication—a recognition of the difficulty of adequate prediction and the adoption of a more or less "open admissions" policy. Here the candidate, self-selected, faces a test of survival in the training period. This has the disadvantage of an expensive, cumbersome, and often painful delay of ultimate rejection in the unsuitable. But some people feel that the odds would not be that different from our usual procedure, which, in addition, "selects out" some applicants who might have developed into superior analysts.

Many years ago, Therese Benedek, at the Chicago Institute, proposed, only partly in jest, a year of such open admission as an experiment. Her suggestion was not followed, but such a procedure was employed at that time in Switzerland, and there was an interesting variation in one South American locale, a Kleinian stronghold. In this group, an aspiring analyst was advised to start his own analysis, then find private supervision and begin doing analytic work on his own. After a time, the results of this experimental period were assessed by the analyst and supervisors and used in the selection process at the institute. This ingenious method has one serious, and to my mind insuperable, drawback: the exposure of patients to the possibility of treatment with an inexperienced, incompetent, perhaps destructive therapist. It is as if they were being used as guinea pigs in the service of selection.

There is yet one more theoretical possibility of eliminating the burdensome task of a searching, depth-psychological evaluation of the future analyst. I refer to the perfection of our scientific knowledge to the point where, although reasonable intelligence, training, and professional honesty would still be required, the special qualities of talent and personality in the analyst would be minimized and asymptotically reduced. Science would reduce art to technology. Eissler (1953) listed the three crucial elements in any analysis as (1) the personality of the analyst, (2) the structure of the personality of the patient, and (3) the external situation. By assuming optimal external conditions, and heuristically eliminating the role of the analyst's personality, he arrived at a series of technical postulates that became almost sacred text to a generation of young analysts. Of course, Eissler never seriously underestimated the personality of the analyst, but the dream of constructing a science of psychoanalysis long preceded him, reaching its height in the triumph of ego psychology in America in the 50s.

In the Collected Papers of David Rapaport (1967) there is much about cognition, but the index contains not one reference to empathy. Waelder (1962), also a physicist by training but, unlike Rapaport, an eminent clinician, actually minimized empathy as a criterion for selection. However, here Waelder used empathy in the sense of a premature deep intuition into the unconscious. It was this attitude that led Kohut, disturbed by a sense of increasing dehumanization of psychoanalysis, as well as the inappropriate intrusion of both biological and social psychological methods, to write a paper (Kohut, 1959) in which he delineated the method and boundaries of psychoanalysis in terms of introspection and empathy. He thus defined psychoanalysis as a science sui generis, in a way that both narrowed it and broadened it: narrowed it by the extrusion of the biosocial contaminants, broadened it by the inclusion of a whole range of human interactions loosely employed, like "therapeutic alliance," into a rational framework that could be largely explained by the later concept of selfobject. But although he claimed fresh ground of human interaction for rational scientific thought, he never neglected the humanly artistic side of analysis. Heinz had his own surgical metaphor for analysis—not the dispassionate attitude toward pain—but the often expressed idea that of all the healing fields the special talent of the doctor was most crucial in surgery and psychoanalysis.

But what is the special talent of the analyst? Clearly, impending changes in the psychoanalytic world are going to place far greater demands on our powers of effective selection than ever before. All the current signs indicate that an organizational revolution is taking place in American psychoanalysis, that the established institutes, which have overwhelmingly been the bulwark of psychoanalytic advancement and education in this country, will move progressively in the direction of admitting nonmedical applicants. The entry of this new class of applicants—hardly a class, since they will show a much greater diversity and heterogeneity than the medical group—will pose even more difficult problems for evaluation than the ones I have mentioned. After all, the medical requirement greatly simplified the labors of selection committees—not just in reducing the numbers, but in working with a population that had passed many tests of stability, industry, and clinical responsibility and moreover resembled their selectors.

The newer applicants will pose problems of identification and empathy even, or especially, in seasoned medical evaluators. I recall in a recent group studying the prerequisites for analytic training, one member saying plaintively, "They [the nonmedical applicants] are very bright people with a fine education, but they're so different from us. It's hard to explain—they just don't seem to have the clinical feel."

Obviously, such applicants would receive remedial clinical training—but they *are* different. That does not mean they could not become first-rate analysts. They are just harder to judge. Surely in time, and with experience, good working criteria will be threshed out, especially when carried out by existing institutes, which have an elaborately developed, albeit imperfect, apparatus for this activity. But the crucial factor here will still be so-called psychological sensitivity, so essential to our work. Perhaps this is the lingua franca that will link people from very diverse fields. Here is a challenge to self psychology, which has the strongest theoretical equipment to address this issue and not only make a contribution to the practical solutions, but perhaps shed new light at the heart of psychoanalysis.

To return to some of the specific issues that the self-psychologically informed analyst could investigate. One of the questions Kohut raised before the Study Commission was, in effect, what are the genetic factors that would impel a man to spend the bulk of his working day immersed in the inner life of another person? The question itself suggests many answers: the usual ones of voyeurism, substitution for relationships, vicarious affective experience, Pygmalion motives. One that may be central and what I think, in retrospect, Kohut possibly had in mind, is a need in the analyst to firm his own self through vicarious mirroring; that is, there is a certain vulnerability of cohesion in a relatively intact self, so that constant repetition creates a rhythmic reaffirmation of the analyst's self while giving functional pleasure in helping another person move toward self-recognition and self-cohesion. Often this resembles the experience of an artist or writer who feels whole or integrated when practicing his art but restless and uneasy when not at work. This formulation, which in some ways seems obvious—in fact, an extension in systematized form of normal daily human intercourse—is at variance with another view of analytic work—that it is depleting, and the analyst should have ample sources of gratification and supplies outside of his profession, or perhaps periodic analysis to replenish himself. Both factors are of course present in varying degrees. I alluded earlier to the tendency of candidates to search for the ideal analyst. Among aging analysts the question is often instead, Who is an analyst? because, contrary to folklore, age does not necessarily increase tolerance, especially among analysts. But in my private inventory I think the majority, though not all, of good analysts would fall into the first category, people who find the work sustaining, but at such a deep, internalized level—neutralized if you will—that it is a source of strength, like a smoothly running ego function not an intrusion, which would be felt as exploitative by the analysand.

We are told with solemnity that an analyst must not use the patient for his own need or gratification, and this is certainly true for the most part; but at the deeper, neutralized level I am postulating, I think it goes on all the time. In optimal form it is less a question of "physician—heal thyself" than, to quote the poet Gerard Manley Hopkins (1948), "this seeing the sick endears them to us, us too it endears."

The analysts I have in mind may not be outstanding theoreticians— some do not publish—may not be politically or socially active, may not even have the broad cultural interests that everyone says an analyst should have. But there is no question about their dedication and analytic skill. Incidentally, I am not referring here to the myth of those analysts who allegedly "analyze by the seat of their pants" but are weak in theoretical explication. The analysts I have in mind can articulate very well their conception of the process in terms of clinical theory.

Perhaps we can focus the examination of the postulated "good analyst" a little better if we correlate his qualities with the task at hand. Kohut (1984) distilled the work of the analyst into a two-stage process of understanding and explanation. Stage 1 depends on the empathic receptivity of the analyst but is of course not by itself sufficient. There has been some controversy over the role of empathy as a curative factor, and there are occasional grotesque distortions of so-called empathy used as technical maneuver. Kohut's stand was unequivocal—although there is certainly a self-strengthening effect of feeling empathically understood over a period of time, the interventions that are helpful, mutative, perhaps curative, depend on how the analyst communicates his understanding.

In this conceptualization, he claimed for self psychology bona fide status in the classical tradition of psychoanalysis—even according to the strict rules of Eissler—of empathic listening and data gathering followed by interpretation, particularly of the transference. Yet he (Kohut, 1984) conceded in the final pages of his last book, as we all must, that

> a modicum of psychotherapeutic impurity will often, if not always . . . [I would say always] be present even following analyses that have been satisfactorily concluded. . . . Although the self psychologist knows that self psychology, by allowing the analyst to recognize and analyze the selfobject transferences, has enormously reduced this psychotherapeutic admixture, he also knows that the ideal zero-point of such admixtures is still out of reach. (This recognition probably means no more than that there are still transferences—that have not yet been discovered and which, therefore, remain unanalyzed) [pp. 209–210].

While abjuring perfectionism, he then distinguished between the harmless impurities and those which have resulted in permanent restrictions, presumably due to gross identifications with the analyst, as in certain training analyses.

This portion of persistent psychotherapeutic admixture is perhaps the most important area for future self-psychological investigation. I believe it is the area in which the really "good analysts" excel while maintaining optimal empathic contact and an analytic stance. It also has been a cause of bitter conflict from the very beginnings of psychoanalysis, related to the permissible activity of the analyst and the so-called unobjectionable transference.

The approach to this problem caused early dissension between Freud and Ferenczi (see Jones, 1957) and has been a burning source of controversy ever since. How much alloy turns the analyst into a psychotherapist? Classical analysis tried to resolve the problem by limiting analysis to those conditions amenable to this kind of treatment, first the transference neuroses, later the good enough ego. This is the area in which Kohut always maintained that classical theory was valid and relevant.

The widening scope was an embarrassment. Gitelson (1962) addressed this issue when he raised orthodox eyebrows by proposing a necessary diatrophic attitude in the analyst during the first phase of treatment. Influenced by Spitz's (1956) pioneer studies of nurturant mothers in the preverbal stage, he saw this as an essential psychotherapeutic measure for strengthening the patient's ego and making it possible to conduct analysis in the standard fashion. There is a formidable number of contributions on this issue, but it was one of Kohut's greatest achievements to reclaim this area for analytic understanding and systematic treatment by the delineation of the selfobject transferences.

The "widening scope" includes not only more pathological or primitively organized patients, but those same elements in healthier patients who are amenable to standard analysis, albeit with certain remnants of deficit. So the "widening" scope is also a "deepening scope" with the hope of more successful and complete analyses. And just as Gitelson was inspired by the pioneer work of Spitz 25 years ago, the analyst of today has at his disposal the fruits of the extraordinary explosion in infant research and developmental studies of the intervening period, work summarized so brilliantly, for instance, by Lichtenberg (1983, 1987) and Stern (1985).

But there are difficulties. Many of the findings, theories, schemata, are not exactly in agreement with each other and in fact often are strenuously opposed. Analytic clinicians have always had a certain reserve about the observational findings of child researchers. No matter how rigorous or sophisticated these studies are, they still suffer from the lack of direct contact with the inner experience of the mind of the child. Nevertheless, the work cannot help but widen the span of our empathic inventory and, at the very least, remind us that fixed positions of developmental theory are not sacrosanct. The clinician faced with the bewildering mass of data must inform himself as best he can, letting the ideas filter through his analytic instrument, and thereby experience fresh resonances of which he was previously insufficiently aware. But to adhere too strongly to any schema immediately makes the clinician a partisan and cuts off alternatives. Of course, there are times when such partisanship is both inevitable and desirable—when there has been a major breakthrough, as in Kohut's self psychology—but such events are rare. One of my favorite quotations is from the great Paganini, who, when asked by a young violinist how best to develop himself, replied, "Listen carefully to every good violinist you can, but don't imitate any of them!"

But to return to the man on the firing line, the postulated good analyst who must deal with these issues *in situ*: In all these areas that are being uncovered, the analyst must respond to his analysand with his existing equipment, conscious and unconscious, and this equipment has somewhere experienced everything that the researchers find and much more. The analyst cannot by introspection recognize and articulate it in its archaic form but in favorable instances can still use it. This is perhaps the "seat of the pants" aspect of analysts who are otherwise quite aware of themselves. It has always seemed to me that in addition to presenting themselves as empathic listeners, as targets for transference, as nonjudgmental witnesses, and then as appropriate responders with well-timed, effective interpretations, good analysts, even when they refrain from gratuitous action, still give their patients an unusual measure of confidence, strength, enhancement of self-esteem, just by being who they are. The gleam in the eye, the warm tone of voice, the compassionate murmur, all these are external markers of an extremely complex inner response that functions almost automatically and optimally operates and calibrates itself, not only in the first phase, as Gitelson (1962) recommended, but appropriately throughout the analysis, according to the developmental stage and need presented.

All these things are well recognized and often discussed, perhaps in other terms, but I would like to stress that part of being a good analyst that is not a specific response or countertransference but something added, almost like an organic emanation. Formerly considered a manifestation of libido, it was this kind of phenomenon that led Wilhelm Reich in his approaching fragmentation to detect actual quanta of libidinal energy streaming toward the patient, so that he concretized a metaphor and devised a box to supply the needed orgones. A sad ending for a brilliant clinician, whose earlier work on character analysis once fascinated our generation, including the young Kohut. Good analysts are generally not charismatic or gurulike, but work quietly in a one to one setting. If pressed, I would venture at least one hypothetical determinant: a benign enmeshment in the narcissistic system of the analyst, whose unconscious feeling is, "I am wonderful and anyone tied to me is wonderful." But there would have to be a very highly developed transformation of that motive, with no intrusion of values and expectations and no hostile disappointment if the patient fails to respond. Closely related to basic trust, the holding environment, the "borrowed strength," the process of benign narcissistic enmeshment furnishes a preverbal matrix for analytic work and interpretation at a higher level. In favorable cases, much of the strength is retained, presumably owing to the correction of a developmental deficit by a silent reparenting, at an archaic level. I wish to stress again that this is most effective when the foregoing process is not a conscious technique, but is an inherent quality in the analyst. Perhaps this quality represents the zero point of psychotherapeutic admixture. But further study might make still further technical inroads, or at least give us clues on the recognition of such qualities in future analysts.

I should interject here that the good analysts I am discussing are analysts for analyzable patients; that is, I am not considering therapists who work analytically with severe borderlines and psychotics, for whom many other considerations enter in and who I feel are generally quite different from the analysts I am describing. And analyzability is defined here as the capacity to form at least a cohesive selfobject transference and in a sense could still fit in with Freud's original definition. This, of course, raises the issue of analyzable by whom?

You will recall my description of the controversy in the 1967 Pre-Congress about the suitability of homosexuals as candidates and that it devolved on the issue of an intractable narcissism. At that time, the question about applicants was whether their instinctual conflicts could be resolved in the direction of reasonably mature sexuality, object relations, and neutralization of aggression. Narcissism was considered a resistance against the development of an object-instinctual transference, and a high degree of narcissism was a very negative factor in selection.

But Kohut (1968a) saw the narcissism as the ore for transformation to empathy, wisdom, and maybe creativity—the very stuff of which analysts are made. In a sense, one could almost say that the practice of analysis is a transformation of narcissism—provided, of course, that it was successfully analyzed, that is, according to the principles of the analysis of narcissistic disorders that he was then developing and would be presented one year later in New York. And so, every time the crucial issue of analyzability came up, Kohut's question was always there, either voiced or implicit—analyzable by whom?

Whenever individual applicants were described, he would look for the specific remnant of archaic forms of narcissism and wonder if it could resume its development through analysis of the specific narcissistic transferencelike configurations. (The concept of the selfobject was still germinating.) If these ideas were carried through in evaluation, the selection base would be considerably broadened in terms of diversity, talent, and creativity and might include good, potentially empathic analysts who formerly would have been rejected. Perhaps even the very good analysts I described, in addition to having natural gifts, were products of such analyses in the hands of unusually empathic analysts of the classical variety. But in the statement, "In whose hands?" Heinz meant not so much as artist of empathy as someone who had mastered the new theory and principles.

To move to a later vicissitude of self that I consider of vital importance for analysts who never stop developing, and especially for those with the rare, truly creative gift, a self-psychologically informed biographical vignette will be useful. In our 1967 discussion group, Anna Freud strongly suggested the biographical examination of the lives of earlier pioneers who were generally recognized as great contributors to the field. This idea was very appealing to me because of my own biographical interests. Kohut often used this method persuasively, especially in his paper (Kohut, 1978) on the transference of creativity, where he explored the meaning of Freud's relation to Fliess during Freud's self-analysis. Of course, the method has the same drawbacks as applied analysis in general compared to analytic work *in vivo* with patients in a transference situation, but there are also certain advantages, particularly when used with empathic sophistication enriched by the insights of self psychology.

The time between the Copenhagen Congress of 1967 and the Rome meeting in 1969 was a very critical period for Kohut. During that interval he was planning seriously to run for the presidency of the International Psychoanalytic Association. I have no doubt that this was one of the major life goals he had set for himself—to occupy the office once held by Jung when he was still Freud's favorite, by Karl Abraham, by Ernest Jones, by Heinz Hartmann, the highest official honor in the psychoanalytic world. It was a burning ambition. He had already played an important part in the International as a vice president, and I believe his dominant role at the 1967 Pre-Congress was considered by many as a prelude to his elevation to the Presidency, as if this were a foregone conclusion. He even received affectionately jocular messages "to the future President of the IPA."

But the years between 1967 and 1969 were also a period of enormous internal creative ferment in Kohut. "Forms and Transformations of Narcissism" (1966) had already been published, and the accumulated experience of his developing clinical insight with his patients was leading to a systematization that soon took shape in his Freud Anniversary Lecture in New York in 1968, "The Psychoanalytic Treatment of Narcissistic Personality Disorders" (1968). With all these ideas germinating in Kohut's mind, there still persisted some lingering adherence to the theoretical principles that had formerly been so precious to him and were held by nearly all of his old friends, among whom he had been "Mr. Psychoanalysis." At the 1967 Congress, most of his offerings were still made in the language of ego psychology, although the underlying thinking was more self-psychological, and when he spoke spontaneously his words were increasingly couched in a new conceptual frame. Clearly, he was conflicted between the drive of burgeoning new conceptualizations and an adherence to cherished old goals and relationships. In the midst of this turmoil, he withdrew his candidacy.

I suspect this was one of the most painful decisions of his life; when he spoke of it, with a certain attempt at wistful humor, it was one of the rare times I had ever seen him really downhearted. But not for long. The period that followed was one of unprecedented creativity in the development of the psychology of the self, leading to the publication of *The Analysis of the Self* (Kohut, 1971) and all that followed. Now, I would not suggest for a moment that the construction of the Psychology of the Self was a creative repair to Kohut's injured self. It was the inevitable development of everything he was searching for, beginning with the Introspection paper (Kohut, 1959). But I do think that the conflict situation and Heinz's manly decision were extremely important in his deploying his energies full time to what was the core of his central program, to the fulfillment of his true self, if you will. For although he was capable of enormous efforts to keep several projects going at once, I wonder what would have happened if he had become the president and, for the next two years at least, at that stage of his life, been obligated to travel to the far reaches of the globe, giving speeches, evaluating remote training centers, guiding the affairs of the international body.

Self psychology would undoubtedly have continued its development, but who knows how much of Kohut's legacy would have been lost but for that decision.

Actually, I never felt that Kohut had much of a gift for political activity (although at times he took a boyish pleasure in the goings-on of the smoke-filled room, American style). He had high qualities of leadership and could function effectively as an administrator, but organizational activity was really not his forte. He reached his highest potential as a superb teacher and clinician, and especially as a creative analytic thinker. In making his choice, he followed the voice of a self-righting function, a capacity to make painful decisions, to mourn and emerge with a stronger, undamaged self. His decision and it sequellae illustrate the possibility of a growth spurt at any stage of life while maintaining fidelity to the nuclear program. Of course, the move involved an unhappy estrangement from old friends and associates, but he found new sources of selfobject support in the growing circle of younger disciples, as he poignantly describes in *The Search for the Self* (Kohut, 1978). Most of his disciples are today leaders of the field. And during this period he liberated himself from the strictures of an overrigidified classical theory.

But true liberation does not mean separation from one's past. He made this very clear:

I felt that in order to create a satisfactory new framework, I had to outline a theoretical structure that would be adequate to fulfilling three demands, which I will now set down in order of their increasing importance: (1) the new psychology of the self must remain in an

unbroken continuum with traditional psychoanalytic theory to preserve the sense of the historical continuity of the group self in the
psychoanalytic community; (2) the new theoretical system must, at this
point in the development of psychoanalysis, not disregard the fact that
the classical theories, especially as expanded in the form of modern
ego psychology, though applicable only in a restricted area, are neither
in error nor irrelevant; (3) the new theory, while clear, must not be
dogmatic and definitive, but open to change and capable of further
development [Kohut, 1978, p. 937].

In other words, Kohut saw the psychology of the self as a stage in
development of the mainstream of psychoanalysis. This was in 1977,
close to the end of his life. In 1981, when he wrote his final book, a
work destined for posthumous publication, he reiterated essentially
the same position. I believe this affirmation performed a dual function: 1) it created, at a new level, an inner sense of rapprochement
with his former mentors and friends and a personal feeling of
continuity with the great tradition, and 2) in this consistent attitude,
which many lose sight of because of his criticism of certain theoretical
shortcomings in traditional theory and the penetration of an implicit
moralistic element, Kohut reaffirmed the essential continuity of the
new psychology of the self with the entire history and growth of
psychoanalysis.

THE THRUST OF THE NEXT DECADE

The last dozen years have been a period of enormous fruitfulness and
productivity of self psychology in every area where human psychology counts—not only in clinical work, but in the arts, sciences,
literature, humanities—reminiscent of the way that earlier Freudian
thinking pervaded the civilized world. This is a cause for pride and
celebration, and there is every indication that this momentum will
continue, at an even accelerated pace. But, to use a military analogy,
the forward thrust has to be accompanied by an adequate supply-line
to the rear. In regard to the nonclinical applications, Kohut especially
prized this area, much as Freud often felt his main legacy was a new
Weltanschauung, but for both men the wellspring of knowledge and
insight derived from the psychoanalytic situation. This remains the
fountainhead of one man's comprehension of another in depth. Even
self-psychologically informed psychotherapy of a high order, though
valuable and indispensable, is a form of applied analysis. I do not
believe that self psychology has blurred the distinction.

I also do not believe that self psychology can be properly understood without a solid classical analytic background. Kohut felt this way too and always emphasized the historical method of teaching analysis. In other words, the study of self psychology should repeat its history. Nearly all the leaders in self psychology have such a background and sometimes perhaps take this for granted, since it has become a part of the self and silently pervades their thinking.

But what of the future cadre of teachers and leaders? Where will they gain the deep and thorough education essential for this role? I hope that these future leaders will continue the traditional training, encouraged by self psychologists who will themselves draw closer, at all levels, to the established centers of psychoanalytic learning and continue to exert a wholesome influence on the course of psychoanalytic education. I personally have always favored introducing self psychology to more advanced students, and I can envision institutes where, after a basic core program, different elective tracks could be followed.

I realize that many of the established institutes have been less than friendly to self-psychological thinking. Strong issues of pride are involved; but as I have pointed out, powerful winds of change are blowing, and the same forces that soften the rigidity of the medical model may create a climate more amenable to friendly dialogue and a closer relationship. In the troubled future that psychoanalysis undoubtedly faces, the best minds need each other. In a close relation, self psychology could assume its rightful place in the mainstream of psychoanalysis, and, through a fruitful collaboration, there could emerge new developments and new discoveries that would fulfill both the vision of the founding father and the nuclear program of self-psychologically informed psychoanalysis. A salute to the next decade!

NOTE

This paper was delivered as the Kohut Memorial Lecture on October 24, 1987, at the Tenth Annual Conference of The Psychology of the Self, Chicago.

REFERENCES

Eissler, K. R. (1953), The effect of the structure of the ego on psychoanalytic technique. *J. Amer. Psychoanal. Assn.*, 1:104–143.
Gitelson, M. (1962), The curative factors in psychoanalysis (part I). *Internat. J. Psycho-Anal.*, 43:194–205.

Hopkins, G. M. (1948), Felix Randal. In: *Poems of Gerard Manley Hopkins*, ed. R. Bridges & W. H. Gardner. New York: Oxford University Press, pp. 91–92.

Jones, E. (1957), *The Life and Work of Sigmund Freud*, Vol. 3. New York: Basic Books.

Kohut, H. (1959), Introspection, empathy and psychoanalysis: An examination of the relationship between mode of observation and theory. In: *The Search for the Self*, Vol. 1, ed. P. Ornstein. New York: International Universities Press, 1978, pp. 205–232.

———— (1966), Forms and transformations of narcissism. In: *The Search for the Self*, Vol. 1, ed. P. Ornstein. New York: International Universities Press, 1978, p. 427–460.

———— (1968a), The evaluation of applicants for psychoanalytic training. In: *The Search for the Self*, Vol. 1, ed. P. Ornstein. New York: International Universities Press, 1978, pp. 461–475.

———— (1968b), The psychoanalytic treatment of narcissistic personality disorders: An outline of a systematic approach. In: *The Search for the Self*, Vol. 1, ed. P. Ornstein. New York: International Universities Press, 1978, pp. 477–509.

———— (1971), *The Analysis of the Self*. New York: International Universities Press.

———— (1976), Creativeness, charisma, group psychology: Reflections on the self-analysis of Freud. In: *The Search for the Self*, Vol. 2, ed. P. Ornstein. New York: International Universities Press, 1978, pp. 793–843.

———— (1978), Conclusion: The search for the analyst's self. In: *The Search for the Self*, Vol. 2, ed. P. Ornstein. New York: International Universities Press, 1978, pp. 931–938.

———— (1984), *How Does Analysis Cure?* ed. A. Goldberg & P. E. Stepansky. New York: International Universities Press.

Lichtenberg, J. (1983), *Psychoanalysis and Infant Research*. Hillsdale, NJ: The Analytic Press.

———— ed. (1987), *Psychoanal. Inq.*, 7(3). Hillsdale, NJ: The Analytic Press.

Rapaport, D. (1967), *Collected Papers*, ed. M. Gill. New York: Basic Books.

Spitz, R. A. (1956), Countertransference. *J. Amer. Psychoanal. Assn.*, 4:256–265.

Stern, D. (1985), *The Interpersonal World of the Infant*. New York: Basic Books.

Waelder, R. (1962), Symposium: Selection criteria for the training of psychoanalytic students. III—The selection of candidates. *Internat. J. Psycho-Anal.*, 43:283–286.

Author Index

A

Abraham, K., 266
Aichhorn, A., 191, *207*
Angyal, A., 110, *118*
Antrobus, J. S., 21, 22
Armstrong, J., 170–71, *184*
Atwood, G. E., xiii–xv, xvii–xxi, *xxv,*
   xxvi, 18, *22,* 34–38, *39,* 50, *53,*
   76,*102,* 106, 115, *118,* 121, 125, 126,
   140, 141, 221, *252*
Axelrod, R., 234, *250*

B

Bacal, H., xv–xvi, xviii, *xxv,* 99, *101,* 116,
   118
Baker, L., 93, *102*
Baldridge, B., 52, *54*
Balint, M., 149, *166*
Bandura, A., 178, *184*

Barraclough, B., 170, *184*
Basch, M. F., xii–xiv, xv, xviii, *xxv, xxvi,*
   123, *140*
Beebe, B., v, *xvi,* 19, 22, 112, *118*
Benedek, T., 258
Bergman, A., 59, 60, *72,* 77, 85, *102,* 213,
   252
Bergmann, M., 52, *53*
Beskow, J., 170, *184*
Bibring, E., 219, 239, *250*
Block, J. H., 77, *101*
Blum H., 148, 150, *166*
Boden, R., 77, *101*
Bohm, D., 204, *207*
Bokert, E., 51, *54*
Bonime, W., 28, *31*
Boskind-Lodahl, M., 75, *101*
Boskind-White, M., 75, *101*
Bosman, H. B., 170, *184*
Bowlby, J., xv, *xxvi,* 238, 239, *250*
Brandchaft, B., xiii, xvii, xviii, xix, xx,
   xxvii, 37, 38, *39,* 76, *102,* 106, *118,*

269

SUBJECT INDEX